T0354816

Hello, Marvelous You

Activate Your Inner Apps to
Power up Your Life

Jocelyne F. Lafrenière

BALBOA.
PRESS
A DIVISION OF HAY HOUSE

Copyright © 2015 JFL International Inc.

All rights reserved. No part of this book may be used or reproduced by any means, graphic, electronic, or mechanical, including photocopying, recording, taping or by any information storage retrieval system without the written permission of the author except in the case of brief quotations embodied in critical articles and reviews.

Balboa Press books may be ordered through booksellers or by contacting:

Balboa Press
A Division of Hay House
1663 Liberty Drive
Bloomington, IN 47403
www.balboapress.com
1 (877) 407-4847

Because of the dynamic nature of the Internet, any web addresses or links contained in this book may have changed since publication and may no longer be valid. The views expressed in this work are solely those of the author and do not necessarily reflect the views of the publisher, and the publisher hereby disclaims any responsibility for them.

The author of this book does not dispense medical advice or prescribe the use of any technique as a form of treatment for physical, emotional, or medical problems without the advice of a physician, either directly or indirectly. The intent of the author is only to offer information of a general nature to help you in your quest for emotional and spiritual well-being. In the event you use any of the information in this book for yourself, which is your constitutional right, the author and the publisher assume no responsibility for your actions.

Print information available on the last page.

ISBN: 978-1-5043-2833-3 (sc)
ISBN: 978-1-5043-2835-7 (hc)
ISBN: 978-1-5043-2834-0 (e)

Library of Congress Control Number: 2015902854

1st edition, April 2015

Balboa Press rev. date: 02/27/2018

Acknowledgements

In this book, I share my personal stories, as well as those of people I have met during my life. For privacy reasons, names have been changed. I wish to thank all of you who have inspired me to write this book. Your life experiences and wisdom have touched my heart, and have been a great source of inspiration in my own journey.

My loving thanks to my wonderful husband, Yvon, for your support and encouragement. You are my greatest supporter, and your love is a warm blanket over my heart. Your true love is a gift I cherish each day. Thank you for believing in me.

Thank you to my close friends and family for your kind support. I truly cherish your friendships. A special thank you to my mother for your prayers, love, and encouragement to pursue all my dreams.

Thank you to my mentors and performance managers who over the years have inspired me to become the best that I can be. Through you, I discovered the meaning of excellence, teamwork, perseverance, and creativity.

My deepest thanks to my dear friend Linda, and to Lee Ann from FirstEditing for their valuable editorial insights. Thank you to the Balboa Press team: Wendy Herrington, David Yoder, and Keelyn Walsh, for making my dream come true with professionalism and dedication.

My gratitude goes to all the authors whose writings have been a source of inspiration and guidance in my life since my teenage years. As a teenager, I was looking for an instruction book that would explain the meaning of life, and how to best live my life. Each of your books was a chapter of this instruction book.

Most importantly, thank you to God, the driving force behind this book. Thank you for your unconditional love. Writing this book was such a pleasure, and truly a gift to myself as well.

Dedication

There is not a day that goes by when we do not hear about wars, threats of wars, terrorism, religious oppression, violence, civil unrest, political turmoil, and economic challenges, leaving many people feeling gloomy, discouraged, and even scared of living life.

I felt it was the perfect timing to remind ourselves that our true purpose in life is to be the *Marvelous You*. When chaos is created in the world, it means we are drifting away from our true nature and shifting toward the *Powerless You*.

By choosing to activate our inner apps, we can realign ourselves and allow our true essence to rise from within and flow freely, thus replacing darkness with light in the world.

This book is dedicated to all of you who wish to empower your lives and make a positive difference in the world. May the reading of this book encourage you to actualize your *Marvelous Nature*. May you experience fulfillment, joy, and well-being each day for your own fulfillment, and the betterment of those around you.

Awareness is the spark to the
creation of your best life.

A desire is an exciting vision of the
great opportunities that lie ahead.

Believing is the key that unlocks the
door to these possibilities.

Actions are the little feet that give life
to your desires.

Positive expectations are your
springboard as you journey.

Faith transforms the impossible to
possible.

Life is waiting for you. Get going
now, *Marvelous You*!

Contents

Introduction

The fact that you were intrigued by this book and started reading it shows that you are ready to power up your life and discover who you truly are, the *Marvelous You*.

This is not a quick-fix book to learn how to become a millionaire. But as you read through the pages, you will understand that your life is worth a million. You will find amazing resources to help you become all that you can be. You will cause your life to flourish for your own fulfillment and the betterment of others. You will rise beyond your current level of awareness and *learn* to be more, rather than *trying* to be more.

You are a spiritual being in the midst of a physical experience. You were uniquely designed with inner apps to fully express your *Marvelous Nature*. By activating your apps, you transform your life with abundance at all levels—physically, emotionally, intellectually, financially, and spiritually.

Let me introduce you to the *Marvelous You*!

Endowed with freedom, you choose to actualize your *Marvelous Nature* for complete glee. You are imbued with talents, skills, and abilities to bring more beauty into the world. With good-feeling thoughts and inspired actions, you aim to create a purpose-driven life. With great determination, you reach new heights of success in your career or business.

You are part of this grand universe, connected to God, the Life Force that sustains it all. He co-creates with you, orchestrating your success. As you journey, you are attuned to Infinite Wisdom that inspires and guides you.

You are hopeful for tomorrow and excited for the abundant possibilities that each day brings. Lasting joy lives in your heart each day. You bring passion and happiness into all areas of your life. You stand strong as you go through the storms of life, finding peace in Him. You welcome challenges as experiences to fully actualize your *Marvelous Self*.

You are grateful for life, and you are rich in talents, friends, love, and all good things. With wisdom, you create more wealth for you and those around you. You are love in action, and you radiate kindness, patience, forgiveness, and compassion. Your love brings more joy and peace into the world.

You appreciate life and take time to savor moments of quietness, respite, and recreation. You care and nurture yourself each and every day for increased fitness, vitality, and well-being. You cherish the utmost respect for planet earth, and you care for tomorrow and the generations to come.

When you connect with your *Marvelous Essence,* you discover your true self in all its beauty. In this inner transformation, you experience the fullness of who you are.

Why wait any longer? Activate your inner apps today to power up your life for lasting fulfillment and bliss. Soon you will live your best life. You will shine, and leave your footprint in making this world a better place.

 # Part I

Discover the
Marvelous You
and the
Wonders of Your
Manifestation Power

CHAPTER 1

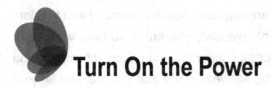

Turn On the Power

Let yourself be surprised by life. In each day,
there is a moment to grow and discover life's great beauty.

Say Hello to the *Marvelous You*

You are the *Marvelous You*, an eternal spiritual being in the midst of a time-bound physical experience. You are part of this beautifully organized universe, connected to the Life Force and orchestrating Power—God, Infinite Consciousness, Divine Intelligence, Infinite Wisdom, All-That-Is, and Spirit—that sustains it all. You are a living expression of God. Through you, He brings great beauty, love, and light to the world.

> *Like a caterpillar, all is in you to become a*
> *beautiful butterfly free to rise to new heights.*

Realizing ever and ever more fully your *Marvelous Self* is your true purpose in life. By gently awakening to your real essence, serenity flows from your heart as springs of living water. When your life lacks love, respect, confidence, passion, strength, and courage, it means you have forgotten—or were not aware—that you are the *Marvelous You*, thus drifting away from your true nature and shifting toward the *Powerless You*. By activating your inner apps, you can realign yourself and allow your true essence to rise from within and flow freely.

3

You were not created to be undiscovered and unfulfilled but to flourish, express your creativity and passion, and experience fulfillment with a sense of confidence, delight, and harmony. You are endowed with freedom to create your best life. Richly blessed, you are a nurturer who never ceases to love and care for others. Inner joy and peace accompany you each day. Now say hello to the *Marvelous You* that you are, and let your greatness be an inspirational source for others.

United to God – You are from God and in God. You are in continuous connectedness with Him, whether you acknowledge it or not. In the stillness of your heart, you hear His voice and feel His power all around you. In His love, you find self-esteem and worthiness. Under His wings, you learn, grow, and become all that you can be. In His presence, you experience pure bliss and inner fulfillment. In faith, you follow His path of true love.

Endowed with Freedom – Each moment is a moment of freedom and choice. Your mind is free to choose positive thoughts and create a purpose-driven life. Your heart is free to be hopeful, love, and cultivate peace. Freedom is yours to listen to the voice of Spirit, and actualize your *Marvelous Self* without limits.

Powerful Creator – You are pure creativity, greatly inspired, and enthusiastic for new opportunities in your life. With good-feeling thoughts and focused actions, you create your heartfelt aspirations with commitment, self-control, and perseverance. Attuned to Infinite Wisdom, you are intuitive and directed with knowingness on the path of fulfillment.

Passionate – Driven by your life purpose, you move towards your desires with passion. Gifted with talents, skills, and abilities, you add unique beauty to the universe. Your great enthusiasm inspires others to cause their lives to flourish.

Confident – You are confident and hopeful for the abundant possibilities that each day brings. You fear not for today or tomorrow. You know that the Life Force that sustains the universe holds you in His hand, and He has the power to transform the impossible into the possible.

Unbounded Joy – Each moment is a moment to rejoice. Life's annoyances have no grip on you. You are not troubled by rainy days.

Blissful joy colors your soul like a rainbow. You embrace glee by creating happiness for yourself and those around you.

Courageous – Your journey is a thrilling adventure, with challenges and new beginnings for your greatest transformation. You are not afraid of setbacks, trusting in the grander plan of life. You are armed with courage, strength, and resilience, fully equipped to bounce back quickly from adversity.

Richly Blessed – Richness flows in your life with talents, friends, love, and all good things. You are grateful for all the pleasures and wonders of life. You are content and humble, conscious that your talents are true blessings. You enjoy creating growth for your own pleasure and the betterment of all.

Loving – You emanate love, generosity, patience, forgiveness, and compassion. You embrace high ethical values. You are a companion, a listener, a comforter, a teacher, a guide, and a provider who uplifts everyone around you. By spreading your wings of love, you bring more love and peace into the world.

Playful – You are playful and fun to be around. You appreciate and savor the beauties of life. You have a great sense of humor, and your life is filled with laughter. By living a harmonious life with playtime, quietness, and relaxation, you experience great well-being.

Nurturer – You are beautiful, just perfect the way you are. Deep within, you know you are worthy of a great life. You cultivate self-love, and appreciate all that you are. You care and nurture yourself and others each and every day. You live a green life for today's generation and those to come.

Expressing your *Marvelous Self* is a transforming process that gradually takes place as you experience life. At a very early age, you discovered your creativity. You were curious, and explored the world around you. In your teenage years, your instincts, passions, and aspirations became stronger. You were hopeful and confident for the future. Now you are fearless, not shying away from new experiences. Love is smiling at you, and you smile back. Happiness is your pursuit. Through life experiences, you discover your unique gifts and talents. You joyfully create your own life experiences with inspiration and wisdom. You discover the beauties of life, and your heart is filled with gratefulness. Facing challenges, you activate the power of courage, resilience, and hopefulness.

By cultivating spiritual awareness, you attain conscious oneness with God. From that place flows true love that you freely share with humanity. You see the world as your home and mankind as your brethren. Connected to Infinite Consciousness, you expand your mind, and you are directed in life with divine inspiration and intuition. Through this transformational process, you discover your true self in its full beauty, and you find deep-seated peace at the core of your being. You are in complete harmony with All-That-Is.

Activate Your Apps

You were uniquely designed with inner apps to fully express your *Marvelous Nature*. By activating your apps, you transform your life with abundance at all levels. You actualize who you truly are: creative, passionate, courageous, joyful, loving, blessed, playful, and nurturing.

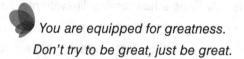
You are equipped for greatness.
Don't try to be great, just be great.

"Wow! Does this mean I can transform my life from good to great?" you might ask with interest. Totally. With your inner apps activated, you let the seeds of greatness that are in you flourish to realize your *Marvelous Self*. Let's have a look at how they empower your life.

Marvelous You Apps

True Inspiration	With *True Inspiration,* you light up the powerful creator that you are. Inspiration flows abundantly to help you become all that you can be. You master the ability to tune in to your intuition. Gone are limited beliefs and chaos in your mind.
High Drive	*High Drive* puts little feet under your dreams by helping you craft a plan to bring action into your passions. With commitment, you move towards your vision. You unlock your full potential for the manifestation of fulfilling life experiences.
Dynamo	Managing your emotions is so much easier with *Dynamo.* This app alerts you when your emotional temperature is going down and you are moving away from your well-being zone. You can swiftly take action and bring more passion into your life.
Higher Power	With *Higher Power,* you ignite an interactive relationship with God. In oneness with Him, your soul is enlightened. You experience acceptance, wholeness, and harmony. In this communion, bliss and praise are in your heart each day.
Be Happy	With *Be Happy,* your mind is filled with good-feeling thoughts. You speak words of possibilities. You embrace a positive attitude. You live life with enthusiasm and passion. Your heart is grateful for life, for today, and tomorrow.
Fit and Fab	By turning on *Fit and Fab*, you automatically activate your membership to the *Fit and Feeling Fabulous Club*. You commit to nurturing and caring for yourself. You say yes to a life transformation with more fitness, vitality, and wellness.
Love Power	With *Love Power,* you embody love, patience, forgiveness, kindness, and humility. You forgive your own faults, understanding that you are on a journey of growth.
Financial Tycoon	*Financial Tycoon* helps you create financial growth in your life for your own pleasure and the benefit of others. You become a channel for richness to flow in the world.
Go Getter	*Go Getter* helps you land your dream job. You are disciplined and well-organized. You are passionate in your work. You are a leader who does not shy away from responsibilities. You communicate positively and are well-respected by your peers.
Fly High	With *Fly High*, you are a strategic thinker and successful entrepreneur. You welcome change to drive growth and improve performance. You strive for success. You create a culture of excellence, and are an inspiration to your team.
Fun and Play	*Fun and Play* brings more leisure time into your life. You say good-bye to stress, and say hello to more playtime, relaxation, and quietness that energize your body, ease your mind, and increase your well-being.
Green Thumb	*Green Thumb* helps you de-clutter, complete the incompletes, and transform your home and work area into an inspiring oasis. Home hygiene and economics are no longer a burden. You happily green your life.

Each morning, take a few moments to activate your apps. Your day ahead will be as you have never seen before. Enthusiasm, inner joy, and harmony will be your faithful companions. With inspiration and intuition, you will move in the direction of your desires with passion and intensity. Love will shine through your eyes and embrace your words and behavior. In unity with God, you will awaken to a continuous sense of well-being, no matter what.

As you go about your day, keep your apps activated. On occasion, we press the deactivation buttons and shift away from our *Marvelous Nature*. If you feel the strong pull of the *Powerless You*, press the reset buttons and reactivate your apps. Each of your days will be a celebration of life, growth, and accomplishments, small and grand.

See the Invisible

Throughout time, many religious, mythological, psychological, and philosophical traditions have suggested that humankind is much more than what the eyes can see. God, life after death, consciousness, soul, and spirit still remain great mysteries, and they have led to different interpretations, speculations, and even divisiveness.

A frequent view is that mankind is body, soul, and spirit, with the latter two being immaterial. According to this concept, the body is the material aspect of man. The soul encompasses the will, mind, and emotions, and it is essentially your essence and personality. The human spirit is the channel through which you are in a continuous relationship with God, and it is seen by many as God's breath of life.[1]

Others suggest we have a bipartite, not a tripartite nature, where the soul and spirit are the same entity.[2] As a result, many see the terms *soul* and *spirit* as interchangeable. The non-visible is often referred to as the heart of a person, with many suggesting it survives human death. The expressions *higher conscious mind*, *higher self*, *true self*, and *divine ego* are other names used by many to refer to the spiritual part of man.

You are a spiritual being with a soul,
living a physical experience.

Austrian neurologist and psychoanalyst Sigmund Freud used the terms *conscious*, *pre-conscious*, and *unconscious* to make reference to different aspects of the mind. Freud explained that the conscious mind includes what is currently in your focal awareness. The preconscious mind accumulates information that is easily accessible to your conscious mind. For example, answers to the following questions are stored in your preconscious mind: Where did I leave my car keys? What movie did I watch last week? The unconscious mind stores your hidden beliefs and values, as well as your past memories and feelings, good and bad, that are not easily accessible to your conscious mind.[3]

Several philosophers, psychologists, and scientific researchers have critiqued Freud's definitions of what is in your current awareness and what is not. Some have used different terms or provided different explanations and definitions for the different functions of the mind.[4]

As Dr. Tad James wrote in *Lost Secrets of Ancient Hawaiian Huna*, the ancient Hawaiian Huna teachings explain that we have three non-visible minds (conscious, unconscious, higher conscious) residing in the three respective immaterial bodies (mental, emotional, spiritual) they control. The conscious mind bears a similar definition as the one presented by Freud. The unconscious mind encompasses many of the above aspects. It includes other functions as well, such as health and life preservation, and control and maintenance of perception. The higher conscious mind is your personal connectedness to God, where all knowing resides. It is through the higher conscious mind that one may experience extrasensory perception such as telepathy and remote viewing.[5]

In psychology and everyday speech, the term *subconscious* is widely held to refer to knowledge and past experiences that are not in your current awareness.[6] It is touted that the subconscious mind can manage thousands of events at the same time, while the conscious mind can tackle just a few.[7]

For many, the subconscious mind also embraces the higher conscious mind, the channel through which you experience personal connectedness to God, who guides you towards the actualization of your *Marvelous Nature*.

 You hold the power to create, love,
forgive, and be hopeful and joyous.

As you grow in awareness of your *Marvelous Nature*, your path will light up for your heart to see the beauty of the invisible. You will be inspired to activate your apps and live to the fullest with your body, soul, and spirit. In doing so, you will invite abundance into your life at all levels: physically, emotionally, intellectually, financially, and spiritually. All this is for you to experience greater fulfillment, joyousness, and well-being.

While there are different views and terms to explain all that you are, there is one common truth, and that is, you are truly a magnificent being, meant to actualize your *Marvelous Nature* for greater fulfillment and well-being. Is your head spinning with all this information? Don't worry, I have it all summed up in the table below for easy reference.

Glimpse of Human Nature Views

Parts	Bodies	Purpose
Body	Physical	The physical body houses your organs, various types of cells, body systems, body parts, brain, and more.
Soul (will, mind, emotions)	Mental and Emotional	The conscious mind includes your emotions, perceptions, sensations, and memories in your current awareness. It is where you create thoughts, and where you calculate and reason. Your intellect understands, memorizes, and processes your thoughts.
		The preconscious mind consists of learned skills, past memories and feelings, values, and beliefs that you can easily pull into your conscious mind.
		The unconscious mind stores information your conscious mind cannot easily access: early childhood memories, repressed memories, hidden values and beliefs, and past traumatic events. It regulates your physiological body functions without effort.
Human spirit (connection with God)	Spiritual	The higher conscious mind is the channel through which you experience personal connectedness to God and higher plains of consciousness. Through Spirit, you are guided and inspired to fully realize your *Marvelous Nature*.

Let the Light Shine

In past decades, in-the-brain consciousness, brain function, and energy fields have been of great interest to science. While we have made advances and gained a better understanding of these concepts, there is much to be discovered as research continues in many different countries around the world.

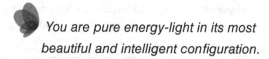

You are pure energy-light in its most beautiful and intelligent configuration.

Largely covered by the media, American Dr. Andrea Stocco, PhD, Research Assistant Professor at the University of Washington Department of Psychology and the Institute for Learning and Brain Sciences (I-LABS), along with two colleagues, Dr. Rajesh Rao, MD, and Dr. Chantel Prat, PhD, recently demonstrated the possibility of transferring simple information directly between two brains using non-invasive brain stimulation devices.[8]

Dr. Rao and Dr. Stocco were playing a video game. Dr. Rao was hooked up to an electroencephalogram (EEG) while Dr. Stocco was connected to a brain-stimulating coil above his left motor cortex. Dr. Rao imagined moving his right hand to push the spacebar trigger but stayed still. It was Dr. Stocco, sitting on the other side of the University of Washington campus, who moved his hand to push the trigger.[8]

"I am impressed!" you might say with astonishment. You are right. This experience is truly amazing. In my view, this study demonstrates that while the brain and mind are inter-connected, the mind is not restricted to one's own brain. Who knows? This may bring more light to telepathic events, where mind-to-mind communication without physical interaction or known sensory channels is being reported. While telepathy has been largely studied, it still has not been definitely confirmed.[9]

Research of the mind continues actively, and science now recognizes the existence of energy fields associated with our body. Neuroimaging (a relatively new discipline within medicine and neuroscience/psychology) uses various techniques to image the structure and function/pharmacology of the brain. Advances in functional neuroimaging show that certain areas of the brain light up when processing information. This is a result of increased blood flow and neural activation.[10]

The EEG test allows for the measurement of brainwaves, which are essentially the electrical activity in the brain produced by signals sent at once by millions of neurons.[11] Brainwaves vary vastly from high to low frequency depending on what the person is doing: highest state of focus (gamma wave), wide awake (beta wave), relaxed or in a meditative state (alpha wave), light sleep with dreams or extreme relaxation (theta wave), and deep and dreamless sleep known for its energizing and restoring properties (delta wave).[12]

The electrocardiogram (ECG) measures the electrical activity of the heart over a period of time. Using the SQUID magnetometer (superconducting quantum interference device), scientists are now in a position to detect bio-magnetic fields associated with physiological activities in the body.[13]

Furthermore, Russian bio-physicist, scientist, inventor, author, and pioneer of the scientific field of electrophotonics, Dr. Konstantin Korotkov, PhD, is known to have developed the EPC/GDV technology (electrophotonic capture/gas discharge visualization). This technology uses a special camera to capture the physical, emotional, mental, and spiritual energy, known as the auras, emanating to and from an individual, plants, liquids, powders, and inanimate objects, and it translates this into a computerized model.[14]

Certified in Europe, the EPC/GDV technique is approved by the Russian Ministry of Health as a medical technology. It allows visualizing imbalances in the energy fields that may influence a person's well-being. Displaying the area of the body and organ systems involved, it greatly facilitates the diagnosis of causes of such imbalances.[14]

Why do I tell you this captivating information? Simply to reiterate that you are more than your eyes can see. You are unified into a collective ocean of energy, where each one of us is a wave. We are one, connected to each other and to the Life Power that sustains this beautiful and grand universe.

Let the Great Minds Speak

The brain is a sending/receiving station that facilitates your soul's expression. As the seat of the mind, your brain enables consciousness and controls numerous functions, including mental thinking, learning, remembering, movement, and feelings. With billions of neurons that communicate with each other, the brain gives meaning to electrical signals it receives from neurons through the nervous center as you experience the world with your senses. This process in turn influences the biochemistry of your body and feelings.[15]

To sum it up, the mind is an activity of the brain. No brain, no mind in the physical world. It's as simple as that. "Where is the mind located? Where are my past thoughts and emotions stored?" you might ask out of curiosity.

The location of the mind still remains a mystery for science. Many proponents of energy medicine (energy healing) believe the human aura is made of successive layers of energy fields that permeate, surround, and sustain the body. Frequently called bodies (mental body, emotional body, spiritual body), these energy fields are believed to be interconnected. They store past memories, emotional responses, beliefs, behavioral patterns, and much more information.[16]

*As you awaken to Spirit, you find a new
state of consciousness.*

*As you discover Spirit, you see the
invisible.*

*As you embrace Spirit, you realize
oneness with Him.*

*As you feed from Spirit, you experience
wholeness.*

While we await further discoveries on our magnificent nature, we can certainly acknowledge that our body, soul, and spirit are inextricably woven and communicate with one another. Let's look at some examples of their dialogue.

Conscious and Subconscious Minds

- In an instant, you can bring into your conscious mind past memories and feelings that reside in your subconscious mind.

- Skills are transferred to your subconscious mind once learned, and can be accessed by your conscious mind at any time. For example, you can go years without riding a bicycle, and within a few minutes of practice, you can excel again.

- Beliefs and thoughts must be congruent for manifestation. Assume you want to lose twelve pounds in one month, but don't really believe you can succeed. What will ensue next is you will not follow your nutritional plan. On the other hand, if you set a realistic and believable goal of four pounds in a month, you will likely succeed.

Body and Soul

- Thoughts are the basis for sensations and emotions. If you think for a moment that you are drinking lemon juice, you will feel the sour taste in your mouth. If you think that you were wrongly dismissed from your job, you will instantly be upset and feel stress in your body.

- If you are overworked and your physical body is tired, you may feel depressed and lifeless. You may become very nervous, and your immune system may likely weaken.

- If your child or your husband dies, you may feel a huge hole in your physical body, as if a part of yourself was taken away.

- If you are scared, nervous, or anxious, your heart may start racing uncontrollably.

Body, Soul and Spirit

- Spirit communicates with you through intuition and inspiration. Communication comes to your awareness through thoughts and feelings (positive or negative), which in turn cause corresponding biochemical reactions in your body.

- People with strong faith generally keep their thoughts, words, behavior, and values captive in positivity, which makes them feel good physically and emotionally.

As you delve into the awareness of your body, soul, and spirit connection, you open yourself to better health. It is touted that the release of negative emotions moves you on a path of wellness. For many, forgiveness has led to emotional freedom and improved physical health. A positive outlook on life helps people face challenges with less stress, which in turn keeps them in better emotional and physical health.[17]

Mental rehearsal, also known as visualization, guided imagery, or motivational imagery, has been found to improve people's physical and psychological functions in certain situations, namely their focus, well-being, confidence, motivation, creativity, and performance. For this reason, many athletes have incorporated mental rehearsal techniques as part of their overall training regimen to perform with more ease.

American physiologist Edmund Jacobson, through the use of sensitive detection instruments, discovered in his study that people practicing physical exercise visualization showed increased electrical activity in their muscles.[18]

Australian psychologist Alan Richardson also conducted a similar experiment, which was published in *Research Quality*. He took a group of basketball players, divided them into three groups, and tested each player's ability to make free throws. One group would practice 20 minutes every day. The second group would only visualize shooting perfect baskets every day for 20 minutes, but no real practice was allowed. The third group would not practice or visualize. The results were quite amazing. There was significant improvement in the group that only visualized; they were almost as good as those who had practiced.[19]

Olympic athletes participated in the Visual Motor Rehearsal Program of American psychologist and respected author Dr. Denis Waitley, PhD. As Dr. Waitley explains in his audio album, the *Psychology of Winning*, the same muscles were fired in the same sequence whether the athletes were rehearsing the event in their mind or competing in real-life. Quite impressive, right? By embracing your body, soul, and spirit connection, you will experience greater wellness, enabling the manifestation of your desires with more ease.

Play Beautiful Music

You are unique, and science has proven it. Your iris and retinal patterns, hand geometry, and voice have become secured methods of identification.[20] No one else is exactly like you. With your unique gifts, talents, passions, and all that you are, you are meant to play beautiful music in the orchestra of life. Greatness is in you, and you are called to let it shine.

The main reason for your existence is to unfold your *Marvelous Self*. All the seeds of the *Marvelous You* are in you, and your task is to activate your inner apps for the seeds to flourish for more abundance in your life. In being all that you can be with your unique gifts and skills, you bring more beauty to the universe. Life is truly yours to create with all that you are. In your own unique ways, you leave your imprint on this world.

You are creativity when you are inspired with ideas. You are passion when you get excited about your new projects. You are pure joy when you rejoice for no reason. You are courage when you bounce back from adversity. You are wisdom when you take actions for the betterment of all.

You are generosity when you lend a helping hand in times of need. You are compassion when your heart listens and grieves. You are peace when you forgive. You are playful when you laugh out loud. You are a nurturer when you are kind to yourself and others.

From the moment you were born, you never cease to experience the world. As a young infant, you discovered your surroundings with your senses, looking at objects and toys, hearing sounds, touching, and smelling. As a child you were curious, trying to understand the world around you. Growing older, you became aware of the polarity of life within your body, mind, and soul: health and sickness, richness and scarcity, love and hate, peace and war, success and failure, joy and sorrow. As you become wiser, you recognize that you are the author of such polarity within your thoughts, beliefs, actions, and feelings.

Each moment is a learning experience, an opportunity to choose, learn, grow, be inspired by others, plant seeds of love, and transform your life and the lives of those around you. Each day is an opportunity to become who you want to be, maximize your potential, and most importantly, experience serenity with a heart filled with gratitude. You are endowed with the power to bring to life your *Marvelous Essence.*

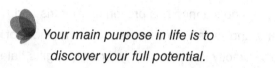

> *Your main purpose in life is to*
> *discover your full potential.*

Looking to soar to new heights? Pay attention to define your reality not only with your senses and conscious mind, but with your higher conscious mind. When you feed yourself from God, the Source of life, you breathe and live a reality that is beyond your conscious mind. You are born into life from God, and He knows all about you today, tomorrow, and eternally. He knows your aspirations, feelings, and all that you can be. He made you unique and special as a celebration of the diversity that He is.

From this place of understanding, you awaken to a deeper connection to others. Your soul seeks to respect and allow others to realize their *Marvelous Nature.* Love is the best symphony; you can play along with people from all ethnicities, cultures, and religions of the world.

Take Ownership of Your Life

When I was fourteen years old, my world shattered when my parents divorced. I was born into a middle-class family. We had a good life, with summer camps, vacations, and private schooling. Suddenly, my new reality was financial scarcity. So from a very young age, I worked my way through high school, college, and university, working at different part-time jobs, from being a mathematics tutor, babysitter, and salesperson to a telephone operator and accounting clerk.

I found out early in life that I had to take ownership of my life. This realization kept me away from drugs and alcohol, as I needed to be alert and mindful to tackle the challenges in front of me and stand strong in the face of life's disappointments. Some truths of my *Marvelous Nature* came to light during those years: creator, courageous, forgiving, and hopeful. However, I was not very good at mastering my emotions, so my heart was in limbo. I felt so sad and alone. It was a difficult time, yet a blessing in disguise, as I don't believe I would be who I am today if I hadn't been through that hardship.

Taking ownership of your life involves being responsible for what you create with your thoughts, emotions, actions, and faith. It equates to having faith in your ability to create a better future.

Being responsible for your life means looking at yourself in the mirror and answering truthfully these questions: Am I responsible in any way for where I am? Can I do things differently? What can I do today to move closer to my vision of success?

If you want changes in your life and don't see much happening, search inside of you, as the answers lie there. If you always get the same negative outcomes, it means you are not on the right path, and you need to change the way you do things. For some people, their fate is always caused by someone else other than themselves. They blame their father or mother, they blame their spouse or ex-spouse, or they blame their employer or their peers. Any reason are used to shun facing reality, taking responsibility for their actions, and changing what needs to be changed.

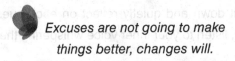

*Excuses are not going to make
things better, changes will.*

"I am stuck in a rut." These were the words Louis and Barb told me when we first met. Both had their wheels spinning but were going nowhere near where they wanted to be. Louis always returned to the bottom of the ladder, and Barb was stalled in the middle of the ladder. They were both looking outside themselves as to why they were in a rut. Once they finally understood that they were letting past events influence their today, they were able to take charge of their lives and were back to climbing the success ladder.

Louis couldn't hold a job for very long. His father was an alcoholic who left him with the feeling of never being good enough. As a child, that feeling caused him to silently rage. As an adult, he became a roaring lion in response to criticism or any threat to his judgment. He would just charge like a bull. As a result, he was left wandering from job to job for years, unable to respect authority. With proper coaching, Louis was able to change his belief about himself and take mastery over his own insecurities. This led him to engage in more positive communication.

Insecurity was also the cause of Barb's difficulty in climbing up the corporate ladder. Barb is a very ambitious, intelligent, and hardworking person. Her mother left when she was young, leaving her very insecure. To find a sense of security, she became a perfectionist. When her perfection was threatened, she would become very condescending and arrogant with her spouse and peers. Once Barb recognized her pain and insecurity and chose to let it go, she became more at ease to collaborating in a positive manner.

You are who you are and where you are because you have created it with your thoughts and actions. No one coerced you; you chose it all. If you don't like what you see, step out of your pity party, stop blaming and complaining to those around you, and take positive action. Say to yourself, "I can create change. I can turn things around. I am the *Marvelous Me* and nothing can stop me."

You may want to use the *Transformation Power Tool* to help you address issues and roadblocks that hinder you from engaging in the change process. Sit down and quietly reflect on each question with all honesty. In stillness, listen to your inner voice whispering the answers.

Transformation Power Tool	
1.	What is the issue at stake? What does it mean to me to have it resolved?
2.	What are my inner and outer roadblocks?
3.	What actions am I willing to take to address these roadblocks? What talents, skills, tools, and resources will help me take positive actions?
4.	Are there any beliefs about myself that I need to reprogram?

You may consult with family, friends, and peers with an open heart. Listen without judgment. Accepting responsibility for where you are today is the first step in a true transformation. When ready, you will engage in crafting an action plan to nudge you towards a new destination.

Don't let life pass you by. Take ownership and create an outstanding life with focused thoughts, positive feelings, and disciplined actions. Be willing to take a risk. Dare to dream bigger dreams. Surprise yourself with how much more you can do and be.

Learn the Three Cs of the Manifestation Process

Like a caterpillar, all is there inside of you to become a butterfly. You are the *Marvelous You,* fully equipped with inner apps to live your best life and soar to new heights of abundance and success. Each aspect of the manifestation process—conceive, commit to action, and celebrate—involves all that you are.

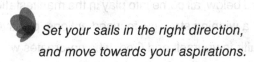

Set your sails in the right direction, and move towards your aspirations.

Conceive – Your thoughts are the sparks that ignite the manifestation process. With *True Inspiration* activated, you bring to life the powerful creator that you are. Inspiration and intuition flow abundantly, and your heart is filled with desires that create a chain reaction that will turn them into reality.

Gone are limited beliefs and chaos in your mind; your desires are well aligned with your inner beliefs. With *High Drive,* you craft an effective strategy that fires you up into action. By activating your *Be Happy* and *Higher Power* apps, you are in a state of positive expectedness. Embraced by good feelings and faith, you are grateful for what is to come, yet detached to the outcomes.

Commit to Action – With commitment, self-discipline, and dedication, you pursue your journey with excitement and passion. Plagued with moments of doubt? You realign your beliefs with your desires. With *Be Happy* activated, you are empowered by good-feeling thoughts that keep you flying high. You stay in a high-vibration energy space where well-being resides. As you journey, you assess your progress and reevaluate your strategy for the best results.

Focused and determined, you stand strong in the face of adversity. With daily affirmations and creative visualization, you move forward with confidence in the direction of your desires. With *Higher Power* activated, faith moves you to an even higher vibration of energy, where you find pure bliss. You are grateful for what you have, and for today and tomorrow.

Celebrate – With a joyful heart, you celebrate your accomplishments, small and grand. You cherish all your successes in the treasure chest of your mind. You let feedback be your friend. You are grateful for the seeds of your *Marvelous Essence* that you have discovered through the process.

You feel joy in having co-created the desires of your heart with the Highest Power of the universe. You recognize that He has aligned people and events to ease the journey.

As summarized below, all come into play in the manifestation process: inspired thoughts, a winning strategy, focused actions, positive emotions, and unwavering faith in yourself and God, who co-creates with you.

The Manifestation Process

Conceive	Commit to Action	Celebrate
The Power of Your Thoughts		
• Activate your *True Inspiration* app and express your desires without attachment to the outcomes. • Align your desires with your inner beliefs.	• Realign your beliefs as needed. • Shut up the *I can't* voice and maintain positive thoughts as you allow your desires to become reality.	• Celebrate all your accomplishments, small and big wins. • Keep your success memories in the treasure chest of your mind.
The Power of Your Strategy		
• Activate your *High Drive* app and craft your action plan and contingency plan.	• Keep *High Drive* activated to carry out your set strategy. • Assess your progress and realign your strategy as needed.	• Let lessons learned be an opportunity for growth. • Reflect on the seeds of your *Marvelous Essence* that have flourished.
The Power of Your Emotions		
• Activate your *Dynamo* app to shift from low- to high-vibration feelings. • Feel the joy of what is yet to come.	• Keep *Dynamo* activated for better-feeling thoughts as you move ahead.	• Feel the joy, happiness, and empowerment of having created your desires.
The Power of Your Faith		
• Turn on your *Higher Power* app and expect great things to happen, yet without attachment. • Have faith in your gifts, talents, and ability to create.	• Stay in a state of abundant gratitude. • Believe in the impossible. • Let the Highest Power of the universe surprise you with more than expected.	• Let your heart be filled with gratitude for all your successes. • Praise the Infinite Power of the universe who co-creates with you.

Perhaps you have lost your job, or your husband, and you are overwhelmed by disappointments. You think that life was not rigged in your favor. Your dreams were shattered, and you don't want to dream anymore. Shake off your sorrows—you are not a victim.

Each of your experiences, good and bad, is an opportunity for growth. Challenges are opportunities for your creativity to emerge, and for you to learn what works and what doesn't. In addition, roadblocks may hold a message that there is a faster or better path ahead. Wake up your desires again and let the world see that you are the *Marvelous You*, a powerful creator destined for greatness.

It is better to have dreamed and lost,
than never to have dreamed at all.

Just like driving a car, you are going nowhere until you release the brake pedal and move the transmission's selector lever out of the park position. Constantly doubting yourself will not get you very far. If you keep moving the transmission from drive to reverse or neutral, you will essentially go nowhere. Don't settle for inaction; take ownership of your life, and let today be a turning point where you choose to manifest the life you want.

Get your wings ready to fly higher. Activate your inner apps today to give yourself power to move in the direction of your desires. Get ready to transform your life and the lives of those around you.

Make the decision to say, "I choose to realize my *Marvelous Self,* and I allow my true essence to be. I take full responsibility for my life. I am ready to fly higher in a space where inner joyousness resides, and where the clouds of life can't pull me down. I let my heart be filled with enthusiasm and passion."

Own Your Freedom Wisely

You were born with free will as your birthright. You bear full responsibility for what you create with your thoughts, beliefs, emotions, and actions. As you engage in the manifestation process, you will experience life's duality in your mind and emotions: love and hate, confidence and fear, hopefulness and discouragement, glee and sorrow.

When you choose love, forgiveness, confidence, and joy, you bring to light your *Marvelous Essence.* By choosing disrespect, hate, anger, despair, and worry, you are drifting away from the *Marvelous You* and becoming the *Powerless You.* With your mind inspired by Spirit, you can renew your thoughts, emotions, and actions to shift away from the *Powerless You.*

 Free will is a powerful tool to be used wisely to avoid spinning out of control.

Gifted with free will, you can either create goodness and beauty, or you can create oppression, violence, war, chaos, and suffering. Thus, you are called to choose wisely and responsibly, with love as your ultimate guidance. Free will with love is powerful, but free will without love is disastrous. Not choosing love has dire consequences for you and those around you.

Wars, environmental issues, and economic crisis are created out of fear, not out of love. They are born from a place of limited understanding of life and abundance. It is only in the actualization of our *Marvelous Nature* that we will resolve the chaos we have created.

We create war by ignoring the sacredness of life and the right to freedom. We create famine by protecting ourselves first and letting others take care of themselves. We wrongly believe that wealth is limited, and spreading it around would leave us in a precarious position. We create air and land pollution, global warming, and resources depletion by focusing on today's gain with no respect for tomorrow. All around the world, it is feared that our human activities are the cause of loss of biodiversity and the extinction of some species.

"What do we do now?" you might ask.

All of us need to choose wisely and recreate our lives in a spirit of love for the betterment of our families, communities, countries, and those to come after us. All it takes is a conscious and collective shift towards love, reverence for life, unity, peace, freedom, international cooperation, and earth preservation.

It all starts with you and me choosing wisely and radiating love at home, at work, and in the community, creating social bonding, developing friendships, sharing our gifts, and serving others.

CHAPTER 2

Power Up Your Thoughts

*With small successes in tow, dare to
have bigger dreams.*

Activate Your *True Inspiration* App

Whenever you have a desire in your heart, know that you have the will
to turn it into reality. Heartfelt aspirations are an expression of the great
beauty that resides within you. They are messengers of possibilities for
your life. They are true expressions of who you can be. They make you
feel alive and empowered, and they ignite passion and a zest for life. They
are sparks that give you energy in the morning to nudge you into action.

*A desire is an exciting vision of
the great opportunities that lie ahead.*

Let me ask you: what are your true desires? What is your heart longing
for? Where are you right now? Where do you want to go? Who do you
want to be? What do you want to achieve in life? What would you do if you
were assured of success? Perhaps you don't have a vision for your future,
living day by day without any passion or excitement. In essence, you feel
stuck, unable to move forward, as your past failures have paralyzed you.
If you are ready to give your life another chance and experience greater
fulfillment, turn on your *True Inspiration* app today and fire up your mind
with inspiration to create an amazing life.

With *True Inspiration*, you consciously engage in a self-reflection of what you want to bring into your life. You let your imagination flow with creative ideas. You ask yourself some fundamental questions: What do I like? What are my skills? What ignites passion in my life? Who do I want to be? What things do I want? What does it mean to me to live my desires?

You rediscover who you are, your life purpose, and the true aspirations of your heart. You are inspired by thoughts that enliven excitement, passion, and hopefulness. You are ready to create your best life and step out of your comfort zone. You believe in the power of your desires. Your heart is filled with joy, hopefulness, and passion. You rejoice at the thought of today and tomorrow.

Deeply attuned to your intuition, you trust your inner guidance to set the stage for a powerful transformation in your life. Excited and motivated by your aspirations, you can't wait to see the beautiful surprises that await you. To sum it up, *True Inspiration* fires you up with creative ideas that will bring about great realizations in your life.

Let Inspiration and Intuition Flow

You are the *Marvelous You,* born to be a visionary, an influencer, and a powerful creator, not an observer of the universe with no control over your life. If you think that only a few are destined for greatness, you have it all wrong. God planted seeds of greatness in you. You are fully equipped with inner apps to become all that you can be.

If a desire is lingering in your heart and is associated with positive emotions, it means it is yours to fulfill. Know without any doubt that Infinite Wisdom is behind your desire. Desires from the heart are blessings coming towards you and those around you.

Don't wait any longer; choose to live your best life. Start with a reflection of who you want to be and what you want to achieve in life. Activate your *True Inspiration* app to listen to your inner voice, and let the seeds of greatness that have been planted in you flourish. Get ready to embrace your full potential. Don't be afraid of big dreams that speak of your greatness. You deserve to express your *Marvelous Self* and manifest the desires of your heart in synergy with God, who co-creates with you.

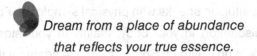

*Dream from a place of abundance
that reflects your true essence.*

"I don't think I have an inner voice. I don't hear anything," you might say.

We all have an inner voice. Inspiration may come at any time during the day, but mostly when your mind is quiet and free of pressure, thus producing low-frequency alpha and theta brainwaves. Oftentimes changing your usual surroundings for a while is all you need to escape from the chaos of your busy life and let inspiration flow from your heart. Try some of my favorite inspiration activators, which are mostly tethered to stillness.

Inspiration Activators	
1.	Relax in bed (about to sleep or just awakening).
2.	Take a bath or a shower to relax your body.
4.	Take a leisurely walk outside and connect to nature.
5.	Do fitness exercises to calm your mind.
6.	Listen to your favorite music at home or while going to work.
7.	Go shopping and enjoy walking and looking around.
8.	Read inspiring literature and various magazines. Be inspired by others.
9.	Quiet your mind and pray in stillness.
10.	Close your eyes and take deep breaths to reconnect with the serenity within.

Some of our greatest inventors got their amazing ideas through an instant flash of knowledge. It is said that an apple falling from a tree was the source of inspiration for the theory of gravity of English physicist Sir Isaac Newton.[1] Legend has it that the Greek mathematician Archimedes jumped out of his bath and shouted "Eureka!" when he realized that solid is denser than water, and he subsequently wrote Archimedes' principle.[2]

With your *True Inspiration* app activated, not only are you divinely inspired, but you are gifted with discernment, inner wisdom, and knowingness. You tune into your intuition and let it be your trusted friend. For some, intuitive guidance manifests itself through a strong inner sense of direction. For others, it is expressed through pictures that form in their mind. Many times, intuition speaks with physical symptoms. For example, you may feel a discomfort in your body, mainly in your stomach area, signaling that something is wrong. Some others are adamant that dreams experienced during sleep have been a source of direction in their life.

While different theories surround sleep dreams, there is no consensus on their purpose and function.[3] Some suggest they do not serve a real purpose. Others praise their benefits in maintaining emotional well-being. Obviously, be cautious in using your dreams as a source of guidance.

For a long time, I did not listen to my inner voice. I was all ears to the voices of others. I had relinquished my freedom to others. Then one day, I chose to be divinely guided by my own inspiration and intuition. My whole life turned around, with aliveness and inner joy flowing in my heart for simply allowing myself to be. Intuition is my trusted friend, and it has never failed me. When I feel inner peace and joy in my heart, I know I am going in the right direction.

Now, it's your turn to activate your *True Inspiration* app. Relax your mind and tune in to listen to your inner voice. Like Isaac Newton, be inspired as you look at the apple falling from the tree. Pay attention to the omens scattered along your path that provide divine guidance. Most importantly, follow your heart, and you will find happy surprises coming your way.

Express Your Wants with the *W. D. Factor*

As the *Marvelous You*, you want to realize yourself to the fullest in all areas of your life. You want to create a bright future for yourself and those around you. With a harmonious and meaningful life comes fulfillment and well-being. With your *True Inspiration* app activated, reflect on what you aspire to achieve in your life, the relationships you would like to develop, what you want to accomplish in your career and in the community, and what truly moves you. To help you develop your vision of success, take a look at the table below and be inspired by desires expressed with the *W. D. Factor,* meaning with detachment.

Vision of Success with the *W. D. Factor*	
Life Areas	**Desires**
Physical	▪ Great physical health ▪ Energy and vitality
Spiritual	▪ Deep spiritual connection ▪ Greater understanding of life
Professional/Business	▪ Fulfilling and inspiring career ▪ Prosperous business
Financial	▪ Wealth and financial abundance ▪ Peace of mind at retirement
Relationships	▪ True companionships and relationships ▪ Family harmony
Leisure Time	▪ Work-life harmony ▪ Recreation and relaxation ▪ Self-growth and self-acceptance
Environmental	▪ A heartfelt home ▪ An inspiring work setting
Legacy	▪ Be a giving channel to others ▪ Happily serve others to better their lives

To voice your deepest aspirations without attachment means you are open to different paths. You acknowledge that God, the orchestrating Power that sustains the universe, co-creates with you. You have faith that He may surprise you with *hows* beyond your imagination. In this state of awareness, your heart is uplifted and full of praise for His awe-inspiring magnificence.

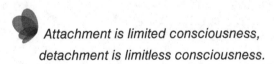

Attachment is limited consciousness,
detachment is limitless consciousness.

Just as different roads can lead to the same destination, different *hows* can lead to the achievement of the same desire. As you journey through life, your goals may change, but your deep aspirations may remain the same unless you choose otherwise. If one plan fails, prepare another plan. If a door closes, open another door.

When you express your desires with the *W. D. Factor*, your eyes are focused on the ultimate outcomes. You have great expectations that your desires—or something better—will come to pass. You gladly expect the unexpected, allowing Infinite Consciousness to surprise you with His greatness.

Build Treasures with Your LEGO®

Let the fun begin! Get your LEGO® bricks out and create your best life. For those of you who are not familiar with the construction toy LEGO, it is a creativity game for children, and it comes with interlocking colored plastic blocks, gears, mini figures, and various other parts. There is no limit to what your imagination can create with them, from vehicles, houses, pet houses, and necklaces to buildings.

You are endowed with your own LEGO pieces that are your creativity, personality, talents, skills, and capacities to add beauty to the world. No one else is exactly like you. We each have a different LEGO box with which we create our life. You hold the freedom to choose what you will do with your LEGO set. Seeds of greatness are in you, and you are embedded with freedom to create an outstanding life.

Activate your *True Inspiration* app and give thought to your life mission. Ask yourself what you want to do with your gifts and talents, and how you can best contribute to the world. If you struggle to crystallize your life mission and purpose, take a look at the following tips to gain clarity.

Uncover your Life Mission and Purpose

1.	Have an honest look at your natural abilities and skills. They say a lot about how you can best contribute to the world.
2.	Think of times when you felt joy in your heart. What were you doing, and with whom? These are hints of roles and settings that may bring you great life satisfaction.
3.	Look at past decisions that made you happy, and the drivers behind your choices.
4.	Remember tasks you have done where you simply lost track of time and felt energized.
5.	Consider activities, hobbies, magazines, or books that you enjoy.
6.	Pay attention to the reasons your family, friends, and colleagues call on you. This tells much of the greatness they see in you.
7.	Participate in a career orientation program to gain more information on career options.
8.	Ask family, friends, and colleagues what they think your life purpose is. Be inspired by their insights, but most importantly, listen to your heart.
9.	Consult an inspiring coach or mentor who can help you gain clarity.
10.	Volunteer, take a class, practice a new sport, or find a new job. Quite often, it is through action that we find our life purpose and direction.
11.	Unwind your mind and listen to your inner voice. Oftentimes answers are hidden in your heart.
12.	Reflect on values that are most important to you. These could include acceptance, care, cooperation, faith, generosity, health, integrity, learning, and service.

A flower is a joy to behold, but a bouquet

of flowers is magic. You are the flower,

the world is the bouquet.

By answering why your mission matters, you have just stated your life purpose. Know in confidence that not only has God placed aspirations in your heart, but He has given you the power to achieve them. Your co-creative powers can turn any desire into reality. By following your heart, your life will be less about struggles, and more about manifesting who you are meant to be and what you are meant to do. With soulful purpose, you will be heading towards a path of passion and success.

In the eyes of God, you are a being of great value, a divine expression of His life. In you resides a unique aroma that is meant to be a delight to those around you. When you fulfill your life mission and purpose, you release your sweet scent into the universe. You live with enthusiasm, passion, and energy. Not only do you happily transform *your* world, but you transform *the* world.

If you don't like what you have created so far with your LEGO building blocks, start all over again. If you haven't played with your LEGO set in a long time, take out the box, shake off the dust, and be creative. It's time to inject some passion into your life. You might say, "Well, I don't have a lot of LEGO varieties in my box. I can't create anything out of the ordinary."

Having five or twenty LEGO bricks, doing grand or small things, being tall or short, with brown or blue eyes, is not of the greatest importance. What matters is for you to connect with your *Marvelous Nature* and be all that you can be. If you have lots of LEGO pieces in your box, you can always share some pieces with others and help them build treasures in their lives. Sharing is love in action. So simple, yet so powerful.

Share a smile, a laugh, information, knowledge, and financial resources. Sharing replaces disappointments with hope. It speeds up recovery from tragedies and provides responses to unanswered questions. When you connect and reach out to someone else, you open the door to new possibilities in other people's lives. To sum it up, you are gifted with talents, skills, and capacities, and you hold the power to build treasures with your LEGO set and create a better world for you and others today and tomorrow. You are the rays of light that brighten the universe. Open your LEGO box and start creating your best life today.

Empower Your Life

Greater clarity on your vision of success, mission, and purpose empowers your life with better direction to move you into action with inspiration and passion. It drives how you live your life, the career choices you make, the attention you give to your spiritual growth, your community involvement, and how you care for your relationships and yourself.

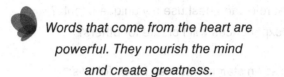

Words that come from the heart are powerful. They nourish the mind and create greatness.

Writing down your vision, mission, and purpose statements and reading them each day reminds you of what you are in the process of creating in your life, and why it matters. It truly gives you momentum to direct your actions towards your desires. In just a few words, you express your aspirations, what you intend to do and why. Clear, concise, and value-driven, each of your statements should be short and easy to remember. Covering all areas of your life, your vision of success may have more than one or two lines. Below are questions to refresh your memory and help you compose them.

Vision of Success – A statement of your aspirations for each of your life areas. Remember to end your statement with the words *"this or something better"* to signify your vision has the *W. D. Factor.*

 –   What are my aspirations?
 –   What outcomes am I striving for?

A sample statement of a vision of success for all areas of life may look like this:

> *I live a healthy life and nurture myself daily. Embraced by God's love, I help others create their best life and experience greater well-being. I create richness in my life and in the lives of those around me. Driven by the desire of work-life harmony, I cherish my personal relationships. I care for planet earth, and I am determined to create a better today and tomorrow. This or something better.*

Life Mission – A statement of what you intend to do and the experiences you want to create.

- In what role can I best use my unique talents?
- What experiences will I create for others?

Sample mission statements may be as follows:

- Be a caring parent for my children to live happy and fruitful lives.
- Provide inspiring coaching services for people to gain clarity and live a fulfilling life.
- Deliver valuable nutrition advice to enable people to make healthy choices.
- Provide medical expertise with care and devotion for patients to feel comfortable and be encouraged.
- Build wealth by providing wise investing services.

Life Purpose – A statement of the reason why you are motivated to serve your mission.

- Why do I want to do this?
- Why does it matter?

Sample life purpose statements may look like this:

- Empower my child to be all that he can be.
- Learn and help people be the success they are meant to be.
- Educate people for them to live a healthier life.
- Nurse people back to health for them to enjoy life.
- Help people create wealth.

As you journey through life, your views may change. Your vision may change, and so may your life mission and purpose. Revisit each of your statements as needed to align them with who you want to be and what you aspire to achieve. Well-defined vision, mission, and purpose statements act as lighthouse keepers as you navigate the sea of life with enthusiasm.

Shut Up the *I Can't* Voice

You are the movie writer, director, and producer of your destiny. If you have a desire in your heart, it means you have the resources to create it. Flirt for a moment with the idea of your desires becoming alive. Close your eyes and see your new reality on the screen of your mind. How does that make you feel? Do you feel the excitement?

A simple positive thought is the spark that ignites the manifestation of your desires. It ignites the transformation process and creates a chain reaction that produces positive results. By focusing on what you want, your thoughts produce high vibrations in the energy space, with feelings of excitement, passion, and hope in your body that move you into action.

If you don't like your life as it is now, challenge your thoughts and beliefs. Do you believe you hold the power to pursue your dreams? What is constantly in your mind? Your wants, or your do not wants? Are you constantly bullied by barrier thoughts that say: *I don't have what it takes to be a success, I don't have skills and money, I am doomed to stay where I am, or I once failed and I will fail again?*

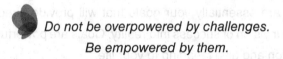

Do not be overpowered by challenges.
Be empowered by them.

With your *Be Happy* app, you become a master of the mind, and you easily shut up the *I can't voice*. You choose better-feeling thoughts and beliefs about yourself. You say good-bye to hopelessness, boredom, discouragement, frustration, resentment, failure, and fear, and say hello to your aspirations, fulfillment, deep joy, and appreciation. Your whole being offers high vibrations in the energy space.

You are the *Marvelous You*, and you are armed to live your best life. By keeping your thoughts in alignment with your desires, you gain better control over your life. You are no longer a victim controlled by life, circumstances, or actions of others. You are a conqueror living victoriously in full freedom and control over your thoughts and actions.

In this state of consciousness, you wake up these desires of yours, and you shout out loud: "I can bring to pass my wish list! I am the *Marvelous Me* and I have what it takes! I have talents and I am open to developing new skills! I am strong in Him and I am a success!" With your mind captive by good-feeling thoughts, you move with great momentum towards your dreams. Your life is filled with hope, enthusiasm, passion, courage, and love.

Get ready to shake off your negative and limitless thoughts and rise up! It's time for your best life to flourish, and for you to become the best that you can be. Get excited about living your aspirations. Let me hear your *I can* voice.

Move to the Creative Plane

Being from God and in God, you are connected to Pure Creativity, Infinite Knowledge, and Divine Wisdom. You hold the power within you to allow your life to flourish and live your deepest aspirations. Now, take your brush and design your *hows*.

Your *hows* are essentially your goals that will provide direction and focus to turn your vision of success into reality. Goals are powerful, as they spur you to action and give meaning to your life.

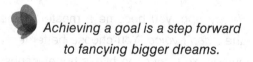

*Achieving a goal is a step forward
to fancying bigger dreams.*

With your *True Inspiration* turned on, take some time to assess your personal strengths and weaknesses in each area of your life: physical, spiritual, professional, financial, relationships, personal growth, environmental, and community involvement. This reflection will help you define areas around which your goals will be developed.

Ask yourself the following questions:

- Am I happy with my life? What do I really want?
- How is my work inspiring?
- How can I better myself? What new skills can I learn?
- How can I best contribute to society?
- Do I experience work-life harmony? Am I physically healthy?
- Is my future financially secure?

By using the goal-setting *S.I.M.P.L.E. Criteria*, you will set stretch goals that are a true reflection of who you are meant to be. Easy to measure, they will drive positive actions. Inspiring and aligned with your life purpose, you will likely move in the direction of your wants. Not only will you transform your life, but you will bring betterment into the lives of others. As a result, your goals will keep you excited and engaged.

Goal-Setting *S.I.M.P.L.E. Criteria*		
S	Stretching	Dare to be all that you can be, and set goals that are challenging and will cause growth and improvement.
I	Inspiring	Listen to your inner voice to choose meaningful goals that reflect what you truly want.
M	Measurable	Let your goals be measurable and time-bound to help you monitor your progress.
P	Purpose-Driven	Set goals that are well-aligned with your life purpose.
L	Life-Changing	Choose goals that bring novelty to your life and make a positive difference in the lives of others.
E	Engaging	Make sure your goals instill passion and are engaging.

There is much power in *S.I.M.P.L.E.* goals to move you in the direction of your vision of success. Stretch goals allow you to discover who you truly are: a being of expansion. They enable you to unleash the many truths of your *Marvelous Nature,* your own uniqueness, confidence, courage, and passion.

Heart-inspired goals are those that matter most to you. By calming your mind and listening to your inner voice, you hear guidance from Spirit. In conceiving from the heart, you will create greatness with more ease. With measurable goals that are time-targeted, you will better monitor progress and celebrate mini-successes along the journey.

By paying attention to your inner voice and the omens scattered along your path, you receive divine guidance on your life purpose. Purpose-driven goals are those that align with your mission and life purpose. Choosing fulfilling goals that transform not only your life but the lives of those around you translates into a more fruitful life. Passionate about creating your best life, you set engaging goals that will ignite the spark of success.

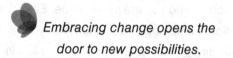

Embracing change opens the
door to new possibilities.

Some find the goal-setting exercise relatively easy to do. They follow their heart and have great clarity on what they want to achieve. Some others struggle a little more; they simply need to connect to their *Marvelous Nature* to get momentum and be the success they are meant to be. Remember that you are the owner of your life, and you have full responsibility to live your best life. If you are lacking ideas for goal setting, let yourself be inspired by the following vision of success goals.

Vision of Success Goals

Life Areas	Goals
Physical	<ul><li>Exercise twice a week.</li><li>Make healthier food choices daily.</li><li>Reduce calories to lose eight pounds in two months.</li></ul>
Spiritual	<ul><li>Read one inspiring book every two months.</li><li>Attend an inspirational lecture once a month.</li><li>Read daily motivational quotes.</li></ul>
Professional/ Business	<ul><li>Be promoted to supervisor in the next year.</li><li>Improve performance with the use of technology tools.</li><li>Attend a writing class in the fall.</li></ul>
Financial	<ul><li>Contribute to a savings plan each month.</li><li>Find a second job in the next month for extra money.</li><li>Diversify investments for a better rate of return.</li></ul>
Relationships	<ul><li>Meet new people each week by participating in an activity or attending an event.</li><li>Take personal time twice a week with my spouse.</li><li>Spend one-on-one time with my children each week.</li></ul>
Leisure Time	<ul><li>Enjoy a trip once a year.</li><li>Learn or practice a sport twice a week.</li><li>Spend time with friends each week.</li></ul>
Environmental	<ul><li>Buy a home in two years.</li><li>Clean up my drawers over the next two months.</li><li>Build a patio during the summer.</li></ul>
Legacy	<ul><li>Get involved with a charity four hours per week.</li><li>Donate money each month to humanitarian causes.</li><li>Make a humanitarian trip during the summer.</li></ul>

Let me answer some questions you may have surrounding goal setting. How many goals should I have?

I suggest you develop a five-year goal plan, which will become the basis for your annual goal setting. Your five-year plan may include short-term goals to be completed within a year, and those that span over a longer period. With the identification of a timeline for each goal, you will be able to define in which year the goals will be on your radar.

It is better to have fewer goals and achieve them than to have several left uncompleted. Take the time to assess the level of effort associated with your goals. This will give you a better sense of how many goals you can pursue each year based on your available time.

Prioritize the areas of your life that need development or more attention. For example, your health and finances may need more attention and may require more than one annual goal.

Someone moving up the corporate ladder may require focusing on at least one goal for each of the career development pillars such as performance, excellence, uniqueness, and growth. To sum it up, be realistic, and set a number of goals that you truly believe are reasonable and attainable.

Why not prepare a 10-year plan?

There is nothing wrong with nourishing a long-term vision for your life in your heart. Ten years is a long time, and in a fast-paced and changing environment, your goals and plans may change drastically over time. Considering the time investment needed to prepare a life plan, it is best to assess every five years or so where you are, what your next destination is, and how you will get there.

How about stretch goals; how difficult should they be?

You want to become all that you can be, yet resist the urge of setting goals that are too easy. Stretch goals allow you to discover your full potential. Set learning goals if you note skill deficits that limit the achievement of your desires.

How do I handle long-term goals? What is the best way to achieve them?

It is best to break down goals that span over a number of years into smaller goals that will be included in your annual action plan to carry you to your destination of success. As you succeed in smaller goals, you will build confidence and momentum.

Now that I have set my goals, what's next?

You will activate your *High Drive* app and design a successful action plan that aligns with your goals to move towards your vision of success with good-feeling thoughts, positive beliefs, and well-planned actions.

What can I do to reinforce my commitment and consistency to pursuing my goals?

You need to understand that you deserve all the best. You have probably heard this old English proverb: "Where there's a will, there's a way." If you believe in the power of your *Marvelous Nature*, you will commit to your goals and transform your life. Reading or mentally reciting your vision, mission, and life statements, as well as your goals, at least once a day, will bring about feelings of excitement for what is to come and reinforce your commitment. Don't forget to empower the process with daily visualization. With the eyes of your imagination, you give life to the manifestation process. You see yourself moving in the direction of your desires. You sense the experience and feel the joy and appreciation of manifesting your vision. With visualization comes more confidence, motivation, and well-being.

In being focused and engaged, you will direct your energy to the achievement of your goals and will reach your destination of success with more ease and in less time.

Step Out of Your Comfort Zone

The stretch goal concept was introduced by American Jack Welch during General Electric's golden years as he asked workers to reach beyond what they had achieved the year before. Historically, the stretch goal concept was not used solely to drive growth, but to incite workers to think outside the box. The concept was to force people to look at issues from different angles and become more creative.[4]

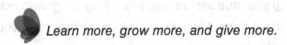 *Learn more, grow more, and give more.*

Stepping out of your comfort zone forces you to collaborate with others, be creative, and find new ways of doing things. When you expand out of your comfort zone, you see yourself growing and deepening your skills, talents, and creativity. With expansion comes new discoveries, excitement, and satisfaction.

Many companies have now embraced stretch goals as part of their employee performance measurement process. Setting stretch goals was key for me to move up the corporate ladder. It forced me to focus on what I wanted to accomplish in the year, and to lay out my strategy to reach my mid- and long-term goals. It allowed me to grow as a person, deepen my knowledge and skills, discover my gifts, tackle challenges, reach bigger goals, and learn perseverance, teamwork, quality work, and so much more.

Many very successful people did not have immediate success in their lives. Some started with just very small businesses and worked really hard to grow them. Others were told they would never succeed. Some others went broke a few times. What paid off was their commitment, self-control, and tenacity in pursuing their desires.

Oftentimes the fear of failure or the unknown keeps us from setting stretch goals. The antidote is to dream big. Don't be afraid to take a leap of faith; you were born to learn and grow. Reflect on the character traits you would like to develop, what you would like to achieve this year, in five, and ten years.

Learning a new skill, changing a behavior, or starting a new venture is not always easy, but enthusiasm combined with commitment makes perfect. As written by German philosopher Johann Wolfgang von Goethe, "Everything is hard before it is easy." Don't let a negative experience stop you from trying again and again.

Be daring with your goals. Let the unknown be an exciting challenge. You will discover secrets about yourself. You will experience life to its fullest. By fulfilling your true aspirations, you will create growth not only for yourself, but for those around you. From now on, choose to let your seeds of greatness flourish. In achieving more, you become more.

Reprogram Dysfunctional Beliefs

The subconscious mind stores your hidden beliefs, past memories, learned values, good feelings and bad ones. These include pain, anxiety, or conflict. Past memories and hidden beliefs continue to influence your behavior, even though you are unaware of their influence. While not visible to the eyes, your beliefs are made visible by the fruits of your life. What you believe drives who you choose to be and what you create in your life. Setting goals is initiated in your conscious mind, but implementation is largely dependent on your subconscious mind, where your hidden beliefs reside. Both your conscious and subconscious mind must be in coherence for you to create your wants. If not in alignment, the powerful force of your subconscious mind will keep you from moving ahead. Dysfunctional beliefs and negative emotions will paralyze you and prevent you from being all that you can be.

 Only a clear intention well aligned with your beliefs moves you into action.

Limiting beliefs can range from thinking life is hard and money is scarce, to not being good enough, not lovable, and not intelligent, and so many more. If you don't like what you have become and created in your life, dig deeper into your beliefs to see if they are well-aligned with your desires. You may find all sorts of limited beliefs that hinder change from taking place.

Dysfunctional beliefs may be inherited from your parents, friends, teachers, and even society, or they may be rooted in past experiences that have left you with feelings of unworthiness. They may clutter your subconscious mind, leading you to be disengaged, stumble day after day, fail, or be stuck in a rut. They may hinder you from fully affirming your *Marvelous Self*, keeping you away from the great life you are entitled to live.

You deserve to step beyond disempowering beliefs and false concepts and be all that you are. Have the courage to say no to a life that is not a testimony to your greatness. You owe it to yourself to live on a path of wholeness, engagement, excitement, and passion. You deserve to live to the fullest and contribute constructively. When you gain awareness as to who you truly are, the *Marvelous You*, you will empower yourself with new beliefs about yourself and the life you can create.

You are endowed with freedom to choose your beliefs and values. If you are plagued with beliefs and values that no longer resonate with you, then take charge and choose to counteract their effects. While past beliefs can't be removed, you can create new ones to actualize the exciting life you deserve. By keeping your conscious mind busy with good-feeling thoughts, you are giving wings to your life to soar to a place of creativity, passion, happiness, love, peace, success, and wealth.

Start by reflecting on new beliefs that would move you in the direction of your desires. Then plant these new beliefs in your mind with the help of any of the following techniques: positive affirmations, visualization, subliminal messages, self-hypnosis, hypnosis, and *One Step Plus One*.

Positive Affirmations – By reading aloud or reciting mentally positive affirmations about your *Marvelous Nature* each day, renewed thoughts are transferred to your subconscious mind and stored as your new beliefs. For example, you may want to say, "I am the *Marvelous Me*, embraced by God's divine love. Seeds of greatness are in me and I am making them grow. I am creativity, wisdom, and passion. I am courageous in the face of obstacles. I aspire to be all that I can be. My life is abundant in every way. I am delighted to be a channel for financial prosperity."

Your words should not feel forced, and they should flow easily from within. The process is even more powerful when your affirmations resonate and vibrate within you, and they trigger positive emotions such as glee, confidence, and excitement. If you prefer, you may use words that reflect your engagement in the creation process. For example, "I am actualizing my *Marvelous Nature*. The seeds of greatness that are in me are growing each and every day. I am living each day with creativity, wisdom, and passion. I am creating richness in my life and sharing with those in need."

Let your heart be rich in praise. With a grateful heart, thank God for all your blessings and what is to come. With faith comes the power of transforming the impossible to possible.

Visualization – Empower the benefits of reading your *Marvelous You* affirmations with daily visualization. Close your eyes and visualize each attribute of your *Marvelous Nature*. With more awareness of who you truly are, you experience wholeness and well-being.

46

With new beliefs about yourself, both your conscious and subconscious mind are restored. Attuned to the voice of Spirit, your life choices bring you closer to the *Marvelous You* that you are, and away from the *Powerless You.* Your tiny inner spark becomes a radiant star that shines in the universe.

Subliminal Messages – Subliminal messages are words, images, or sounds that your mind receives without consciously being aware of them, but your subconscious mind notices them. Easy to use and practical, subliminal audio-recordings are the favorite technique of many to add new beliefs. They can easily be found in bookstores and on the web. If you worry about the messages hidden within the recordings, you can create your own messages.[5]

Self-Hypnosis – Self-hypnosis is reported by many as another effective way to reprogram your beliefs and strengthen your self-esteem. Some use the technique wide awake, while others prefer to induce their subconscious mind with positive affirmations when entering a sleepy state, when their mind and body are more relaxed.

An alternative to buying recordings is to create your own messages. While some people report success with self-hypnosis audios, others may find only a partial change. In such cases, hypnosis may be another option to explore.[6]

Hypnosis – Hypnosis is a technique similar to self-hypnosis but involves the interaction of someone else who provides the suggestions. The technique has been proven beneficial in treating anxiety, eating disorders, sleep disorders, compulsive gaming, post-traumatic stress, smoking, and weight management. Hypnosis works differently on people. For some, change is rapid; for others, not as sudden. Should you consider working with a hypnotist, inquire on their qualifications and accreditation with a relevant professional organization.[7]

One Step Plus One – *One Step Plus One* is the name I have given to the technique of reprogramming beliefs through small success actions. Mini-goals set a path towards small victories that become a great source of inspiration to dream and fulfill bigger dreams. Each step with a positive outcome creates a change in belief that the impossible is possible. They create an *I can* attitude that in turn motivates people to accomplish more.

I have known Mary for a little more than 10 years, and for a long time she had difficulties losing weight. When she was a little girl, she dreamed of being a ballerina. But her dream was crushed when her teacher told her she would never be a ballerina because she was not thin enough, and it was not in her genetic makeup to be naturally thin.

This thought found a place in her subconscious mind. So diet after diet, Mary could never lose weight, until one day when she understood that this belief was untrue, and her subconscious mind needed to be reprogrammed. Since then, she has reached a healthy weight.

When you soar to a higher level of consciousness and choose to replace limited beliefs with a vision of new possibilities, you allow your true essence to rise from within and flow freely. With renewed thoughts, you realign yourself with who you truly are, the *Marvelous You.* You choose to believe that you are pure creativity, connected to God, who co-creates with you.

With new beliefs in your heart, you boldly pursue your true aspirations with courage, confidence, and passion. You free yourself from self-doubt, discouragement, and turmoil, and you are hopeful for tomorrow. You swiftly close the box when old negative beliefs try to peek out.

By reinforcing your new beliefs, your behavior, your life, and the world around you will change. Loneliness will be replaced by new friendships. Financial scarcity will be replaced by wealth. Failure will be replaced by success. Unhealthy relationships will be replaced by great ones. Don't let your past define your future. You deserve to be the best that you can be, and you hold the power to do it.

Embrace Who You Are

As you engage in your goal-setting process, embrace who you are—your values, and what you really want in life—not what others have, are, or want you to be. Reflect on your life, where you want to go, what is important to you, what you want to achieve, the experiences you want to create, and the material possessions you would like to have.

Ask yourself: What do I really want out of life? What does it mean for me to have this or do that? Do this exercise for each area of your life. Take time to write the answers down, as it makes the goal-setting process real. You might say: "I am not good with goals. My New Year's resolutions are always out the door in no time."

You are a born creator. You are the *Marvelous You*, with all that is needed to create a great life for yourself and those around you. When your life lacks passion, accomplishments, and results, it's simply because you have forgotten or were not aware of your *Marvelous Nature*.

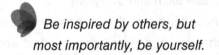 *Be inspired by others, but most importantly, be yourself.*

To achieve faster and greater success, your goals need to be meaningful to you. They need to align with who you are and your values. Look at your strengths, weaknesses, skills, interests, and areas for development. Embrace who you are with your physical features, intellectual capacities, and personality traits.

Sometimes career aspirations do not manifest themselves because we can't change who we are. You may be able to enhance your appearance, learn new skills, improve your mental skills, or change personality traits, but it may not be enough. Some careers are very selective, with efforts and abilities being two different things.

For example, some people are just not tall enough or do not have the physical traits that modeling agencies are looking for. While really good, some young hockey players do not make their dream team as there are better scorers or faster skaters available at that particular time.

Rejection is hard because you have to let go of a dream not meant to be. It's a loss that can deeply affect you, and you need to give yourself time to heal. Emotional healing comes when you accept your limitations but see your own beauty, unique talents, and abilities.

To accept who you are with all your gifts and limitations will free you from the pain of rejection. Rejection is not a message of failure. Oftentimes it is a door that closes for something better to come into your life. Focus on what you have, not on what you do not have. Moved by a spirit of gratefulness, you will let yourself be excited by another dream and keep a positive outlook.

Open Your Treasure Chest

I like to say that life is a treasure chest filled with riches that are your aspirations, experiences, successes, loved ones, and all those simple little joys of life that you create each and every day.

As you experience life, bury all your positive experiences in your treasure chest. Each day, open your treasure chest and celebrate the growth you've made, your successes, special moments with family and friends, the knowledge you've gained, the gifts you have, the better control you have over your finances, and the love you share and receive.

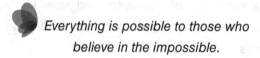 *Everything is possible to those who believe in the impossible.*

When you look into your treasure chest, you reinforce your beliefs in success, reminding yourself of your past wins, the possibilities that are in you, and the beauties of life. Self-confidence is key to personal success. With confidence comes positive emotions that move you forward. Believing in yourself is a powerful choice that allows you to accomplish great things and be a success. Celebrating small and big wins is a great way to build self-confidence.

With your beliefs well-aligned with your aspirations, you are moving towards goal achievement at a faster pace. Nothing will stop you, not even an obstacle. As you move into action, insecurities, self-doubt, and limiting beliefs have no power over you the moment you open your treasure chest. Positive memories are there to remind you that you are a wonderful being with great potential—creative, confident, and fearless. Past successes are in front of your eyes, reminding you that you can succeed, and reinforcing your beliefs that your desires can become reality. You have showed success in the past and you will show it again.

Take time each day to be grateful and celebrate your day's victories, small and big. My favorite time to do this is before going to bed or before closing my computer for the day. Write down in your success journal all that you are grateful for, tell a friend, treat yourself, and thank those who support you.

Sometimes life may appear unfair, and some events just can't be changed. Faced with dark plights, acceptance is the way to freedom and lightness. Smile even if you are acting. Smiling makes your heart smile. By developing a positive attitude, you face challenges with more grace. You welcome life's surprises with more ease. You see each moment as an opportunity to learn, grow, and improve. By letting your predominant thoughts be positive, you accept that everything is there for a reason. You see life with a brighter lens.

So many people fail to recognize that they are here to express their *Marvelous Essence,* and they forget that they are resilient, courageous, and never alone. With a positive attitude, challenges become opportunities to improve, advance, expand who you are, and enrich your life, not oppress it. From this state of positive expectations blossoms success.

There is no such thing as failure, only a better understanding of what works and what doesn't. Standing on past successes, you build confidence and accelerate your next success. You move on to bigger dreams. Below is my *Up to The Top Technique* to increase confidence, tackle great challenges, and celebrate your achievements, one step at a time. I have used this technique many times in managing large projects and had great success with it.

Up to The Top Technique	
1.	Learn everything that will make the climb easier.
2.	Get all the material resources you need.
3.	Surround yourself with a great and enthusiastic climbing team.
4.	Map out the expedition in mini mountain climbs.
5.	Stop at base camps to celebrate all successes.
6.	If you face obstacles, stay calm and committed.
7.	Let your mind be filled with feel-good thoughts at all times.
8.	Keep your eyes on the mountaintop, and continue the climb.
9.	Celebrate your victory.

So, get ready to climb and reach the top. I'll see you there soon!

Be Ready to Expand

Life is all about expansion. As you expand your horizons, you grow. As you live new experiences, your subconscious mind expands. As you expand your awareness, you soar to new heights of consciousness.

As I live new experiences, my subconscious mind expands. As your neighbor lives new experiences, his subconscious mind expands. According to some cosmologists, even the universe is designed to expand.[8] We are interconnected. We all expand.

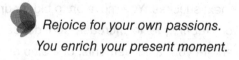

Rejoice for your own passions.
You enrich your present moment.

As you are from God and in God, goodness is in your spirit. You are wired for more goodness and less hardship. Look at how you relate to money. Do you want less money? Of course not; you want more. How about health and free time? Do you want less? The answer is no and no; you want more. You are joy and goodness in expansion.

You are pure potential ready to expand. You are a powerful creator equipped to create the desires of your heart. You have the key to releasing your full potential. All is there inside of you to develop, pursue your goals and interests, and improve your life.

You are born to expand your capacities, blossom, and realize your *Marvelous Nature*. Do more of what you love. Be grateful for who you are, for all that you have accomplished so far. Be proud of yourself. Turn the power on and expand your life for more glee, love, success, and well-being.

You no longer need to compare yourself with others and feel threatened, superior, or inferior. You are the *Marvelous You*, secure and free to be all that you are. Appreciate the accomplishments and great beauty you see in others, but most importantly, love yourself and be grateful for your own gifts. Be excited for today and tomorrow. Be a source of inspiration.

CHAPTER 3

Power Up Your Strategy

*Strategic thinking is what moves you
from second to first place.*

Activate Your *High Drive* App

Many people have wonderful aspirations for their future, but far too many do not pursue them. Unlike visionaries who are driven to create, grow, and expand, many are passive observers of life, waiting for change to materialize with no effort. Not actively involved in creating their desires, their lives lack fulfillment, enthusiasm, satisfaction, and passion. Why is that? Simply put, their *High Drive* app is not turned on.

 Success becomes alive with action.

Who do you want to be: a visionary, or a passive observer of life? If being a visionary is your answer, then activate your *High Drive* app today and stop going around in circles. With *High Drive* you are no longer waiting for your life to change. You are fully present in creating your life, leaving the past behind. You claim your full power, leading you to actively pursue the desires of your heart. You are motivated to craft a roadmap to get you to your destination in less time. You are passionate about using your gifts and skills to better your life and the lives of those around you. You figure out ingenious initiatives to achieve your desires. With your contingency plan in hand, you are not intimidated by proadblocks.

With *High Drive*, you release the hand brake and move into action with commitment, self-control, and perseverance to live your best life. You are excited to be alive, speeding ahead with high productivity and effectiveness. You increase power when going up a hill, and celebrate each milestone towards your destination.

Buckled up, you enjoy the ride. With a positive outlook on life, you race ahead and maintain your vision. Why wait any longer? Turn on your *High Drive* app and get ready for an amazing ride. See you soon on the road to success!

Craft Your Vision of Success Plan

Now is the time to be confident and say, "I am ready to craft my action plan and manifest my desires." Developing an action plan is the key that opens the door for all possibilities to come alive.

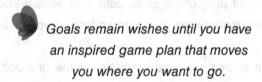

*Goals remain wishes until you have
an inspired game plan that moves
you where you want to go.*

Start by challenging your vision of success goals and be truly honest in answering these questions: Am I motivated by my goals? What do they mean to me? Are these goals relevant to where I want to go in my life? Do they align with my beliefs and values? If your goals don't deliver excitement and passion, simply change them. If they fire you up, move on to the next step of developing a five-year action plan.

With your goals well-identified and prioritized, you are now ready to answer the *what, by when, and how many* questions that will help you create your five-year action plan.

What Activity – There may be more than one path to achieve your goals. Start by weighing in possible actions and choose activities/tasks that best resonate with you. Pay attention to how you feel about each possibility.

As said earlier, guidance can be found in feelings. Actions to consider may include people to contact, courses to take, books to read, or any other activities that may bring you closer to your goals. Consider breaking down tedious tasks in sub-activities to render them more manageable.

What Resources – Now, have a look at the resources—financial, material, and human—required to perform the chosen activities. If some goals involve the participation of other people, write down who will be responsible to perform the activities under your supervision.

By When – Then, indicate the expected start and completion date of your goals.

How Many – Lastly, write down how many times per day, per week, and per month you will carry out the activities/tasks.

Once your five-year plan is completed, you can now focus on the last step, which is to prepare your annual action plan. Derived from your five-year plan, your annual action plan details your goals for the year to come; activities to be completed and their frequency, needed resources, and time frame. Assessing your progress against both your annual and five-year plans helps you define your next-year plan and revisit your five-year plan as needed.

You may want to use a simple template as the one John used to capture key elements of your next-year plan. John is a university student who works part-time. He is single, and would love to meet his dream girl. Living a healthy life and having financial success are his two areas of focus.

PHYSICAL	
Desire	Great physical health and vitality.
Goal	Lose eight pounds in two months.
Activities	Exercise more regularly at the gym.
Resources	$80 for a two-month gym membership.
Time Frame	October and November.
Frequency	Three times per week.

PROFESSIONAL	
Desire	Fulfilling career.
Goal	Complete a bachelor of commerce degree in three years' time.
Activities	Attend university classes, work part-time to pay tuition fees.
Resources	$10,000 per year for tuition.
Time Frame	Next three years.
Frequency	Fall and spring semester weekly classes.

FINANCIAL	
Desire	Wealth and financial abundance.
Goal	Contribute $25 monthly to a savings plan.
Activities	Arrange for fund transfers to a savings plan.
Resources	-
Time Frame	Over the next year.
Frequency	Monthly.

RELATIONSHIPS	
Desire	True companionships and relationships.
Goal	Meet new people each week.
Activities	Do various activities: sport, gym, museum, etc.
Resources	$25 per week to cover activity costs.
Time Frame	Over the next year.
Frequency	Weekly.

With your *True Inspiration* and *High Drive* apps activated, listen to your inner voice for creative ideas, insights, and guidance to formulate your plan. Get ready to map out your itinerary for an exciting journey on the path to success.

Develop a Contingency Plan

Having an action plan does not mean there will be no roadblocks along the journey. No need to get overwhelmed by a flat tire or little bumps in the road. Do not get bitter or discouraged if you face obstacles or if things don't happen as planned. What looks like an obstacle may be an opportunity to grow. Stay strong and motivated. You are fully equipped to cope with and handle life's surprises, as you have set a contingency plan designed to resolve problems swiftly to get to your destination safely.

I remember when I was a university student, interested by the business world. I was studying to become a Certified Professional Accountant (CPA), and my back-up plan was to study for a master of business administration degree if I was unsuccessful in the exams. I knew that being a CPA was not the only way for me to have a rewarding business career.

Having a back-up plan kept my mind at peace, giving me an option to fall back on if my dream did not materialize. It allowed me to focus all my energies on my goal without worrying. With hard work, my dream of becoming a CPA became reality.

While you journey, you may encounter roadblocks simply because others have different intentions than yours. For example, you may be a layoff survivor because your past employer underwent a reorganization or downsizing. In addition to having to deal with feelings of sadness, guilt, or fear, you are now left to find a new path to your destination.

Back-up plans are great to avoid turmoil internally and externally. They provide different paths to reach your destination and make the journey more flexible. They allow possible barriers to be mitigated by developing solutions that can quickly be activated.

Some might ask, "Isn't this self-defeating thinking?" If you concentrate 20 percent of the time on the problem and 80 percent on the solution, you are in creation mode. If you find yourself thinking about the problem 80 percent of the time and the solution 20 percent of the time, you are in negative mode, likely heading toward stagnation.

 What matters most is to reach your destination, not the path you travel.

Having a contingency plan is part of an effective strategic thinking and planning exercise. It allows you to reflect on possible problems and obstacles, explore alternatives, and prepare yourself for different possibilities. It makes you feel stronger and in better control. The world is changing at a fast pace, and a proactive attitude will move you faster to your destination. If the road is blocked, you can still get to your destination by choosing another path.

Now you are all set to go with your roadmap and contingency plan on hand. Let's get you on the road. Release the hand brake and move the selector lever out of the park position. Each day, drive a few miles towards your goals. Have a nice trip. You have all that it takes to address any urgencies.

Manage Your Day for High Productivity

Moving towards the achievement of your vision of success goals is a step-by-step journey. "There is always so much to do in a day, how can I get better organized?" you might ask with a feeling of discouragement. Planning the week and days ahead is an effective strategy to stop procrastination, accomplish your goals, better schedule your time, and maximize your productivity. Keep your *High Drive* app activated, stay on course, and travel at a good pace using my seven steps to successful weekly and daily planning.

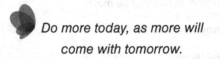

Do more today, as more will come with tomorrow.

With the help of a weekly activity planner, complete Steps 1 to 5 to have a glimpse of all the activities/tasks you wish to achieve in the week, and their respective timing. Working down from your weekly activity planner, follow the instructions at Step 6.

With a daily activity planner, identify activities for each day of the week, with their estimated time and priority. Prioritization is essential for effective time and conflict management. Complete Step 7 to record in your electronic or paper-based day planner prioritized activities, their timing, and estimated time.

With activity planners, you will remain focused and committed to your daily tasks. You will gain greater efficiency and accomplish more of what you want. You will move towards the achievement of your goals at a faster pace. To facilitate your time management, consider using the free weekly and daily activity planner templates offered on my company's website, www.jflinternational.com, in the Tools & Resources section.

		Successful Weekly and Daily Planning
W	1.	Review your vision of success plan for all areas of your life, as well as your detailed career or business plan, if you have prepared one. Write down all the activities you plan to do during the week.
E **E** **K**	2.	Think of what you need to do at home, at the office, in the community, and write down additional activities you need to tend to. Review appointments and meetings already recorded in your electronic or paper-based day planners.
L **Y**	3.	Block some time for unexpected events, requests, and glitches. Each day brings new requests and things to do, and planning for unexpected events allows for more flexibility in your schedule.
	4.	Indicate on which day of the week you plan to engage in the activities, meetings, and appointments.
	5.	Set a time for each activity, meeting, and appointment. Keep at least half an hour each day for unexpected events.
D **A** **I** **L** **Y**	6.	Too many activities in a day? Prioritize them with the following system: A. Urgent and cannot be moved. B. Urgent but can be moved. C. Not urgent. Align your most difficult tasks to times of the day when your energy level is at its peak. Make arrangements to move B and C activities into the next day or week, as necessary. Reconvene to an agreeable time frame with relevant parties.
	7.	Input your prioritized activities, timing, and estimated time in your electronic or paper-based day planner.

Sketching the week and days ahead can easily be done before leaving the office for the weekend, or during the weekend, as you see fit. As the day goes by, add new meetings and appointments in your day planner. At the end of the day, identify your non-completed tasks, and adjust your daily planner accordingly.

Be careful on how you manage *Time Stealers*. They can easily take you off course. These include looking at e-mails, reading the news, browsing on the Internet, sending messages on social media, and chatting with friends and colleagues. Each interruption steals five to ten minutes of your day, a few minutes to care for the activity, and a few minutes to get back to your work and refocus your thoughts. By weaving the following tips into your day, you will be proactive in managing *Time Stealers* to stay on schedule and limit delays.

- Set 15-minute break times two to three times a day for *Time Stealers* activities.
- Close your office door and use a *Do Not Disturb* card. Communicate to your team that you are not answering e-mails for the next two hours.
- If someone comes in your office, first determine if this is a time-sensitive or crisis issue. If the matter is not urgent, let them know you are tied up at the present moment, and set a time for a future meeting. Don't be shy to say no or delay a conversation until a later time, followed by the proper explanations.
- Have a voice mail on your business and private cell phones.
- Have an assistant go through your e-mails.

In addition, maintain a daily action and improvement log where you write down lessons learned, and two things you did during the day to advance towards your vision. A daily gratitude journal is another great tool to celebrate your successes and be grateful for your life. These tools are offered in the free Tools & Resources section of www.jflinternational.com, and they will help fill your life with a great sense of accomplishment and satisfaction.

Assess Your Progress

With *High Drive*, you move towards your vision with commitment, self-control, and perseverance. Assessing your progress towards your vision of success are mile markers on your journey. While traveling to your destination, rest at the pit stop each week to replenish and enjoy the satisfaction of your small and big wins. Write down your progress-to-date against each goal. Maintain distinct lines in your journal to track each week's progress or simply update your progress line week after week, as illustrated in John's progress report. Don't overlook rewarding yourself for all your successes, small and grand.

PHYSICAL	
Desire	Great physical health and vitality.
Goal	Lose eight pounds in two months.
Activities	Exercise more regularly at the gym.
Resources	$80 for a two-month gyms membership.
Time Frame	October and November.
Frequency	Three times per week.
Progress	Lost eight pounds in the two-month period.
Completed	Yes.

PROFESSIONAL	
Desire	Fulfilling career.
Goal	Complete a bachelor of commerce degree in three years' time.
Activities	Attend university classes, work part-time to pay tuition fees.
Resources	$10,000 per year for tuition.
Time Frame	Next three years.
Frequency	Fall and spring semester weekly classes.
Progress	One semester completed.
Completed	No.

FINANCIAL	
Desire	Wealth and financial abundance.
Goal	Contribute $25 monthly to a savings plan.
Activities	Contact financial institution and arrange for fund transfers to a savings plan.
Resources	-
Time Frame	Over the next year.
Frequency	Monthly.
Progress	Set aside $80 in four months.
Completed	No.

RELATIONSHIPS	
Desire	True companionships and relationships.
Goal	Meet new people each week.
Activities	Do various activities: sport, gym, museum, etc.
Resources	$25 per week to cover activity costs.
Time Frame	Over the next year.
Frequency	Weekly.
Progress	Able to do only two activities per month over the past four months.
Completed	No.

If you are not getting the results you were expecting, don't give up on your desires and goals. If you hit a roadblock, readily accept the obstacle. Look your fears right in the eye. Don't let your emotions stop you.

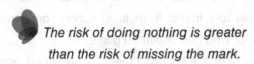

The risk of doing nothing is greater than the risk of missing the mark.

Keep your *True Inspiration* and *High Drive* apps activated. Look at your contingency plan, and explore new ideas and possibilities. Notice any skills that may be lacking, and what needs to be done differently. Once you have done this exercise objectively and positively, choose a new path and move forward.

Don't get stuck in a rut; get going, and take some new steps. Change is good. Embrace it and own it, with all its new experiences. Complaining without actions will get you nowhere. With resolve, motivation, and discipline, commit to your destination, even if you have to slow down your pace. Update your action plan to reflect new priorities, and change goals that no longer meet the *S.I.M.P.L.E. Criteria.*

Do not pressure yourself with time. Time will always be there; it's not going anywhere. It is better to achieve a goal than leave it incomplete. Goal accomplishment is a great confidence booster. You are the powerful creator. Take action, take risks, and be your best cheerleader.

Be Accountable

A research study on the effectiveness of goal setting was initiated by Dr. Gail Matthews, PhD, clinical psychologist at the Dominican University of California. The study was completed by 149 participants, recruited from businesses, organizations, and networking groups from the United States, Belgium, England, India, Australia, and Japan, and included a variety of entrepreneurs, educators, health care professionals, artists, attorneys, bankers, marketers, human services providers, managers, vice presidents, directors of non-profits, etc.[1] The study concluded that:

- Those who sent weekly progress reports to a friend accomplished significantly more than those who simply sent their action commitments to a friend, formulated action commitments, wrote their goals, or who had unwritten goals.
- Those who sent their commitments to a friend accomplished significantly more than those who wrote action commitments or did not write their goals.
- Those who wrote goals accomplished significantly more than those who did not write their goals.

*Celebrate your successes, stay focused, learn
from your experiences, and keep on going.
You will reach your destination over time.*

The combination of writing goals and accountability has been shown to be highly effective in goal achievement. Before you leave for your new destination, let a friend, a family member, a coach, a mentor, or a counselor know about your goals and your roadmap. The moment you let someone else know of your goals and commitments, you engage yourself on the road to success.

There is power behind public commitments. They bear energy that gives you drive to move to action. Even goals that seem frivolous, foolish, or larger than life should be shared with close friends. Who knows? You may find an ally who also believes in your dream and will collaborate to make it happen.

Celebrating your progress helps you remain positive during your journey. Sharing your progress with a friend, family member, coach, mentor, or counselor is a great way to keep you motivated and accountable.

Stay close to like-minded, empowering people who believe in your aspirations. We all need people in our lives who say, "If you need help, don't be afraid to ask. I am here for you." They are your greatest supporters who will encourage you and keep you motivated. There is so much power and momentum in asking and letting others use their gifts to contribute to our desires.

Own your creative power and stay motivated as you journey towards your vision of success. Turn the music on and enjoy the ride!

Shut Down Your Critical Voice

What kind of music do you listen to on your soul radio? Songs of hope, or songs of despair? If you want to hear songs of hope that inspire you with great ideas and excite you for life, then turn your radio to the *ICAN* radio station. You will get in the groove of creation and be excited about life. You will not be afraid of challenges; on the contrary, you will see them as

65

opportunities for growth and creativity to emerge. What you thought were dark moments will become moments of enlightenment where you will actualize your *Marvelous Nature.*

If you want despair in your life, then turn your radio to the *ICANT* radio station. On that radio station, you hear the same old "Life is so Hard" song that goes like this: "Life is so hard. I can't find a job. I can't make money. Life is so hard. I can't find a spouse. I can't find love. Life is so hard. I can't get healthy. Life is so hard. I can't go to college . . ." and it goes on and on like this.

While "I can't" is a short statement, it has a powerful influence on your feelings and the way you create your life. With self-defeating thoughts come negative feelings. When you sing the "Life is so Hard" song, your mind, soul, and spirit paralyze. You no longer have creative and positive thoughts. You do not dare to dream of a better tomorrow. You feel desperate. You do not take action. You are not inspired. Your heart is filled with fear and anxiety. If you want a shift in your feelings and are looking for change in your life, you need to turn your radio to the *ICAN* station and be empowered by the rhythm of the "Life is Good" song. You will soon become the best that you can be and express the *Marvelous You* that you are.

 First comes change in your mind,
then comes change in your life.

With the "Life is Good" song on your lips, there is no room for negative self-talk, and you sing: "Life is good. I climb mountains, one step at a time. Life is good. I forgive and let go of the past. Life is good. I enjoy life and live in the present. Life is good. I love with an open heart. Life is good. I am disciplined and committed to success. Life is good. I am the *Marvelous Me.* Life is good."

When you hear the "Life is Good" song, you can't help dreaming about your next projects. You are inspired, and have ideas on how to manifest your desires. You are not afraid to try and explore. You have faith in yourself, your desires, gifts, and talents. While in action, you are enthusiastic, knowing that all is good. You stand strong in your faith and you guard it in your heart.

Whenever your heart dances to the "Life is Good" song, you feel good about who you are and what you want. You are passionate and excited about life. If you commit a mistake or did not choose the right path, you are not overly critical of yourself. You learn what needs to be learned and you move on. You see setbacks for what they are: opportunities to learn and identify new paths to travel by, moments to make better choices, and occasions to be creative, confident, and perseverant.

When you keep the "Life is Good" song in your heart, you think beautiful thoughts about yourself, those around you, and life in general. There is joy, peace, and laughter in your heart. You have faith in God, and you trust that the impossible is indeed possible. You are not afraid to take a leap of faith.

Turn your soul radio to the *ICAN* radio station today, and enjoy inspiring and motivating music. Get in a creating groove, believe in your aspirations, be good to yourself, rejoice for tomorrow, trust in God's power, and be excited for all the good moments to come.

Let Feedback Be Your Friend

Asking for feedback from people you trust can provide you with valuable information, not only when you set your action plan, but when you assess your results. Asking for feedback from your peers, superiors, mentor, coach, spouse, kids, clients, and friends can make your personal and business relationships flourish. Nothing is off limits with feedback. You can ask for comments about a career choice, financial strategy, business process, client service, and behavioral aspects such as communication, leadership, strategic skills, or team-building abilities.

 Feedback is a meeting of the minds, where no one is right or wrong. It's a moment of reflection on the next best thing to do.

As part of their continuous professional development program, several companies use sophisticated feedback or appraisal tools to help their managers gain insights on their competencies and improve their performance. They either design their own tool or purchase feedback templates. I have used sophisticated performance feedback tools in the past and found them quite useful.

Yet, I like to complement the feedback exercise with my own *Do and Don't Feedback Questions* that generate substantial information for reflection, change, and growth. Easy to use, you can ask these two questions to people who are close to you: spouse, family, friends, and colleagues.

Do and Don't Feedback Questions	
1.	Is there anything that **I do** that you want me **not to do**?
2.	Is there anything that **I do not do** that you want me **to do**?

Get yourself a treasure with a mastermind group. I am blessed with a dear group of advisors whom I can reach out to at any time for input. I cherish their opinions, as they have my interest at heart. They provide me with great insights and ideas. Feedback is to be welcomed as an opportunity for growth. By paying attention to the positive feedback rules, you will enrich the experience.

Positive Feedback Rules	
1.	Be clear on the nature of the feedback you are looking for.
2.	Listen and remain open to both positive and negative critics. There is no need to start arguing your position at this time.
3.	Take time to ask for clarification as needed.
4.	Don't get angry at your advisors if you disagree with their comments.
5.	Thank people for their input.
6.	Reflect on the information and insights gained from the experience. Take the answers for what they are—a message towards something better.
7.	Be still and listen to the small voice in your heart. Follow what you think is right for you and change course as required.
8.	If something is not working, don't blame your advisors. Take full responsibility.
9.	If you messed up, apologize and make amends, then move on.
10.	Do not ignore your advisors if you don't agree with them. Explain your position calmly and politely. There is no need to be defensive as you face a different opinion.

Look around for people who do care and are ready to support you in an advisor role. Surround yourself with people who are successful, objective, non-judgmental, uplifting, and have your interests at heart.

Learn from Your Experiences...
Good and Not So Good

Don't be turned off when you face obstacles and glitches. They are just small bumps in the road that will not keep you away from your destination. When you face problems, disappointments, or frustrations, activate your creative process with a positive outlook to address the issues at hand. Don't let your problems empower your life, but be empowered by your creative energy. Know that you have all that you need to overcome challenges if they come your way. If you stumble, keep moving.

Constantly looking at your life in a defeated way hinders your growth. Self-doubt, self-pity, and discouragement only keep you from being all that you can be. It stops you from growing and reaching out to your desires. Self-pity may attract you sympathy at first, but eventually, it leaves you a very lonely person, as no one is attracted to negativity.

Roadblocks are opportunities for growth, not signs to quit. Keep moving.

No matter what life throws at you, you have the power to bounce back. Know that you will not sink. You will rise above the storm. Harness your creative energy to conceive positive outcomes, not defeat. Activate the power of your faith and speak words of trust and victory. "I have plenty financially. I take care of myself and I live each day in good health. A great partner is coming into my life. New clients and opportunities are coming my way." Let the sun shine on your life, and peace and warmth will take over your heart. You will discover the *Marvelous You* in all its power.

As said earlier, there is no such thing as failure, only a better understanding of what works and what doesn't. Challenges are opportunities for growth and creativity, not for oppression. It is critical that you grasp this concept to remain in a state of non-resistance and happiness in all circumstances.

What you believe today influences your thoughts and expectations, which in turn have an impact on your behavior and feelings. My question to you is: How do you look at disappointments? Do you move on or are you immobilized? Do you hold a grudge or do you let go? In believing that all events, relationships, and situations, good or bad, are learning experiences, you maintain a positive attitude.

Things happen because you or somebody else made it happen. If you are in a precarious position because of your own decisions, accept full responsibility. Identify how you could have done things differently or have better responded to an event. We are each responsible for our own life choices.

Unfortunately, decisions made by others may become your roadblocks and obstacles. The key is to observe the experience or the situation as it is, not resist it. Look at it objectively. Find what you can learn from it, how it can enrich your life, and move on. In every event, there is a lesson to learn. You are never a victim, you are the *Marvelous You*. You are a powerful creator, resilient, and courageous.

Unleash your creativity, stay in the pursuit of your goals in a relaxed state of mind, and be joyous. Focus on your past and future successes and be excited for what is to come. Be patient; your aspirations will come to fruition in due time. All life's moments are learning experiences. Remind yourself that negativity and guilt have no place in your life.

CHAPTER 4

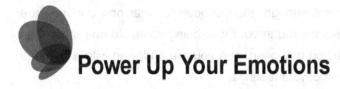

Power Up Your Emotions

Emotions are like a roller coaster ride with speed,
loops, and turns. Exhilaration and excitement when
going up, fear and screams when going down.

Activate Your *Dynamo* App

Imagine for a moment experiencing life with no emotions. You would be a robot, executing tasks with no passion, no excitement, no *va va voom*. Life would be quite boring, with today being like yesterday. On the other hand, living fully with all your emotions, good and not so good, makes you feel alive. Emotions bring color to your life. They are an ally to your intelligence, as they bear messages to help you direct your life.

Positive emotions such as love, glee, confidence, appreciation, and enthusiasm make your eyes shine and radiate. They excite you for tomorrow. On the flip side, negative emotions like grief, depression, fear, hate, anger, disappointment, and pessimism make you wish there was no tomorrow. Under their spell, you are drifting away from the *Marvelous You* and becoming the *Powerless You*.

To live your best life, you need to stay in a high-vibration energy space. There is no better way to shift from low- to high-vibration feelings than by activating your *Dynamo* app. This app alerts you when your emotional temperature is going down and you are shifting away from your well-being zone. By paying attention to your feelings, you can swiftly restore your emotional well-being with techniques that will bring forth good-feeling thoughts. This in turn will help you stay in a state of confident expectation for what is to come.

Don't neglect to turn on your *Be Happy* app to have better-feeling thoughts that will move you back to your well-being zone. If one good-feeling thought is not enough, then choose another one until you are at peace and well-anchored in your well-being zone. No one other than yourself can make you feel good, and you are endowed with a *Dynamo* app to help you control your feelings.

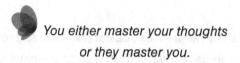

*You either master your thoughts
or they master you.*

Each day is full of external events that impact your life, and your response to these events influences your emotional temperature. It can go up or down as you respond favorably or not to life events and annoyances. Knowing that you have freedom to choose your thoughts blossoms into a feeling of empowerment. You hold the power to radiate more love, joy, enthusiasm, and bliss in your life. You can take control over toxic emotions, and say good-bye to anxiety, anger, rage, bitterness, depression, and despair.

Not knowing how to master your emotions is like being at sea without a life jacket. You will soon drown, swept away by the high waves. There is nothing wrong in feeling negative emotions for a moment. What is wrong is self-oppression where you are constantly rooted in toxic thoughts and dominated by low vibration feelings. What is wrong is sabotaging your life with disastrous choices.

Practice makes perfect, so don't be discouraged if you have occasional negative thoughts and you feel sad, disappointed, fearful, or upset for a moment. Simply replace your thoughts with better ones, and realign yourself with your *Marvelous Nature* for a more harmonious life. With *Dynamo*, you will simply be a great surfer, and you will ride the waves of life with more feelings of joy, confidence, optimism, and passion.

Calm the Storm

No need for alcohol and food to calm an emotional storm. Engulfed by negative emotions, the *Tornado Destroyer Tactics* are your best choice to swiftly move back to your well-being zone where you offer high vibrations of energy. The *Tornado Destroyer Tactics* revolve around understanding the causes of your toxic emotions and physical pain, and releasing them to reclaim your well-being.

Tornado Destroyer Tactics	
Identify the Cause of the Negative Emotions	
1.	Observe any physical discomfort.
	Are you muscles tense? Do you have physical pain? Do you have a headache? Is your stomach upset? Do you lack energy? Is your heart racing?
2.	As you take note of your physical reactions, name the negative emotions you are experiencing: boredom, frustration, rejection, disappointment, sadness, anxiety, worry, discouragement, anger, rage, jealousy, guilt, grief, fear, despair, or any others.
3.	Look within to find the cause of your emotional reaction and physical sensation.
	Is it an event, a comment you heard, a negative thought, little annoyances, something you have seen, or too much or not enough work?
4.	Reflect on the cause of your emotional breakdown. Be objective in your reflection.
	What does it say or mean to you? Is it a message to look for change? A lesson to be learned? Guidance for a new direction? A past emotional wound that continues to cause despair? An unresolved battle?

Tornado Destroyer Tactics	
Release Negative Emotions and Reclaim Well-Being	
5.	Try the following suggestions to release your negative emotions. Don't be shy to cry, throw a pillow, or shout as you open your heart and release negative emotions. Most importantly, activate your *Love Power* app to let the power of forgiveness, compassion, and love for yourself and others clear your negative emotions.
	- Bring to your mind the issue and embrace it with love. Visualize it becoming smaller and smaller, leaving room for only love in your heart.
	- Consider opening your heart by journaling your emotions and their causes.
	- Speak aloud about the issue. Do the exercise a few times until you can recount the issue with better feelings. If you prefer, do it with a friend or someone you trust.
	- Activate your *Be Happy* app to empower the healing process with good-feeling thoughts. You may say: "I am a person of great value. I am blessed and grateful for all the goodness in my life, and for what is to come. I choose freedom and let go of negative emotions."
	- Move forward to become all that you can be. Map out an action plan and take action for a more positive life.
	- Activate your *Higher Power* app. Pray, meditate on God's goodness, praise Him, and be thankful for all that you have.
	- Choose to not linger on painful memories. You cannot change the past. Learn from each of your experiences. Let time and love heal your wounds.
	- Reach out for professional help (physician, therapist) if distress lingers. A number of therapies are available to address different conditions.

While not scientifically proven, you can also look into the *Emotional Freedom Technique*, known as tapping, which has been reported by many as a great tool in the treatment of physical and emotional issues. Tapping is touted to relieve conditions such as migraines, fibromyalgia, phobias, body aches, and post-traumatic stress disorder.[1] The technique, popularized by American Cary Craig, is also taught by other teachers, namely Nick Ortner, Helena Fone, Jack Canfield, and Pamela Bruner.

Emotions are like tornado warnings. Watch them carefully for fear of getting caught in the storm.

You are not built to be a permanent home to negative emotions. With good-feeling thoughts and healing actions, emotional freedom will be yours, and you will reclaim your well-being in alignment with your *Marvelous Self*. You will master distressing emotions and reach greater harmony in your body, soul, and spirit.

You will find that negative emotions have no grip on you. You will become stronger, fearless, courageous, and more in control of your thoughts and beliefs, which in turn will give rise to positive actions. You will see challenges and sufferings as opportunities for growth and strength, not defeat and oppression.

Remember, you have all that it takes to change your outlook on life, tackle challenges, and live a great life filled with glee, excitement, eagerness, and bliss. Activate your *Dynamo* app today to say good-bye to discouragement, depression, and pessimism, and say hello to continuous well-being. Let the emotional healing begin!

Feel Good

Feeling good is at the core of your soul. You are fully equipped for inner joy to be your experience each and every day of your life. If you are looking for lasting joyousness and peace, practice the *Path to Serenity Technique* each day, and you will experience what the word *blissfulness* means.

	Path to Serenity Technique
1.	First, close your eyes, take a few deep breaths, and stop your thoughts for a few moments.
2.	When you inhale through the nose, let glee fill your body. Place your hand on the body area where you feel the negative emotions. Let peace and joy radiate on the body area.
3.	When you exhale through your mouth, let out negative and toxic energies. Let go of all stress, knowing that all is well and good. Simply experience the joy of being, peace, love, and acceptance.
4.	Just breathe calmly and feel oneness to other human beings, the universe, and God.
5.	Now dive in and enter your heart. Imagine walking on a path that leads to a beautiful garden of well-being. Walk around, look at the waterfall, and smell the flowers. Breathe slowly, simply relax, and enjoy yourself in that radiant place.
6.	Let your heart be filled with appreciation. Be grateful for your family, friends, home, work, and blessings. Cherish good-feeling memories.
7.	Sit quietly near the waterfalls and feel God's unconditional love embracing you and filling your heart with self-love. In this quietness, hear His voice speaking to you and guiding you. Feel the wind of Spirit on your skin.
8.	When you are ready, continue to walk around the garden with unbounded joy and lightness in your heart. Open your eyes slowly and you will see that joy and bliss are now engraved in your heart.

The *Path to Serenity Technique* leads you on a road of emotional well-being. It is healing for your soul; moments of stillness, freedom, wholeness, deep fulfillment, and bliss when you experience oneness with God, anchored in His love and grace. There are no words to describe this joyful state of equanimity; it is truly yours to experience.

By inhaling and exhaling, you invite glee and peace into your heart, and you let go of toxic emotions and energies. Your body relaxes, your mind is at peace, and you feel terrific. In a sea of high-vibration energy, you experience spiritual connectedness to other human beings, the whole universe, and God. You are grateful for your life, and experience boundless bliss.

In shifting your thoughts from negative to positive, you increase your emotional temperature and generate positive emotions. In doing so, you feel more joy, excitement, and passion, and less frustration and disappointment. By increasing your positive vibrations, you are moved to take positive actions, and you are excited for what is to come. Your whole self—thoughts, emotions, actions, and faith—is in harmony.

*Once you have found the path to inner
bliss where love, deep joy, and peace
reside, this place is yours forever.*

In the garden of well-being, you blossom and experience the simple joy of being, for no reason; not conditional on events or material things. With your eyes open or closed, you can visit and walk around the garden anywhere and at any moment.

By practicing the *Path to Serenity Technique* daily, you will develop an increased awareness of your value and *Marvelous Self*.

Escape from Fear

Have you ever watched a horror movie? Even knowing that this is not a true story, you are glued to your seat, scared, cringing, and experiencing fear. Did you ever notice how good you are in writing and directing horror movies in your life? You amplify the "what if" in your scenarios to a point where you paralyze, choke, or can't speak, with your heart beating like a drum. You become a prisoner of fear, chained to doubt, worries, feelings of inferiority, or other negative emotions. You cannot create your best life without breaking these chains and rising up out of the fear dungeon.

While fear may be a valid signal alerting you of imminent danger, oftentimes it is a creation of your mind. Hundreds of fears have been identified. For example, some people are afraid of failure, as they start a new project or a new job. Others are afraid to learn a new skill, deliver a speech, leave home for college, or take a school exam.

Others fear their surroundings and are afraid of certain animals, riding a car, traveling, bacteria, heights, darkness, being alone, crowds, or meeting new people. Some have physical fears; they are afraid of sex, being touched, washing, or bathing. Some others fear the future, afraid of losing their job or spouse, lacking money, or being rejected or unjustly judged. Oftentimes fear is hiding behind our daily stress.

A self-sabotaging fear is a message that you forgot for a moment that you are the *Marvelous You*: fearless, courageous, engaged, and in continual connection with God. With the *Mastering Fear Techniques* below, you will counteract the poisonous effects of destructive fears and clear your mind of chaos and turmoil to become all that you can be.

	Mastering Fear Techniques
1.	Start by being mindful without judgment. Express only love for yourself. With an open mind, recognize physical discomforts. Are your muscles tense? Are you trembling? Do you have a headache? Is your stomach upset?
2.	Clearly identify your fears. Ask yourself: What am I really afraid of? What am I running from? As you answer these questions, embrace your fear with love.
3.	Reflect on what is causing the fears. A past experience gone wrong? A false belief about yourself or life in general? A worry about the future?
4.	Reflect on how self-sabotaging fears impact your life. Ask yourself: How badly is this affecting my life? Does it inhibit me from realizing my full potential? Is it worth it? Do I want to continue to live with the fears? Do I want to escape from their chains?
5.	Explore how you can change your attitude (thoughts, beliefs, actions) about your fears. Be objective and realistic. Look at your fears for what they mostly are, a creation of your mind.
6.	Replace self-defeating thoughts and beliefs with good-feeling ones by reading positive affirmations about your *Marvelous Nature*.
7.	Don't overlook adding visualization about your *Marvelous Self* to reinforce new beliefs.
8.	Choosing to face your fears is courage in action. Prepare an action plan that will help you master your fears. Ask yourself: What assumptions am I making? What new thoughts can I have? What small steps can I take? How can I overcome my most dreaded fears if they come true in the future? Who can help me?
9.	With your action plan in hand, get into action. By facing your fears, you will gain more confidence.
10.	Practice daily the *Path to Serenity Technique* described earlier to experience more inner peace and deep joy. Know that you are always safe in the garden of well-being, in oneness with God.
11.	If you do not have success on your own, consult a physician or therapist for personal support.

Fear is the scary monster hiding under the bed. Wake up and turn on the light. With confidence, crush your self-sabotaging fears.

When you lean into your fear, you gain more confidence. Soon you will find your trembling fears being replaced with just a small discomfort. Your heartbeat will slow down, and you will breathe more easily. One step at a time, you will rise to new heights of well-being. You will no longer be afraid of today and tomorrow. You will discover empowerment and freedom.

These victories will become the basis for new beliefs. You will be shouting, "I am Marvelous! I am courageous and strong, and I boldly say that fears have no grip on me! I refuse to let unhealthy fears destroy my life! With good-feeling thoughts, new beliefs, and engaging actions, I crush those fears once and for all. I choose freedom! I rejoice in the present moment, and I trust that tomorrow will be fine."

In oneness with God, you will embrace with love who you are, and the world around you. In awareness of His presence, you will let your conscious mind be filled with the voice of Spirit, keeping your thoughts captive in fearlessness.

Give yourself permission to stumble as you take little steps, try again, and ask a friend for support. You are not meant to be a prisoner of fear, only a prisoner of love. Do whatever it takes to allow yourself to affirm your *Marvelous Essence*. Take a leap and be courageous. You are a conqueror, and you have the armor to conquer your fears. It's all there within you.

Say Good-bye to Anxiety

Anxiety disorders are monsters that are very real to those who experience them. These monsters have different names: generalized anxiety, panic attack, phobia, social anxiety disorder, obsessive-compulsive disorder, post-traumatic stress disorder, and separation anxiety disorder.[2]

For those plagued with generalized anxiety, the monster is constantly under the bed. There seems to be no relief in sight. Fear is so intense and persistent. You can't live in the moment, you can't think and reason properly, and you can't sleep. You worry about everything, founded or unfounded. You expect disaster, and you only see darkness. You cry, and you are desperate. You are totally debilitated, with extreme nervousness and uneasiness day after day. You no longer function at work and at home, and you have serious difficulties interacting with others.

 The anxiety monsters have no right
on you. Slaughter those beasts.

With panic disorder, you have sudden attacks where you see the monster under the bed, and you are embraced by terror with intense physical symptoms such as shaking, being confused, and having difficulty breathing. Prolonged stress, stressful events, or changes can lead to panic disorders.

Phobia is an irrational fear of an object or situation. Social anxiety disorder is characterized by a fear of others. Obsessive-compulsive disorder is recognized by repetitive thoughts or actions that seem to alleviate anxiety. Post-traumatic stress disorder is an anxiety that results from previous traumatic events. Separation anxiety disorder is characterized by high anxiety when being separated from a place or a person.

With your *Dynamo* app activated, you can swiftly take action with medication, a healthy lifestyle, well-being techniques, and therapies to slaughter those beasts.

Medication – First, consult your physician to discuss your condition. Anxiety may result from altered levels of the hormones produced by the thyroid gland, abnormal heart rhythms, or other heart abnormalities. With blood test results on hand, your physician will be in a position to provide the proper medication to allow wellness in less time.

Healthy Lifestyle – Prolonged stress or stressful events can lead to anxiety disorders. A healthy lifestyle will help you become stronger.

Choose healthy food and take a multi-vitamin if your diet is limited in vitamins. Reduce your stress with daily stretches, light exercise, breathing exercises, or other relaxation and nurturing techniques.

Even if you cannot sleep, take naps or just relax in bed. Give your body time to rest and recuperate. Listen to inspiring music, step outside for a brisk walk to witness nature around you, take a warm bath, or get a soothing massage. Calm your racing mind in any possible ways that work for you for a greater well-being. Take *Me* time each day to stay in your well-being zone for a more vibrant life.

Well-Being Techniques – When you are able to breathe with more ease, try the *Mastering Fear Techniques* explained earlier. The techniques help in changing your beliefs and responses to events and the unknown. See if you can change your thoughts, emotions, and behavior by yourself.

Each day, whether you feel like it or not, practice the *Path to Serenity Technique* detailed earlier. As you walk in the garden of well-being, smell the flowers of inner peace and glee. Forget for a moment your outer life, and feel your connection to other human beings, the universe, and God.

Breathe and stay calm, knowing that you are part of this beautifully organized universe. You do not have to worry, knowing that you are connected to the organizing Power that sustains it all. This ever-present Force is always active in your life, always looking out for you while you journey through life. All is well, all is good.

God loves you with all that you are, even with your fears. To increase your awareness of His presence, activate your *Higher Power* app and initiate a personal relationship with Him. Talk to Him each day. Let Him know how you feel and what you need. Feed your heart and mind with His seeds of love and have faith in Him.

Trusting in God creates the highest vibrations of energy, which in turn gives you more ease and confidence to tackle life's uncertainties and disappointing events. When you nurture your relationship with Him, new beliefs and inner joy and peace take root in your heart.

Therapies – If you do not see relief, consult a proper therapist. Psychodynamic therapy, cognitive behavior therapy, and interpersonal psychotherapy are part of effective therapies that can help relieve your anxiety and positively transform your life.[3]

- Psychodynamic Therapy – Helps you understand how your behavior can be affected by unresolved emotions and issues.
- Cognitive Behavior Therapy – Focuses on your thought pattern to help you change dysfunctional thought and belief patterns.
- Interpersonal Therapy – Helps you identify issues in interpersonal relationships for you to take action and minimize stress at work and at home.

Never give up! Your hear me? Never give up! You are born to affirm your *Marvelous Self,* and you will get better. Your future holds so many moments of happiness. Let your heart lead you to this place of well-being where inner joy and peace live.

Forgive to Outweigh Anger

We all get bruises as we experience life, some more than others. You get bruises when you are abandoned by your parents, raped, bullied at school, subjected to verbal or physical abuse from your spouse, or financially duped by people you trusted. You get bruises when you are a victim of a bombing or other terrorist act, or when you lose your retirement plan or job due to your employer's mismanagement.

Bruises can transform you into a powerless and resentful person who is angry toward others and life in general. Some people carry so much anger that it takes significant space in their inner self. As a result, they have a very small inner garden of well-being in their heart. In order to maintain a state of harmony in your body, soul, and spirit, anger needs to be released through forgiveness. With forgiveness comes healing and freedom from past hurts.

"I can't forgive and I will never forgive what this person did to me," you might say to yourself. Forgiveness is an act towards emotional freedom. You make that choice because you yearn for wholeness and well-being.

You forgive those who have wronged or abused you to set *yourself* free. You wish to set others free to make mistakes, experience life, and unfold their *Marvelous Self* in their own time.

Everyone is subject to pain, sadness, and bruises inflicted by someone else. Oftentimes other people's own bruises make them say and do things out of fear rather than out of love. As a result, they bruise those around them and create more sadness and pain. They act from their own level of consciousness, making decisions and speaking words that reflect their current level of awareness. They may not see today how they have wronged you and others, but they may realize it one day as they expand their consciousness about love and life.

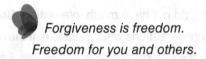

Forgiveness is freedom.
Freedom for you and others.

Forgiveness equates choosing to be the *Marvelous You* who lives on the side of love and stays away from the *Powerless You* who lives on the side of hate. With your *Love Power* app activated, you choose to forgive those who have hurt you, and you cover their faults with love.

In true forgiveness, you allow others to have their own journey and lessons to learn. You open your heart to the positive aspects of their lives and wish them well. In oneness with God, you see them with eyes of love, knowing that He is graciously waiting at the door of their hearts. From this place of greater understanding, your anger diffuses, your pain dissolves, and your wounds heal. You set yourself free from the anger chains, and you make space in your heart for love and compassion.

"What if the person does it again and again?" you might ask.

Communication is key in interacting with others. Let the other person know what it is they do that you dislike, why and how it makes you feel. Clarify comments they said and try to understand the motive behind their actions to come to a positive resolution. If after several attempts the person continues to bruise you, you have different options to choose from: take time away, therapy, avoidance, or cutting ties completely.

Taking some time away to reflect on your relationship may be all that you need to clear your mind, address what needs to be dealt with to avoid future bruising, and rekindle the relationship. Communication and commitment from both parties are essential to make it work. Let the other person know you need time to reflect, and when you are both ready, discuss how you can resolve your differences.

At other times, counseling or therapy may be the best option. You may need an independent party to help you address the issues. There are great therapies and intervention techniques to help both of you heal. As new thoughts and beliefs are adopted, new behaviors emerge.

Avoidance means limiting your interaction with the offender. This may be possible when the offender is a coworker, a school student, or a family member with whom you do not have much interaction. Be nice and polite, but limit meetings and conversations when possible. If the person continues to release venomous arrows, address the matter swiftly. Sometimes people do not even realize what they are saying or doing.

If the abuse continues, and you believe that what needs to be addressed cannot be resolved, then you may be left with no other alternative than cutting ties completely. This is not an easy decision, but sometimes it is the best option. This may mean finding a new job or school, removing the person from your Facebook page, and not taking calls and e-mail messages. It can even go as far as to separate from your spouse. If you are a victim of harassment and/or bullying, inform your family, the school administration, a teacher, a friend, and even the authorities, if warranted.

As much as you are entitled to respect, forgive those who have abused or wronged you. To sum it up, there is freedom in forgiveness, freedom from resentment and emotional pain, and freedom to move on, be happy, and love unconditionally.

Chase Away the Depression Dragon

Depression is not a friendly dragon, and it has no right on your life. Your *Dynamo* app gives you hints that he is coming to chase you. The depression dragon comes with difficulty sleeping, recurring negative thoughts, a lack of energy, and it attacks you violently.

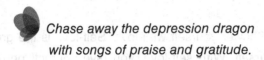

*Chase away the depression dragon
with songs of praise and gratitude.*

A combination of factors can lead to the appearance of the depression dragon. Too much stress can produce chemical imbalances in your brain and body, and it can exacerbate depression. Difficult life events and a troubled family life can be the source of withdrawal and stress. For example, the loss of a loved one, the loss of a job, a scarce financial situation, shattered desires, a divorce, or unresolved abandonment can open the door for the depression dragon to swoop in.

A negative attitude where one sees life with dark lenses can lead to depression. Dreaming without taking actions, with each day being the same, can bring about discouragement. Even low self-esteem may be hiding behind depression. The dragon is fierce and spits flames of sadness, excessive crying, fatigue, trouble concentrating, physical pain, no desire to be around people, no will to do anything, extreme pessimism, no vitality to make decisions, sleeping too much or not at all, extreme nervousness, and suicidal thoughts.

The good news is that you are the *Marvelous You,* and you can claim victory over the depression dragon. You can be free of the chaotic, destructive, and struggling flames he is lashing at you. There is hope, and you can win the battle. A number of options are available, from medication to self-love, a healthy lifestyle, friendly support, well-being techniques, and therapies. The combination of these alternatives is known to be very effective in slaughtering the depression dragon.

Medical Support – Consult your physician to discuss your condition, especially if your condition worsens over time. Physicians can investigate if your condition is the result of infectious diseases, nutritional deficiencies, a neurological condition, or physiological problems.[4] As proper care and medication are provided, you gain a better mood, you feel less pain in your body, you sleep better, and you feel more energized as you gain more appetite for life. It is best to use medical support jointly with other treatment options that address your lifestyle, thoughts, beliefs, and behavior to promote wellness.

Self-Love – Shower yourself with love. Self-love is the greatest gift you can give yourself. With self-love, you give yourself permission to be vulnerable and embrace your wounds with love. You give yourself permission to learn and grow, thus allowing you to make mistakes in the process. You give yourself permission to love who you are today, with your strengths and weaknesses. You give yourself permission to not be discouraged by today and have faith in tomorrow. You give yourself permission to forgive those who have wronged you, living each day with joy in your heart.

Healthy Lifestyle – A healthy lifestyle that includes stress reduction techniques, proper nutrition, and restful sleep is powerful to bring you back to utmost wellness. To calm your racing mind, do stretches and breathing techniques and light physical exercises on a daily basis. Choose healthy food and eat balanced, small meals of protein and complex carbohydrates. Take a multi-vitamin if your diet lacks vitamins and minerals.

Friendly Support – Tell your friends that you are not feeling well. You will be surprised how much their support will greatly accelerate your well-being. They will take steps with you and provide support, even go out for walks or for a little shopping, and mostly they will be a listening ear if you want to open your heart.

Well-Being Techniques – Take naps, listen to music, go outside, take a bath, get a massage, or do anything else that is soothing to your soul. Many report benefits from acupuncture and various relaxation techniques. I also encourage you to read self-help books and use the *Tornado Destroyer Tactics* and the *Path to Serenity Technique* explained earlier.

Activate Your *Higher Power* app – Activate your *Higher Power* app and talk to God. Tell Him what is on your mind including your pains and sorrows. He understands what you are going through. He loves you, and wants you to be whole again. He has fully equipped you to tackle life's challenges. He will guide you to victory. Open your heart and feel His unconditional love. In the stillness of your heart, you will hear His voice saying, "My hand is on you. You will get better. You will be a shining light for all to see. You are my love, today and eternally."

Healing Therapies – Many people with depression work with a team of experts to help them take positive steps. I encourage you to consult a licensed psychologist, psychiatrist, a social worker, counselor, or other therapists who can help you deal with the causes of your depression. Look around to find who would be a good fit for you. Therapy —psychodynamic, cognitive behavior, and interpersonal—can provide great insights on unresolved issues and unhealthy thought and belief patterns.

Give time to your body, soul, and spirit to work together and bring you back to a state of wholeness. Be open to trying different treatment alternatives. If one option does not work, try something else. Don't give up! It may take a few months to get better, but rest assured, depression will dissipate. Soon you will be excited about life again!

As you get better, prevent the depression dragon from reappearing by keeping your *Dynamo* app activated. Listen to your feelings and your body for signs of your emotional temperature going down. Use the *Tornado Destroyer Tactics* to raise your emotional temperature and slaughter the monstrous beast before it inflicts significant damage. Continue to practice a healthy lifestyle and favor well-being techniques like the *Path to Serenity*. Small steps each day will keep the dragon away.

Bye-Bye Loneliness

Have you ever felt so lonely that you wondered why you were put on earth in the first place? I know I did when I was in my twenties. At that time, not having a father present in my life since my early teens left an empty space in my heart that was filled with strong feelings of loneliness. Loneliness was my companion, well-hidden in my heart and behind my smile.

For a few years, sadness was lingering in my heart. Even my inner awareness that I was from God and in God was not sufficient to lift me up. Not even prayer worked. I went to work with a smile on my face, but my soul was aching. And then one day, loneliness was gone; time and love healed my wounds. I awoke to the beauty of my true essence. I felt wholeness, a sense of delight, and bliss in my soul. This was the day of a new beginning for me. As I owned my joy of simply being, a few years later I found my life purpose, a treasure hidden in my heart.

Out of curiosity you might ask: "What is your life purpose?"

At the time, I was volunteering in a youth group on a weekly basis. This experience opened my eyes as to what I do best—helping others blossom and live their best life. Finding my life purpose gave me direction and passion in all my doings, both at work and in the community. It filled my heart with great joy and a zest for life, with each moment filled with gratefulness and hopefulness.

 Time heals, and so does love.

To those who say that you do not outgrow loneliness, I say you are wrong. In my thirties, loneliness faded away, and to this day, it has never returned. Even the storms that I later faced in life did not eclipse my inner joy. In fact, they led me to activate all my inner apps and experience more of the truths of my *Marvelous Nature,* namely inner joyousness, peace, and a blissful feeling that surpasses all understanding.

Is your heart aching today? Do you feel lonely and hopeless? Are you down to the point that you consider taking your own life? Look at all that you are. Hope is in you. Beauty is in you. The power of life is in you. God's love is in you.

Activate your *Dynamo* app and learn to celebrate yourself and the small joys of life. Take care of yourself. Be grateful for what you have. Read inspiring books, forgive your shortcomings, and do whatever makes you feel good. Become your greatest companion. As you love and forgive yourself, His love flows within you, and you are no longer alone.

Look for others ready to help you. Let people around you know how you feel. Talk to someone—a friend, a physician, a parent, a school counselor, or a support group. Know that emotional pain and suffering will subside.

Having been wounded, you need time to heal. As you reach out and receive care, His love flows within you, and you are no longer alone.

Look for love, the great healer. Get involved in the community. Meet people and happily serve others. See the *Marvelous Nature* of each one you meet. As you love and receive love from others, His love flows within you, and you are no longer alone.

Know that there is a light at the end of the tunnel and keep walking, no matter what. Today does not define your tomorrow. As you gain awareness of your true nature and the grand scheme of life, you will see how we are all connected in a sea of energy. You will experience wholeness in Him.

Restore Your Grieving Heart

"My soul aches. My soul is wounded. My soul is bleeding. There is a hole in my soul. A part of me has left and the pain is unbearable. My soul is restless." These are common words of a grieving heart after a divorce, a miscarriage, the death of a loved one, a lost dream, a financial loss, serious illness, or any other loss or sense of loss. Losses can be extremely painful and debilitating. It can freeze someone in time, leaving the person with no ability to move on.

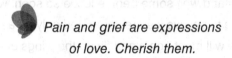

Pain and grief are expressions of love. Cherish them.

Grief signifies your love and attachment to your loved ones and the life that you had created. "How can I heal my emotional wounds? How can I close the hole in my heart? Will I ever be whole again?" you might ask.

Time, love, positive thoughts, actions, the celebration of your *Marvelous Nature* and life, faith, and the remembrance of your loved ones, all help in the healing of your emotional wounds for more wholeness and harmony.

There is no scheduled time to heal your wounds. Grieving varies from one person to another. For some, it takes a few weeks; for others, it takes months. Your faith, attachment, and the significance of events in your life come into play in the healing timetable. When you grasp the concept that nothing is forever and yours to keep, you bounce back from the loss more quickly. As time passes and you embrace your grief with love, your wounds heal.

Don't fight your grief; instead, acknowledge your loss and feelings. Express your grief by writing down your tumultuous feelings. Cry, yell, and open your heart to others. Join a support group, talk to your friends, and surround yourself with love. By releasing your pain and spreading your love, your wounds heal.

Open your treasure chest at any time and remind yourself of all the goodness of life. Look forward to tomorrow. Celebrate life, develop new relationships, help someone find a job, or give a great life to a new pet. By maintaining positive thoughts and engaging in action, your wounds heal.

Visit your garden of well-being each day by practicing the *Path to Serenity Technique* explained earlier. When you remind yourself of your *Marvelous Nature,* your wounds heal.

Losing someone you care for can be quite intense. If you are grieving the loss of a loved one, find ways to celebrate the person's life. Write in a journal about their uniqueness, accomplishments, and willingness to make this world a better place. Cherish all these beautiful memories in your treasure chest. When you celebrate the beauty of a lost loved one's life, your wounds heal.

We don't understand why some people leave so soon, why their lives are cut so short. I like to believe we are separated only for a period of time and that one day, we will meet again and fly on the wings of love together. By activating your faith, your wounds heal.

In honor of your loved one, start a new project that has meaning to you. Set up a foundation or get involved in an organization that pursues a cause that had significance for them. By celebrating your loved one, your wounds heal.

Healing does not mean forgetting your deceased loved ones. Their love will always reside in your heart. With self-love, embrace all that you are, with all your joys and sorrows.

CHAPTER 5

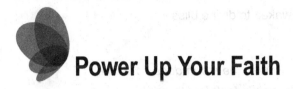

Power Up Your Faith

*Not seeing the mountaintop does not mean
you are not close. Keep climbing.*

Activate Your *Higher Power* App

You are connected to the organizing Power that sustains all there is in the universe. Whether you acknowledge it or not, this Life Force is always guiding you while you journey through life. We are endowed with free will, and God has lovingly intended for you to reach out to Him for companionship.

By activating your *Higher Power* app, you bring to life your faith in God and ignite a spiritual, dynamic, and interactive relationship with Him. You consciously acknowledge Him as the Higher Power, the Source, the All-That-Is, and the Alpha and Omega. You recognize His supremacy over both the physical and spiritual worlds.

In oneness with Him, your soul is divinely enlightened. You gain a better understanding of the grander plan of life. You truly capture that your true purpose in life is to actualize your *Marvelous Self* for more glee and well-being in your life and the world around you.

He becomes your faithful and trustworthy companion. You acknowledge that He co-creates with you. You seek His guidance, and He instructs and inspires you. Together, you bring to life the seeds of greatness that He has placed within you. Your heart is filled with praise each day, in awe of His gracious care and love for you.

Spirit feeds your mind and leads your life with truth, love, compassion, and self-control. In Him, you experience comfort, wholeness, and harmony. In this communion, you awaken to divine bliss.

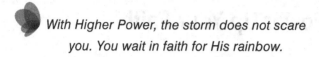

With Higher Power, the storm does not scare
you. You wait in faith for His rainbow.

With *Higher Power*, you are not troubled by challenges. You fear not for tomorrow. You know that God is your protector and armor who gives you victory over challenges. You rejoice in Him, expecting great things to ensue. You believe in divine intervention and miracles. You know that the impossible is possible. You recognize that He aligns people and events for your desires—or something better—to become reality. You never stop being amazed by coincidences and synchronicities in your life. In this state of spiritual awareness, you experience deep joy, peace, and gratefulness.

In Him flourishes self-worthiness. You are His love, enveloped by His blanket of grace. Your heart is thankful for His gift of eternal life to those who seek and love Him.

Have Faith in Who You Are

Are you impatiently waiting for your seeds of greatness to flourish? Do you have constant doubts about yourself? Do you fear the worst? Are you pulled down by challenges? Do you feel lost and alone? If your answers are in the affirmative, then it's time to power up your faith. Today is the day to activate your *Higher Power* app and have faith that the impossible is indeed possible. Today is the day to have faith in who you are, the *Marvelous You,* a powerful and gifted creator endowed with freedom, passion, courage, and hope in the face of adversity.

Faith empowers your life in so many different ways and allows you to unleash the power of your *Marvelous Nature* and experience fulfillment. It moves you to an even higher vibration of energy, where inner peace and joy reside at all times. Your heart is filled with trust and confidence that moves mountains.

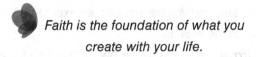

*Faith is the foundation of what you
create with your life.*

Faith in Yourself – It is through faith in yourself that you actualize the powerful creator that you are. Without faith, you are doomed to be a passive observer of life. Faith in yourself activates your creative energy and ability. It opens your eyes to a world of new possibilities for your life. It moves you to dare to dream and be excited and passionate for what is to come.

Faith in Your Desires – Faith in your dreams brings about new accomplishments. It inspires you to get into action for the full flourishing of your life. By gaining more confidence, you dream bigger dreams and realize your full potential. It is through this faith that you persevere and reach new heights of success.

Faith in Your Freedom – With faith in your freedom, you choose positive thoughts and create a purpose-driven life. You know that well-aligned thoughts, beliefs, emotions, actions, and faith create the desires of your heart. It is through faith in your freedom that you listen to the voice of Spirit and actualize your *Marvelous Self* without limits.

Faith in Your Gifts – Faith in your talents, skills, and capacities creates wonders in your life and the lives of those around you. You know that no one else can play the same music in the universe. You are not afraid to explore, learn, and develop new skills, and put your faith into action for your fulfillment and the betterment of others.

Faith in Your Powerful Armor – Faith in your powerful armor is what makes you see challenges as opportunities for growth and learning. You do not dwell on your problems. You are not afraid of setbacks. You are not discouraged. You are strong, courageous, and fully equipped to quickly bounce back. You rise high above your challenges and find creative solutions to optimize your situation. Your spirit remains at peace, knowing that all will soon be well.

93

Faith in the Invisible – With faith in the invisible, your heart is filled with joy and peace, knowing that great victories are on their way. You expect great things to happen. Without attachment to the outcome, you allow the universe to surprise you with more than expected. You keep your head up and rejoice in the waiting.

Faith in Tomorrow – Faith in tomorrow excites you for another day of possibilities. You look forward to new opportunities and experiences. You trust in the grander plan of life. You know that the journey is a thrilling adventure with new beginnings for your greatest transformation.

Faith in Love – It is through faith in love that you spread your wings and love unconditionally. Such faith blooms when your *Love Power* app is turned on. Your heart overflows with kindness, patience, understanding, forgiveness, and compassion. You serve and nurture others for the betterment of the world.

Faith in God – With your *Higher Power* activated, you have faith in God and know His blessings and alliance are with you always during the good and bad times, like a rainbow after the rain. In Him, you never feel alone. You are alive, with your heart and mind being fed by the seeds of His love. Inner joy and peace are with you each day.

Faith in the Power of Praise – Faith in the power of praise makes your heart sing a song of joy. You are grateful for the little joys of life, for today and tomorrow. Praise is on your lips from morning to night. You are inspired to create moments of glee for yourself and others. Nothing takes away your inner joy and peace. All is well, all is good.

Faith is your most precious ally. It moves mountains, and it gets you to fly high and see the invisible. Power up your faith and get your wings back to soar to new heights. Let your true essence, the *Marvelous You,* come to light.

Tie Success Climbing Knots

Now that you are ready to climb to success, with your plan on hand and your heart full of passion and excitement, refresh your mind on how to tie these six essential climbing knots to make your ascent towards your vision of success a fun and safe experience.

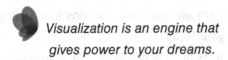

Visualization is an engine that gives power to your dreams.

Faith Climbing Knot – All the loops of faith—faith in yourself, faith in your desires, faith in your freedom, faith in your gifts, faith in your powerful armor, faith in the invisible, faith in tomorrow, faith in love, faith in God, and faith in the power of praise—come together to make the *Faith Climbing Knot.* It is the greatest knot to connect your climbing ropes to your body, soul, and spirit harness. It keeps your ropes from breaking as you climb.

Positive Affirmations Knot – The *Positive Affirmations Knot* ties your thought, emotion, and action ropes together to give you one strong climbing rope. Easy to do, the knot requires just a few twists and turns of daily short, positive affirmations to reinforce your new beliefs about yourself and life.

You can simply say each day, "All is well, all is good. I have the will to manifest my desires. I am connected to Spirit, who inspires and guides me. Everything is possible with faith. I am creativity, passion, confidence, courage, hope, love, and glee, and nothing will take that away from me. I am the *Marvelous Me*." With your thoughts, emotions, and action ropes well tied up and aligned, you keep fear away and feel great climbing up. You reach new heights of success in less time.

Vision of Success Knot – The *Vision of Success Knot* also ties your thought, emotion, and action ropes together to give you one strong climbing rope that empowers you with motivation and confidence. The knot requires a few turns of creating and reading your vision of success statement.

Start by writing down a short vision of success statement. Your statement should lay out how you want to feel physically, who you want to become, how you see your future, the experiences you want to attract, the relationships you aspire to develop, your passion for life, the possessions you would like to have, and any other aspirations.

For a more powerful effect, amplify your vision of success statement with what you experience with your senses, not just your eyesight. For example, write down what you hear, smell, feel, touch, and taste. Power up your written statement with positive emotions that are triggered by the thought of achieving your vision.

You can carry your vision of success statement in your purse or jacket, leave a copy at the office, or place it on your night table. Read it several times per day, when you are on the bus, waiting at your physician's office, or just before going to bed.

Visualization Knot – To reinforce your thought, emotion, and action ropes, you can use a *Visualization Knot* at both ends of your ropes. This is a strong knot that involves the practice of visualization to keep your ropes well-aligned at all times. Like the *Vision of Success Knot*, the *Visualization Knot* helps in keeping you motivated and confident as you climb up towards your desires.

Each day, close your eyes and visualize the actualization of your vision of success statement. See, smell, hear, taste, and touch. Feel the excitement and passion for the images you have portrayed.

Life mapping is another great visualization technique that allows your eyes to see the manifestation of your desires. Easy to do, you simply insert in a scrapbook or paste on a vision board pictures that illustrate your vision of success statement along with inspirational quotes and short positive affirmations about yourself. Every single day, you have a peek at your life map and feel the excitement for what is to come.

You can use props for more fun in your creative visualization. For example, if you want to be a famous model, cut out a picture of yourself and paste it on the cover of a magazine. If you want more money in the bank, add a zero or two to your bank statement and paste it on your fridge. You can play the acting game where you act out your desires with a friend and pretend you have the job you have been searching for or the boat you have desired for so long.

Team Knot – The *Team Knot* is the best knot to tie your climbing ropes to those of your team members. When properly tied up, you and your team members trust each other and climb together. You communicate using positive means, and you help each other while climbing towards your common vision. You work together for the best interest of all. Your minds are creative, and you all climb faster. You learn new climbing techniques from each other and freely share your success stories. You feel safe knowing that someone has your back if one of your ropes breaks.

Progress Knot – The *Progress Knot* is used to tie your rope to anchors as you climb up. Safely secured to anchors, you take time to assess your progress and celebrate your successes. You look for anything that might threaten your climbing plans. You are not turned off by glitches. With your *True Inspiration* app turned on, you are inspired with creative solutions to overcome challenges and climb safely.

Tight Grip Knot – The *Tight Grip Knot* allows you to continue to ascend even when you face obstacles. It is a sliding knot attached to your climbing ropes that allows you to ascend upward by sliding the knot up while you keep your eyes on the mountaintop. You stay calm, knowing that everything you need to succeed is in you. You are strong in maintaining the image of your vision in your mind. You climb up relentlessly, with confidence that you will soon reach your vision of success.

Once you have become an expert in tying all your knots, nothing will stop you in your climb to the success summit. Enjoy the climb. I can't wait to see you at the top!

Rejoice While You Climb

Don't overlook downloading onto your iPod some good tunes from the *ICAN* radio station to empower yourself with good-feeling thoughts as you climb. Rejoicing on your way up is as important as climbing. It makes you a stronger and faster climber. Your heart is confident that your dream—or something better—will come to fruition.

Rejoicing keeps negative thoughts, doubts, and fears away. You know that hard times will pass. Your mind is filled with creative thoughts and new ideas to handle challenges. Your heart overflows with hope, enthusiasm, and optimism. Each step up, whether small or grand, is a blessing. It makes the climb fun and joyful.

As you climb to success, you can't fall very far.
God's hand will swiftly catch you.

Rejoicing has molded me into a more patient, disciplined, and perseverant climber. It has kept my heart from despair and discouragement. It has opened my eyes and made me a believer that the impossible is indeed possible. It has showed me that I can place my trust in Him as I climb safely to new heights.

Looking for other ideas to rejoice as you climb? Weave the following tips into your climb for a joyous heart that will give you momentum on your way up.

Activate Your *Higher Power* App – With your *Higher Power* app activated, you climb with His joy, peace, and serenity in your heart. Praise is on your lips at all times. Frustration, disappointment, and discouragement have no room in your heart. You expect great things in your life, and nothing less. You trust in God's power to orchestrate events, circumstances, and people for your desires to come true at the right time. You trust that all is good and know that in each challenge, there is a lesson to be learned.

Activate Your *Be Happy* App – With *Be Happy*, your mind is filled with good-feeling thoughts. You speak words of possibilities and rise to new heights of success. You embrace a positive attitude with confidence and courage as you climb with enthusiasm and passion.

Practice *Flash Mob Thought* – Practicing *Flash Mob Thought* in your mind several times a day raises your emotional temperature. A little more than a decade ago, groups of people started to do *flash mob* dances where they came together for a few minutes to dance, and then they quickly dispersed. *Flash Mob Thought* is a very similar concept. So easy to do, it can be done anytime, anywhere, and it quickly shifts your vibrations from lower to higher frequency.

The moment a negative thought comes to mind, all you have to do is swiftly respond with a *Flash Mob Thought*. You let your mind dance with good-feeling thoughts that destroy barrier thoughts before they become powerful. By disciplining your mind, you maintain control of your thoughts. You feel deep joy and peace, knowing that all is well.

Read Inspiring Literature – Take time to read motivational self-help books, biographies, and other inspiring writings and teachings. Motivational books are rich with principles, techniques, and success stories to help you as you climb. Biographies of those who triumphed over adversity give you courage and hope in difficult times. They are great allies to boost your confidence in a better tomorrow.

Practice Gratitude – Being grateful for all the goodness in your life raises your vibrations of energy for more well-being. Practiced daily, gratitude brings about more positivity, confidence, and happiness, shifting you away from negative emotions amidst hardships. In conscious awareness of all that you are and have in life, glee becomes your constant companion. Be grateful for all your successes, small and grand, but most importantly, for all the little joys and smiles that each day brings.

Keep an Eye on your Knots – When you climb towards success, you may face high winds and obstacles, and you may lose your grip. Keep an eye on all your knots to ensure that they are tightened up for a successful climb. Faith, positive affirmations, reading your vision of success statement, visualization, teamwork, assessing progress, and commitment all come together to leave you with a merry heart as you manifest your desires. Not only do they keep you motivated and confident as you climb, but appreciative for your progress, collaborative relationships, and the wonderful moments of life.

Climb with Positive Climbers – Keep on rejoicing with like-minded, positive people. Their positive energy is contagious, and they lift up your spirit. They want you to succeed, and rejoice with you while you celebrate successes. Their kind words of encouragement and wisdom are sometimes all you need to keep you motivated as you climb.

Let each of your desires be a breath of new possibilities. Let the winds of hope sustain you. Let the sun keep you warm. Rejoice and enjoy the climb.

Rise on Top of Your Challenges

As you journey through life, you may encounter hurricanes, with heavy winds and severe rains that may cause you serious physical and emotional damage. Adversity, sickness, divorce, and the loss of a job or a loved one may bend you for a time, but these high winds will not break you.

You may bend when your employer lets you go. You may bend when you do not have enough money to pay your bills. You may bend when you become sick. You may bend when your projects fail. You may bend when your loved ones die. You may bend when your spouse leaves you for someone else. The good news is that your *Marvelous Nature* makes you hurricane-proof. You have the ability to withstand life's setbacks, disappointments, and losses.

Like a palm tree, you may bend but will not be broken. You may be disappointed, but not desperate. You may be sad, but not hopeless. You may be scared, but not without confidence. You may be discouraged, but not without resilience. You may feel alone, but not without faith. You may be wounded, but not without a cure. With your *Higher Power* app activated, you are not facing the storm alone. You have faith in the power of God to calm the winds and move you to safety. You heart remains at peace. Your inner joy does not fade. Your heart trusts in Him.

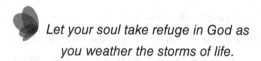

Let your soul take refuge in God as
you weather the storms of life.

The power that gives life is in you. You are the *Marvelous You*. You are creativity, passion, confidence, peace, joy, courage, and rich in blessings and love. With increased consciousness of life's duality, you see challenges as stepping stones for personal growth and transformation. Whenever you face a life hurricane, you are resolute to set a survival plan to move back to your state of well-being.

Stay strong and say, "I have faith in who I am. I am the *Marvelous Me*, resilient, courageous, and never alone. I am inspired, and I have creative ideas to surmount this storm. I am not defeated. I am a conqueror. I have faith in the power of God." Keep your thoughts captive in optimism and know without any doubt that all will soon be well. Read your vision of success statement, be inspired by those images, trusting that they will come to pass in due time as you are fully engaged in the manifestation process. Know that the sun will soon peek out again.

With your thoughts and emotions well-aligned, face your challenges and move swiftly to action. If you lost your job, inform all your friends. Contact employment agencies and attend free networking events. Keep yourself open to accepting a different position or lesser pay for a while. Take a course that may help you.

If you cannot pay your bills, contact your debtors to make payment arrangements. Find other sources of revenue. Rent a room in your home or share your apartment with someone. Limit your expenses. Sell material possessions that you do not need. Find a part-time job if needed.

If you get sick, see your physician and explore complementary and alternative medicines as you see fit. Look for unresolved emotions that may make you sick. Change your eating habits. Get support from friends and family.

If your project failed, look for lessons learned and how you could do things differently. Speak with your coach and mentors. Be inspired by what others are doing well and learn from them. Try again, but differently; do not give up.

If your loved one dies, know that the person is still spiritually alive, and one day, you will be reunited. Love never dies; it remains forever in your heart. Celebrate the person's life and accomplishments, and celebrate yours as well.

With grace and wisdom, rise above your challenges, transform who you are, become an inspiration to others, a comforter for those in need, and a living example of what it means to be a conqueror. Stay in faith and let yourself be captured by thoughts and feelings of hope and excitement. This attitude will give you momentum to conquer all your challenges and feel empowered.

Be Grateful

It is hard to be grateful when you go through hurricane season. When one storm after another hits you with disappointments, losses, break-ups, or scarcity, you may wonder if life is worth living. Your soul may be engulfed with fear, sadness, anguish, or grief.

Your mind may be asking: *Will I get better? Will I get a job? Will I be able to keep my house? Will I have enough to pay the bills? Will the pain ever stop? Will I ever find true love? Why do I have to live? Is it worth it?*

Whenever you go through life's storms, let gratitude be your soul armor against despair. If a storm hits outside, don't let it hit you inside. "What did you just say? How can I be grateful for my miseries? Really, I don't get it. You don't understand. I can't do this anymore. I want out!" you may shout.

You are the *Marvelous You*, rich in talents, friends, love, and all good things. True abundance is in you and around you. By being grateful, your fears, pain, and grief get blown away. You give room to more inner joy and peace.

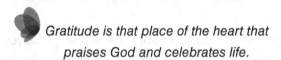 *Gratitude is that place of the heart that praises God and celebrates life.*

There is tremendous power in thankfulness. It wakes up positivity, happiness, hope, and faith. With a grateful heart, you are thankful for:

- Realizing your true purpose and becoming the best that you can be.
- Who you are and your value as a human being.
- Your unique gifts and talents, and how you have used them for your own fulfillment and the betterment of others.
- Your gift of love, respect, and forgiveness, and how you have helped others create a better life and meaningful experiences.
- Your happy moments of the day, such as having a good cup of coffee, a favorite dish, listening to good music, going for a bike ride, or a short drive around.

- What you have—your friends, family, health, work, and material possessions.
- The beauty around you: the flowers, plants, mountains, birds, sunrise, and sunshine.
- Your cherished memories that are alive in your treasure chest.
- The love you receive each day from those around you.
- Your grace for handling challenges in a positive manner.
- How much you have learned and grown over the years.

When you take refuge in gratitude, your mind shifts to more good-feeling thoughts, which in turn create positive emotions that move you in action. Even if strong winds are blowing in your professional and personal lives, you know that hurricane season does not last forever. Keep an open heart, learn and grow, and stay strong in the hope of a better tomorrow while moving forward. There are solutions to all problems. Like a rainbow after the rain, know that love, a new job, more money, and improved relationships will come your way.

Having been through a few storms myself, I learned early in life to practice gratitude. What a blessing! It has kept my heart from drowning many times. There were days when finding three things for which I was thankful was difficult. This forced me to see the great beauty of simple joys in life, such as listening to the birds singing, smelling flowers, or appreciating a smile or someone opening a door for me.

Practicing gratitude for little joys became the base on which I have built my happiness lighthouse. Over the years, I have mastered the art of creating simple magic moments during my day that keep my soul and spirit in a high-vibration energy space where well-being resides. My lighthouse stands strong in the face of high waves, and it is the symbol of courage and resilience.

There are so many ways you can express gratitude. Keep a daily gratitude journal, or simply bring into your mind what you are thankful for while you drive home from work. Send a gratitude e-mail or a card to someone you appreciate. Say thank you for a helping hand, or I love you to your loved ones.

Get going now, and create your happiness lighthouse using the strongest material there is—the small joys of life. Not only will your life shine, but you will be a shining light for those around you who navigate amidst a storm.

Believe in the Impossible

Imagine what your life would be if you would believe the impossible is achievable. That's what happens when you activate your *Higher Power* app. Your faith in God transforms your thoughts, and you believe that you can do so much more than what you are and have done today and yesterday. Most often, we set safe goals that we can accomplish with our talents and skills. By harnessing the Highest Power of the universe in faith, you set yourself up to setting up bigger goals and seeing the impossible become possible.

Miracles are defined as events that are not explicable by natural or scientific laws and are the work of a divine agency. To me, life itself is a miracle, with God being the Source of all that is. You are a miracle; just think how you developed from an embryo to a newborn without intervention. Being alive each day is a miracle, with your unconscious mind regulating your physiological body functions without effort. Creating your life is a miracle, with your simple thoughts being the spark of the manifestation process.

You are connected to the powerful Life Force that sustains this beautifully organized universe. Blessings are bestowed upon you each and every day whether you acknowledge them or not. Are you in survival mode right now? Maybe the past few years have been really hard on you, and you are blind to life's blessings and miracles.

Your spouse left you, you lost your job and your home, and your financial resources are dwindling. If this is your reality, then it's time for you to activate your *Higher Power* app and believe in the impossible and the power of miracles. You are not meant to be a survivor, you are a conqueror. You are meant to affirm your *Marvelous Self*. It's your time to get up every morning and say with eyes wide open, "I was blind, but now

I see. Great blessings are coming my way. New doors are opening. I will fulfill my destiny."

Let hope fill your heart. Let God work with you and direct your steps. Let Him show you His power for your desires to come alive. Allow His goodness to lift you up and give you the courage to be nudged into action. Let your obstacles be a door for something greater. He will open closed doors and do the impossible for you.

I want you to start playing the *Impossible Game* today, as illustrated below. Take a sheet of paper and write down your desires, what you can do to achieve them, and areas where you think you need divine intervention. By co-creating with God, your faith inspires you to believe in the impossible and remain in a state of positive expectations.

Once your list is completed, spend time alone each day and read out loud the actions you will undertake. Then move on to read all the actions where you need divine intervention. Finish your reading by saying: "God, thank you for loving me, for being with me always, for lifting me up, for being my fortress. Thank you for your divine intervention and for manifesting my desires—or something better—for the good of all concerned."

Impossible Game

Your Dream	You	God
To be cured of cancer	• Seek medical treatment. • Stop smoking. • Exercise and make healthy food choices. • Explore energy healing.	• Align the best physicians and other health care practitioners on my path. • Make the tumors disappear all at once.
Find a new job	• Contact employment agencies. • Tell friends. • Send resumes.	• Inform me, a friend, or other acquaintances of a job opening.
Find a spouse	• Attend social events. • Meet people on dating sites.	• Align for the right person to cross my path.

Remember that nothing is too great for the *Marvelous You*. Dare to dream the impossible. After playing the *Impossible Game* for a few weeks, your life will be transformed. Your mind, will, soul, and spirit will be inspired by Spirit. You will be confident that everything will work out for the best interest of all. You will be vibrating at a higher level of consciousness, and experience oneness in Him.

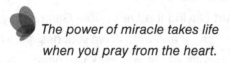

*The power of miracle takes life
when you pray from the heart.*

God is Infinite Consciousness. He is All-That-Is who can align events, circumstances, and people in your life like no one else. He has the power to speak through anyone's higher conscious mind and inspire you and others to do certain things, yet in all respect for your freedom. God can influence, but cannot override the will of another person.

As such, prayers involving others may take longer to come true. God has the power to unbind what was bound, transform losses into gains, and move you to where you want to be in less time, using the most surprising ways. Let Him work in your life in the right season.

Sometimes we are anxious in the waiting and forget the joy of stillness found in the crease of His hand, safe and protected. Open your treasure chest, and remind yourself of your past and current blessings. Let Him lift you up and replace your fears with hope.

Praise Him for all the good that is coming your way. God hears you and is at work. Not seeing the fruits does not mean the seeds are not growing. Let Him grow the seeds of greatness that are in you and transform your life. Hold on and remain strong; your dream is close to becoming reality. Waiting does not mean the answer is no. It may just mean not now. If the answer is no, God will inspire a new prayer in your heart. By remaining in a state of openness, trust, and confidence, He gives you wisdom and grace to accept the answer.

"Does faith healing always work?" you might ask.

I have known people of great faith who had serious illnesses and were healed, and some others who were not kept from death. I do believe in divine healing, and I suggest you pursue divine healing while seeking medical treatment. Having said that, keep in mind that God may not intervene; your journey on earth may be meant to end.

Your true purpose on earth is to unleash your *Marvelous Essence*. A physical setback does not preclude you from realizing each of the truths of the *Marvelous You*. Even more, it transforms you into a shining light and a great source of inspiration for others who are going through challenges and obstacles. In health or in sickness, you are truly alive in Him. He is glorified by your attitude, grace, love, wisdom, courage, glee, confidence, and faith.

Stay in faith and hold tight to His hand. Let His grace and mercy be in your heart, knowing that He is in control of today and tomorrow. In Him, you cannot lose your life; you find life. He is the God of the impossible. In His time, you will see His amazing power, sovereignty, and supremacy.

Look for God Outside the Box

While scientists, physicists, and cosmologists have made significant advances in providing explanations about life and the universe, the mysteries of God and existence still loom large in their minds. It is believed that the universe comprises 200 billion galaxies, containing varying numbers of planets, star systems, and star clusters. Approximately 70 percent of the universe is made up of dark energy, a force that causes the universe to expand at an accelerating rate. In addition, close to 25 percent of the universe is dark matter, non-luminous particles, and the rest is normal luminous matter that we can observe around us.[1]

"How do we know for sure that God exists and created the cosmos?" you might ask.

When we look at the vastness of the cosmos-at-large, the beauty of this world, the various species in the air, water, and on the ground, plus the complexities of the human body and mind, it is difficult to not be in awe and acknowledge a Life Force behind this beautiful creation, a Life Force that is infinitely more than who we are.

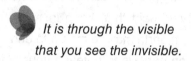

It is through the visible
that you see the invisible.

Some people might ask: "Will faith in God really power up my life?" For some, the answer has been no. Not knowing or understanding God has not hindered their power to thrive for action and happiness. For others, like me, having a glimpse at the whole picture outside the box, scientifically proven or not, has been a real compass in life. It has become a driver to positive actions, love, kindness, compassion, forgiveness, and a great source of joy and hope. Believing in my connectedness to All-That-Is has been a constant source of comfort and empowerment.

It is in the silence and the quietness of my heart that I hear His voice of love. It is in the beauty of others, the world around me, and in the universe that I see His greatness. I like to believe that through His grace, blessings are bestowed upon me, no matter what. Simply put, I enjoy my companionship with Him each and every day.

To me, God is Infinite Consciousness, the Highest Power, and the Alpha and Omega. He is absolute love, peace, forgiveness, righteousness, and guardian. He communicates with each one of us in different ways: through nature, people, experiences, intuition, inspiration, music, prayer, and inspiring writings and teachings. Reach out to Him. His hand is waiting for yours.

See Beyond Death

Life after death has been an ongoing interest for science, philosophers, and theologians of all times. Each year, we hear reports of people who communicate with spiritual creatures, whether light beings, angels, or deceased family members. We hear occurrences of near-death experience

(NDE) and out-of-body experience (OBE), with descriptions of amazing things happening in those moments. These include meeting past known relatives, speaking with an unknown relative, formation of new memories, and traveling in a light tunnel. Science now has evidence that we are composed of energy fields; but what does it say about the NDE and OBE experience? Science has been quite shy to recognize these events as being evidence there is life after death.

Science has provided biological explanations to the NDE and OBE experiences, keeping silent about a possible afterlife and the existence of the soul/spirit outside the body. A study from researchers at the University of Kentucky in the United States of America infers the trigger of a rapid eye movement (REM) intrusion in the brain stem as an explanation of NDEs. The REM intrusion is a disorder where a person's mind wakes up before its body and experiences hallucinations and the feeling of being physically detached from its body.[2]

The brain stem can operate independently from the higher brain responsible for thoughts and actions. So even after the higher regions of the brain are dead, the brain stem, which controls basic functions such as breathing, heartbeat, and blood pressure, can conceivably continue to function and cause a REM intrusion.[3]

Many skeptics just dismiss NDEs, stating they result from abnormally elevated carbon dioxide in the brain, a lack of oxygen in the brain, or brain damage, amongst other things.[4] It is touted that one in ten people may have an OBE in their lifetime caused by either severe physical or brain traumas, sensory deprivation, near-death experiences, dehydration, sleep, or electrical stimulation of the brain.[5]

While NDE and OBE can be explained independently, reports of new memories and conscious awareness when the higher brain is presumed dead is much more difficult to explain. I am not aware that science has yet provided a response to this type of experience. To this day, the afterlife still remains a complete mystery. Perhaps it is meant to be this way for you to experience oneness with God in faith and have the will to fully express the *Marvelous You* that you are.

My personal conclusions? With my *Higher Power* app activated, I say with faith in my heart:

- There is a spiritual world orchestrated by God, Infinite Consciousness. I am from God and in God, endowed with a physical and spiritual nature.
- I am His creature of love and His love power flows through me unless I pull away. His fathomless love for me has no boundaries and surpasses all understanding.
- I am called in the physical world to grow into the perfection of my *Marvelous Self* and be all that I can be.
- I accept the mysteries of God, and I am at peace not understanding it all at this time. While I know little, I know enough to live true love and have faith in Him to be His joy.
- One day, I will be in His presence for eternity. With love and faith flowing ardently in my heart, I will be drawn by grace to His garden of love, like a powerful magnet.
- In oneness with Him, I will continue to grow in perfection and delight in Him.

God is my Source.
He is the wind under my wings.
He is the rainbow after the rain.
He is the sun that lights up my path.
He is the air that breathes through me.
He is the star that makes my life shine.
He is the wave that sweeps me off my feet.
He is the moon where my head rests at night.
He is my ALL.

Part II

Power Up
Your Life for
More Abundance

CHAPTER 6

Power Up Your Attitude

The walk of excellence takes you from
good to great.

Activate Your *Be Happy* App

With *Be Happy*, joy is in the air, and life is like a breath of fresh air, a warm breeze on your neck, or the sun on your skin. You appreciate each moment as a gift. With a positive outlook, you live life with much more ease. You crush negativity. You move in life with more confidence, courage, and passion. You are grateful for today and for what is yet to come, and your heart is safe in true joy. With *Be Happy*, everything about you and your life is enlightened with positivity: your thoughts, words, behavior, faith, surroundings, and values.

 In every moment, you are grateful.

In every moment, you are
happiness.

In every moment, you experience
inner joy.

Keep Your Thoughts Positive – Feeling down, disappointed, or discouraged? With *Be Happy*, you take action to swiftly stop the chaos in your mind and heart. You let go of past negative events and move through life's disappointments with more ease. You nourish your mind with thoughts of hope, abundance, and success. With good-feeling thoughts, you raise your vibrations and move to your well-being zone. You are ready for your seeds of greatness to flourish and live your best life.

You cultivate life mindfulness, where your eyes see the beauty in each moment. A smile, a flower, a sunrise, the smell of fresh coffee, the purr of a cat, a call from a friend, a small victory, a walk outside, the wind in your hair, listening to music, singing a song; all these simple pleasures make your heart expand in gratitude.

Keep Your Words Positive – With *Be Happy,* you maintain a positive outlook and speak words of possibilities. You become your own best friend and reach new heights of success. You control your inner dialogue. There is no more negative self-pity party with negative statements, "I will never have a job. I will never have this promotion. I will never get better. I can't. It never works. Life is hard. The economy is down, and it will be tough to gain new business."

You tame your inner critic and congratulate yourself for your successes, small and grand. You are no longer shy to charm yourself and say, "I can do this. I look great. I am really good. I did well today. I will manifest my desires. I made a mistake, but it's all good, I am learning." Not only does positive self-talk evoke feel-good emotions and heighten your energetic vibration, but it fuels your drive to move forward with assertive actions.

Keep Your Behavior Positive – With *Be Happy,* you are fired up and believe in your desires. You feel alive and ready to be the success you are meant to be. You embrace positive behavior with more enthusiasm, energy, and passion. You allow your wisdom, inspiration, intuition, and guidance to flow as you move into action. There is no room for impatience or frustration. You know that all good things happen in their time. You are grateful for what you have and what is to come.

Keep Your Faith Positive – *Be Happy* keeps you confident that today and tomorrow will be happy days. You choose a positive response to all events. You are not afraid to take a leap of faith. You are comfortable in being uncomfortable.

You are resilient and courageous in the face of challenges. You are armed with courage, inner strength, and resilience, well-equipped to bounce back quickly from adversity. Grounded in God, no challenges can take away your inner joy. You navigate with a happy heart, safely guided by His lighthouse. You see your life as a thrilling adventure with no end, just new beginnings. You are ready to receive more—or something better—than expected.

Keep Your Surroundings Positive – You say good-bye to negative people who do not share or respect your core values, who use you for their own benefit, bring your energy down, and leave you feeling stressed, nauseated, or suffocated. You say hello to those who believe in your greatness. You surround yourself with qualified advisors—friends, family members, colleagues, coaches, and mentors—who look out for your best interest and uplift you.

Keep Your Values Positive – With *Be Happy*, you put little feet under your values and walk the talk. By embracing positive values, you bring to the world more goodness and light. You breathe and live glee, fulfilment, and contentment. You are inspired to create moments of happiness for yourself and others. You let your light shine. You embrace love, respect, integrity, and courage.

Simply put, by activating your *Be Happy* app, you maintain a positive outlook on life and fly to ew heights of well-being and achievement for your personal fulfillment and the betterment of those around you. My husband always says to me: "Fly, little bird, fly." With *Be Happy*, that's what I do. I fly high towards my dreams and like a loon, I run into the wind and let the air beneath my wings elevate me to new heights. I say to you, "Be positive in all that you are—thoughts, words, emotions, behavior, values, and actions. Fly high, little bird!"

Be a Success

Success can be defined in different ways. To some, it is the achievement of something desired or the attainment of popularity and prosperity. For others, it means living their passion or having a good-paying job, a nice house, or other material things.

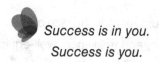

Success is in you.
Success is you.

In my view, success is first and foremost to be all that you can be. This definition implies that we can all have a successful life independently of our social status, the size of our bank account, or how big our accomplishments are. We are all destined to success, and we can all stand tall and be proud of ourselves, our growth, and our accomplishments, small and grand. It doesn't matter if we failed at achieving a specific goal. What matters is that we have grown through the experience.

You might ask, "How can I maximize my potential?"

Remember these four steps: 1) learn more, 2) dare, 3) make positive life-changing choices, and 4) persevere. I have no doubt that you will live up to your full potential and be a success following these steps.

Learn – Each one of us is gifted. You are called to transform yourself and create a fulfilling life for you and those around you. Don't hide your gifts. Develop new skills, open your mind to new ideas, find the creativity within you, try new things, and let your voice be heard. These are all great ways to let your light shine.

Dare – If your heart is filled with desires and hopes, don't ignore them. Desires and hopes are often messages of the direction you should be taking for your life. Most importantly, activate your *High Drive* app and get into action. Desires always come with the power to realize them.

Make Positive, Life-Changing Choices – If you want more in your life, then make choices that will attract abundance. You want more love? Love more. You want more friends? Be more of a friend. You want more money? Give more. You want to feel more invigorated? Exercise more. You want more kindness? Care more. You want more blessings? Be more grateful. In being more of what you want, you become a magnet who attracts more of what you yearn for. As you attract more, give more. In doing so, you are creating a powerful circle of abundance.

Persevere – Do not let a setback stop you from moving forward. Choose a different direction, keep walking, and go all the way to your destination. Failure does not exist, as life is all about learning what works and what doesn't. Growth stems from experiencing life to its fullest, with all its ups and downs.

Success encompasses the whole life transformation process, with you discovering your gifts and talents, learning and growing, being creative, taking action, and adding more beauty into the universe with your own uniqueness. Remember, success is in you; success *is* you. Learn, dare, make positive, life-changing choices, and persevere. Without any doubt, your life will be a testimony of all that you can be!

Get Your Fire Back

Are you stuck in a rut, with no drive and confidence to pursue your aspirations? Do you keep making disastrous choices in your life? Do you feel like the *Powerless You*? Perhaps you wake up every morning saying: "Why bother? I'll never be a success. I'll never find a job. I'll never find a spouse. I'll never be able to pay my debts. I can't do this, it's too hard." And the list goes on and on.

You start the day with no energy and just go about things like a robot, with no life or excitement. Every little task seems like a big mountain to climb. You see everybody else being a success, and doubt the wind will turn in your favor. You wonder if your next song or movie will be a hit, or if you'll have that big contract or promotion to move up the career ladder.

Perhaps life disappointments are so overwhelming that all you see is darkness, and you wonder if life is worth living. Maybe you were betrayed and your spouse left you, and your heart is filled with sadness and feelings of abandonment. Or your inner spark died as a result of too much stress and disappointments.

Whatever reason is behind your loss of enthusiasm and excitement for life, know that you can bounce back by activating your *Be Happy* app. Remind yourself that you are the *Marvelous You,* born to be a visionary and a powerful creator, not just an observer of life. Take time to reflect on what you want your life to be and who you want to be.

Ask yourself: Is my life mission still relevant? Am I on the right path? What do I truly want to accomplish? Do I have new dreams? Am I afraid of failure? Do I lack discipline? Do I love myself enough to make favorable choices? Am I tired of being frustrated? Do I truly want change in my life?

Try to understand how you went from flying high to flying low. With greater clarity on your *spark extinguishers*, you will reenergize yourself. You are pure creativity, fully equipped to live your best life. Don't let self-oppression and self-doubt stop you from creating your best life.

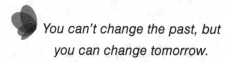
You can't change the past, but
you can change tomorrow.

Long working hours can take a toll on your health and sap your energy. If stress is your *spark extinguisher*, take time to relax your mind and body. A large number of relaxation techniques and exercises are available to reduce fatigue, re-awaken your enthusiasm, and re-ignite your drive.

If not living your dreams is your *spark extinguisher*, then go back to the drawing board. Happiness and success are yours. Set a new vision and inspiring goals. Find the why and how behind what you want to do. Don't be afraid to change your life. Craft an action plan, get in gear, and find satisfaction and fulfillment in your life. You are meant to live to the utmost of your greatness. With commitment, self-control, and determination, you have the power to direct your intentions and actions towards your dreams.

Life's disappointments can be like tsunamis that extinguish your inner spark. From spouse betrayal to wrongful dismissal and shattered desires, life's setbacks can be brutal to withstand, especially when they involve other people who have hurt you. If holding a grudge is your *spark extinguisher*, activate your *Love Power* app, as inviting forgiveness into your heart is the key to get your fire back. Forgiveness means moving forward in spite of your hurts. Letting go of the past heals your wounds and gives you wings to fly.

If your *spark extinguisher* is a lost dream or a roadblock, do not lose sight of who you are, the *Marvelous You.* Roadblocks are challenges to overcome, not to paralyze you. You are courageous, resilient, and hopeful, right? Pull out your contingency plan and get into action. Feed your disappointments with small actions and faith. You will fire yourself back up.

Comparing yourself to others is another *spark extinguisher*. Learn from others, but beware of the negative self-image trap. Don't lose sight that your contribution to the world is unique. Those aspirations of yours will come about as you are true to yourself. Nothing will keep you from your destiny except yourself.

If a lack of discipline is your *spark extinguisher*, you need to understand that only you can change your life. Change takes effort and commitment, but the payback is enormous as you are moving towards your desires. Love yourself enough to create an environment that sustains your efforts. For example, be accountable to someone of your progress, have a mentor or coach, find someone to help out, improve your organizational skills, and celebrate your mini-successes.

It's never too late to ignite your inner spark again. Remember that flowers bloom in all seasons. Be confident and say, "I choose to be all that I can be no matter what. I have great expectations for today and tomorrow. I stand strong in my commitment to live my best life."

As you get your fire back, you will warm up the world with your sparks of energy, excitement, creativity, and love. Be of great faith, and trust the Infinite Power of the universe to do amazing things through you. He holds you in the palm of His hand, and He will open doors for you and ease your way. I know He can do it; trust me. He did it for me, and He will do it for you.

Bloom Where You Are

People tell me all the time how difficult it is to cope with waiting. Perhaps you've been looking for a new job or waiting for a romantic relationship to bloom for some time. Or maybe you doubt that new clients will knock at your door, or you feel overwhelmed by the completion of a large project that spans over months.

As you take action, you await the manifestation of your desires, and it's taking a toll on you. Long delays do test our patience and motivation. While each new job interview, romantic date, or business proposal is a positive action towards change, each day that goes by waiting for a favorable answer is real agony. Doubt and discouragement can easily find room in your heart.

The best antidote for waiting agony is to bloom where you are. Each morning, activate your *Be Happy* app, and with a grateful heart say, "I am happy today. I bloom where I am, and I rejoice in this moment and for what is to come." Blooming equates to being positive, choosing good-feeling thoughts, staying in action, and having faith in tomorrow.

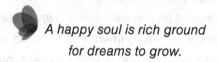

*A happy soul is rich ground
for dreams to grow.*

By remaining positive, you are a great testimony to who you truly are, the *Marvelous You*. At work, with a big smile on your face, you remain dedicated, even if you are looking for a new job. You are on your way to an acting audition? No problem; you are enthusiastic at the prospect of being chosen for the part. You dream of expanding your business? No need to worry; you remain innovative, offering excellent service to your current clients. You are looking for a job? You bless each resume that you send out.

With good-feeling thoughts, you embrace the waiting period. When negative thoughts come to mind, you respond quickly with a *Flash Mob Thought*. You look at all you've accomplished so far; the new friendships you've developed, the new experiences that came along. You see waiting as an opportunity to express courage, resilience, confidence, and be even more creative.

Focused, you happily press on and continue to march towards your vision. By getting into action, you create momentum and celebrate each of your efforts, job interviews, auditions, or business proposals. You are creative and open to new ideas.

You read good-feelings affirmations about yourself and your vision each day. You care for yourself by setting time aside to relax and enjoy life. You are grateful for what you have and where you are in this moment. You surround yourself with positive people who believe in you and uplift you.

You stand strong in your faith, knowing that each positive thought, action, and feeling is a seed that will bear fruit in its time. You trust that God co-creates with you and will show you the way. To sum it up, with your *Be Happy* app activated, you bloom and shine anywhere and anytime. Waiting moments are no longer moments of agony but moments of creativity, hope, courage, and inner joyousness.

Stop Pleasing Everyone

American essayist and poet Ralph Waldo Emerson once said: "To be yourself in a world that is constantly trying to make you something else is the greatest accomplishment." Why is being ourselves so difficult? The answer is simple: we fear rejection. We believe that in living according to other people's expectations, we will be loved and accepted.

From the moment you were born, you craved love, and you needed to belong. From a very young age, you associated obedience with acceptance. You understood that if you behaved, you would receive love. If you didn't, then punishment, days of pouting, or rejection from parents and friends were to come, leaving you in a distressing emotional turmoil.

Many adolescents see their parents pressing their own dreams on them. To please them, they oblige in pursuing a career that is not their choice. As adults, they often carry their need of acceptance in their married lives, and they crush their voice in order to please their spouse.

Years go on, and then one day, they wake up and suddenly suffocate. They reckon they cheated on themselves and did not allow their soul to fly high. Does this sound like your life? Is your soul being held captive? Are you just surviving day in and day out, with no passion and excitement? Perhaps you have given away your life and now you want it back.

You were not born to relinquish control of your life to someone else. You are endowed with freedom to choose who you want to be and what you want to achieve in life. Your life is yours to create. Don't let anyone tell you otherwise. Life is short; live your dreams, not someone else's dreams.

You were born to be the creator of your life, not to dance to someone else's tune. You are gifted with your own life purpose and mission. In silencing who you are, you are depriving the world of your great beauty. It takes lots of courage and volition to stand up for yourself and take your life back. Resolve to fight for your birthright and enjoy your free will.

Change will come with the acknowledgement of who you are, followed by action. Take a stand and say, "I am the *Marvelous Me*, and I am honoring who I am and my aspirations. I deserve to create my best life. I was born to bring beauty into the world. It is my right to fly high."

Strange as it seems, you will be surprised by how much respect people will have for you as you stand for your desires and convictions. You set an example as to what life is meant to be.

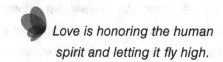

Love is honoring the human
spirit and letting it fly high.

Living an inspired life starts with listening to your inner voice for guidance. Activate your *True Inspiration* app and let inspiration flow abundantly to help you become all that you can be and live the life you deserve. Trust your instincts; they hold the answer as to which path you should travel. In honoring who you are, you are telling the world that your self-esteem is built on the rock of your own truth and acceptance.

Seeking opinions of trusted advisors is different from seeking approval out of fear of rejection. The first one will lead you to growth, while the other will lead you to a road of captivity. As you seek others' opinions, be wise and remember to live your truth. In the end, you are to follow what you think is right and true to you.

Simply put, be yourself, and honor who you are with your unique aspirations, skills, and talents. Don't worry if others do not see what you see. Your desires are for you; not for others to accomplish. So rejoice, press on, and soon you will hear your inner voice chanting: *You did well, Marvelous You. You are on the right path, and I am proud of what you have accomplished.*

Be Comfortable in Being Uncomfortable

Are you ready for some excitement? Let's get you out of your comfort zone to embrace continual evolvement. Don't worry if you are intimidated by change. Being uncomfortable simply means you are on your way to being all that you can be by developing new skills, trying new activities, and meeting new people.

To easily navigate in the uncomfortable zone, first open your mind to who you truly are, the *Marvelous You*, engaged and enthusiastic to explore all possibilities that lie within you. Acknowledge your potential to do amazing things and be ready to replace limiting beliefs with new ones.

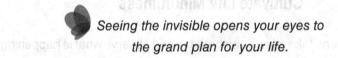

Seeing the invisible opens your eyes to the grand plan for your life.

Next, take mini-steps out of your comfort zone to become more comfortable doing the uncomfortable. Creating change is exciting. See each action, challenge, and experience as an occasion to learn, grow, and be creative. With your *High Drive* app activated, developing skills and abilities, practicing a new sport, learning a new language, adopting new eating habits, or taking on new projects is so much easier.

Your next step is to take control of your emotions and ease discomfort by releasing fears that may capture your heart and mind. How do you do this? Keep your *Be Happy* app activated, and each and every moment, exercise tough love on yourself. Master your thoughts to move to the high zone of the emotion spectrum where you experience inner joy, peace, hope, and enthusiasm.

By choosing to maintain a positive outlook and good-feeling thoughts, you tame the uncomfortable and make it more comfortable. When doubt and fear are around the corner, chase those thoughts with a *Flash Mob Thought* and say, "I honor myself. I choose to be all that I can be. I am abundance. I am creativity. I am joy. All is well and good."

Lastly, cultivate spiritual awareness to heighten your state of well-being. Connected to the organizing Power that sustains the universe, nourish a mind-set that has faith in your abilities and in God to take you to a place of growth and fulfillment.

With these tips in mind, you will happily welcome change and live life to the fullest. You will look forward to pursuing a new direction for your life. Remember—good-feeling thoughts, engaged actions, a positive outlook, and faith are your allies for transforming the uncomfortable into the comfortable. Don't be afraid to show the world how amazing you are. Enjoy the transformation!

Cultivate Life Mindfulness

Stop for a moment, take a few deep breaths, and observe what is happening around you. What sounds do you hear? What do you see? What do you smell? How do you feel? What do you think? By bringing your attention to your thoughts, emotions, body, and senses in this present moment, you have just practiced mindfulness.

To some, mindfulness is strictly present awareness. For others, it also embodies remembering. For me, mindfulness is a calm awareness of life in all its beauty, with its past and present moments. I call the practice *Life Mindfulness.*

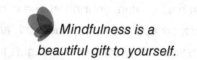 *Mindfulness is a beautiful gift to yourself.*

Mindfulness increases your physical, emotional, and spiritual well-being. It can be practiced as you take a walk during your lunch hour, while on the bus to work, or during your work break. Daily practice of mindfulness brings calm to your mind, body, and soul. The end result is always the same: reviving a sense of awe at life and its mysteries.

By pacifying your fast-paced mind and shifting your negative thought pattern, you halt the emotional storm that is ravaging your heart. As you inhale and exhale, your body releases stress and tension. In these moments of silence, you feel the energy of life within you and around you. You are moved at the thought of oneness with all humanity. You are reminded that you are part of this vast universe, connected to all other human beings, animals, and nature.

With mindfulness, the eyes of your heart open, and you see that all is in you to create an amazing life: abundance, creativity, glee, peace, and love. By embracing unity, you choose to create for the betterment of all.

In observing the blue sky, hearing the birds singing, feeling the wind on your cheeks, and looking at the trees rising to the sky, mindfulness keeps you focused on the beauty of life. With your eyes, you are in awe of the universe. You know with certainty that the power that sustains nature takes care of your life.

Mindfulness energizes your whole life. With a song in your heart, you celebrate life. Your heart is filled with gratefulness for yesterday, today, and tomorrow. You are no longer afraid; you trust that all is well and good. With these benefits in mind, let mindfulness be part of your day. Soon your heart will be filled with wonders, and you will be immersed by a sense of well-being, joy, and fulfillment.

Don't Look Back, Move Forward

Do you wake up each morning with great intentions to improve your life but can't make a lasting change? Do you feel you are dancing around like a puppet with ropes from your past that are controlling you and holding you back? If your past is holding you back, you can sever these ropes that restrict you from dancing to your own rhythm.

You are the *Marvelous You*, and certainly not a puppet. You are in control of your life, and you have the ability to heal, forgive, release negative emotions, and improve your life. You can be the success you want to be. You can start today to live to the fullest and create the change you are looking for in your life.

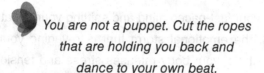

You are not a puppet. Cut the ropes
that are holding you back and
dance to your own beat.

Whether your controlling ropes are past failures, shattered dreams, limited beliefs, romantic heartaches, loss of family members, betrayals, or lost jobs, no ropes are strong enough to keep you from being all you are meant to be. You are fully equipped to triumph from betrayal, pain, and failure.

If you have experienced betrayals, choose to forgive. You are loved, and you have the power to cut this rope. With forgiveness, you free yourself from the pain. You are responsible to live *your* life, not the other person's life. Let things be the way they are and go with the flow, knowing that each one of us is on a path of learning and growing.

If you still feel the loss of loved ones, dry your tears and celebrate their lives and love. Carry them in your heart, in a special place of joy where light abounds. Let them be with you as you move on and continue to honor life. Let your light shine to the world in their honor.

If you struggle with past romantic heartaches, know that it is better to have loved and lost than not to have loved at all. Love is meant to flow, and we can't coerce anyone to love us. When love is not reciprocated, set yourself and the other person free. In keeping an open mind and heart, a true love will find you.

If you have encountered past failures or shattered dreams, activate your *True Inspiration* app and dream new dreams. Learn from past experiences, but don't let them stop you. Every lesson in life is valuable and prepares you for greater things. In action, you will soon feel alive again. There is tremendous potential in you; let it come alive. Work at being the success you are meant to be.

If you are held back by limited beliefs, replace them with new ones that speak to your heart and inspire you. You are responsible to create your own reality. It is your right to say, "No more!" to limited beliefs rooted in past experiences or inherited from parents, friends, teachers, and even society.

Don't wait any longer. Free yourself, and enjoy the life you deserve. Cut the ropes that are holding you back to let freedom come alive: freedom to create, love, and live a life of purpose and fulfillment.

Be Humble, Your Talents are a Gift

You are the *Marvelous You,* born to unlock your full potential and light up the world with all that you are. Being humble does not mean hiding your beauty, talents, and skills. It means being aware that your talents and skills are seeds of greatness planted by God for your fulfillment and the betterment of all.

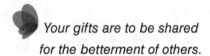

Your gifts are to be shared
for the betterment of others.

You honor yourself when you affirm your *Marvelous Essence.* In spreading your light into the world, you inspire others to do the same. In this gentle awareness, shine confidence and wisdom. In using your gifts wisely, you honor Him. In all humility, you nourish healthy self-esteem.

Focused on watering your seeds, you do not need to compete with others. You appreciate their beauty for what it is—a gift from God. You are inspired and learn from them. You are free from the need to judge them, knowing fairly well that growth is a process. Just like you, they are learning and growing.

In being humble, you develop a love for yourself that is not ego-based, but Spirit-based. You find pleasure in simply being who you are. You forego the need to seek attention and boast of your accomplishments. You let your inner light shine and speak for itself.

With a humble heart, you are generous and give freely, and you are fully aware that all that is in you is for your fulfillment and the betterment of all. You are always ready to give a hand to those in need. You let your presence be soothing to those who hurt, and your words are a balm on their wounds.

127

You value those who have helped you succeed, and you praise their contribution. When you open your mouth, praises are on your lips rather than finding faults in others. You care for and encourage others to live to the best of their abilities. In this kind of humility, you live not only with great wisdom but with appreciation, awareness, and respect for the grand plan of life.

CHAPTER 7

Power Up Your Health

Love is the most powerful anti-aging formula.
An act of kindness a day will keep you radiant
and glowing each day.

Activate Your *Fit and Fab* App

As the *Marvelous You*, you are a lifetime member of the *Fit and Feeling Fabulous Club*. To activate your free membership, you simply need to turn on your *Fit and Fab* app to start your journey towards maximum health and wellness. *Fit and Fab* empowers you with commitment, self-discipline, and dedication to care for your physical well-being and achieve your health and fitness goals. Simply put, it transforms your life with more vitality and wellness. As a member of the *Fit and Feeling Fabulous Club*, you get to enjoy tremendous benefits, namely:

Increased Body-Brain Fitness – You choose from a variety of healthy food that provides you with the right balance of protein, vitamins, minerals, and nutrients. Not only does your nutritional plan protect you from illness, but it improves your overall health and increases your brain-body fitness. You feel fit and fabulous.

 Health is a gift to nurture each day.

Increased Vitality – You take charge and make healthy living changes that allow you to reach your ideal weight, and most importantly, maintain it for more wellness. A healthy weight makes all the difference in keeping your energy level up. You say good-bye to fatigue, bad sleep, and body pain, and say hello to increased energy and vitality.

Fitness Lover – You are committed to a variety of physical exercises that increase blood flow, build strength, and improve balance and flexibility. Not only do you increase your energy level, but you relieve your stress and improve your mood and sleep.

Stress Reduction – You take *Me* time during the day to care for yourself, de-stress, and feel more energized. Try reading inspiring books and positive affirmations, visualization, praising prayer, physical and breathing exercises, and other relaxation techniques.

Sickness Prevention – You are eager to adopt a healthy lifestyle that helps keep the doctor away. Nutritious food, physical activity, reduced stress, and improved sleep are all part of your new reality. You live a healthier life with a stronger immune system that protects you from viruses and illnesses. You carefully listen to the messages your body is sending you, and you care for yourself.

More Laughter – You add more laughter in your day and learn to see the beauty in yourself, around you, and in each moment. Laughter reduces your stress hormones, lowers your blood pressure, and improves your brain functions. It is also touted to increase the response of your tumor-killing cells.

Freedom from Addictions – You have the willpower to change your life and free yourself from compulsive behaviors and unhealthy addictions, including cigarettes, drugs, alcohol, and excessive food, coffee, and soft drinks. You feel at peace with your life, who you are, and what you do.

Constant Support – You are provided with a wealth of information on health matters to make healthy decisions. You understand why fitness matters, and how proper support helps you achieve and maintain your fitness goals. You are inspired by other *Fit and Feeling Fabulous Club* members who also aim for better health and fitness in their lives.

Greater Physical and Emotional Healing – You learn about your body and soul connection, and you are open to different approaches to heal yourself emotionally and physically to experience wholeness and perfect health. Not only do you seek conventional medical advice, but you consider other complementary and alternative medicine approaches.

To sum it up, being a member of the *Fit and Feeling Fabulous Club* brings more health, fitness, vitality, and emotional wellness into your life. Don't wait any longer; activate your *Fit and Fab* app and start your fitness journey today for a thriving life.

Listen to Your Body

Taking care of yourself is a key pillar in taking off to new heights of wellness and creating your best life. With more energy and vitality, it is much easier to manifest your desires and experience life to the fullest. Caring for yourself starts with activating your *Fit and Fab* app to enable you to recognize that you are a person of value who deserves a happy and healthy life.

What you give to your body today, your body will give back to you tomorrow. It's as simple as that. Being kind to your body involves choosing power food and getting enough exercise, rest, and play. It also means listening to what your body is telling you.

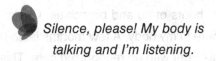 *Silence, please! My body is talking and I'm listening.*

Your body comes with an alert system, telling you when something is amiss and needs your attention. Physical signals may include a lack of energy, pain, tight muscles, shaking hands, memory lapse, a lack of concentration, inflammation, skin redness, splitting headaches, and dizziness.

Most of us are good at activating our *Fit and Fab* app, which enhances our ability to listen to our body's distress signals to swiftly take charge to restore our health. At times, all we need is to add a few better health practices into our life. At other times, we need to get our worrisome symptoms checked out by our physician or health care providers.

Unfortunately, there are far too many people, like my father, who simply ignored turning his *Fit and Fab* app on and paid the ultimate price by losing his life early. Some people have the notion that they are invincible, and they believe that by denying their symptoms, their sickness will go away. Young people are generally very good at the denial game, thinking that sickness is for older people. Others are so busy tending to their work that taking care of their health is not on their priority list.

Creating your best life involves caring physically, emotionally, and spiritually for yourself. As I've always said, "You cannot give what you do not have." There is no output without an input. Likewise, you cannot drive a car without fuel. You cannot be energetic without caring for yourself.

You are the *Marvelous You*, and you deserve nothing less than a wonderful and healthy life. Take charge and turn on your *Fit and Fab* app today!

Eat for Super Performance

Nearly every week, we hear discoveries about the power of food to treat and prevent diseases. Food is a great ally in powering up your health and well-being. I know this from personal experience. Seventeen years ago, following several bouts of flu and bronchitis, I woke up with severe muscle pain everywhere in my body. A few months later, I was diagnosed with fibromyalgia, a disorder with no recognized cure. This disease was a wake-up call for me, reminding me to be more health-conscious.

In less than two years, using a holistic alternative medicine approach, I kicked the disease out of my body. Since then, I have never relapsed, and I am grateful for being full of energy and vitality. Each and every day, just like you, I am faced with the decision to make healthy food and lifestyle choices. Seeing health as a gift to myself helps me stay strong in my commitment to healthy living.

According to the latest *Dietary Guidelines for Americans* issued by the U.S. Department of Agriculture and the Department of Health and Human Services, an adult should aim for 20–35 percent calories from fat, 10–35 percent from protein, and 45–65 percent from carbohydrates.[1]

I have prepared the following nutritional plan by giving consideration to the above guidelines. This will give you an idea of the number of food group portions a moderately active 30-year-old woman and man should be eating each day.

Nutritional Plan			
	Equivalents to One Portion Size	**Woman**	**Man**
Fruits	Small apple or pear (1), banana or grapefruit (½), cherries (10), blueberries, raspberries, or grapes (½ cup), fruit juice (½ cup), dried fruits (⅛ cup) ~ 100 calories	3 portions	4 portions
Vegetables	Salad (5 cups), potato, corn, or carrot (½ cup), other veggies (1 cup) ~ 50 calories	4–6 portions	5–7 portions
Grains	Bread (1 slice), muffin or bagel (½), rice, pasta, or cereals (½ cup), crackers (6) ~ 100 calories	6–7 portions	8 portions
Dairy Products	Low-fat milk or yogurt (1 cup), cheese (1 oz), ice cream (⅓ cup) ~ 100 calories	2 portions	2–3 portions
Protein Food	Eggs (2), beef (2–2.5 oz), chicken or pork (4 oz), fish or shellfish (5–6 oz), nuts (20), whey protein powder (6 tbsp), sesame or pumpkin seeds (4 tbsp), beans or chickpeas (¾ cup), tofu (2 cups) ~ 200 calories	3 portions	4 portions
Oils	Soft margarine, butter, peanut butter, mayonnaise, cream, or oils (⅓ tbsp), salad dressing (1 tbsp), gravy (6 tbsp.), barbecue sauce (2 tbsp) ~ 50 calories	2 portions	3 portions
Total Calories		2,000–2,200	2,600–2,800

Eating a balanced diet is all about consuming the right amount of food from fat, proteins, and carbohydrates. It is important for you to monitor your calorie intake to consume sufficient calories for maintaining a healthy body weight. Keep in mind that fat has a whopping nine calories per gram, while protein and carbohydrates contain four calories per gram. More fat, more calories.

133

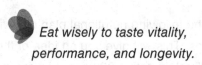

Eat wisely to taste vitality,
performance, and longevity.

Two factors to consider in calorie requirements are level of activity and age. If you are physically very active, you will likely need an extra 200 calories per day for ultimate performance. If you are sedentary, you will need to cut your daily calories by 200. Generally in your forties, you will notice a decrease in your daily caloric needs; your metabolism is slowing down in the face of reduced body mass.[1]

Start today by activating your *Fit and Fab* app and add a little magic into your health. Have fun with your food and choose wisely. Over time, you will see the power of food transform your life with more vitality and longevity.

Learn the ABCs of Nutritious Food

Let's have a closer look at each of the food categories and learn more about their magic power.

Fruits and Vegetables – Fruits and vegetables are rich in vitamins (water and fat soluble), minerals, and other substances needed for the body to work properly. Some evidence suggests that two and one-half cups of fruits and vegetables help in reducing the risk of cardiovascular disease, including heart disease and stroke. They may also protect against certain types of cancer.[1]

Fat-soluble vitamins—vitamins A, D, E, and K—can be stored in fat tissues.[1] Water-soluble vitamins (vitamin C and B-complex) do not last as long in the body. For example, vitamin B3 may last just a few weeks, and vitamin C from one to six months. For this reason, it is best to eat fruits and vegetables every single day or take a daily vitamin supplement. Eating raw fruits and vegetables is preferable, as boiling water and heat may destroy some of the food nutrients and natural enzymes.[2]

Don't overlook adding some green, leafy veggies to your daily diet, as they are rich in chlorophyll, known to alkalinize the blood. Chlorophyll is touted to be an immune system booster, a free radical neutralizer, a blood cleanser, an oxygen booster, and an anti-inflammatory.[3] In addition, fruits and vegetables are also a great source of fiber, which keeps the digestive system healthy.

"I find it hard to eat six servings of fruits and vegetables per day. Any trick to help me?" you may ask with interest.

Six servings seems a lot, but it can easily be reached. Simply eat a big salad at lunchtime, add a portion or two of raw or cooked vegetables at dinner time, and let your snacks be fresh fruits and vegetables. And voila, you're done!

Grains – Grains and cereals are high in carbohydrates and provide your body with glucose, a prime source of energy. Whole grains are much more nutritious and fulfilling than enriched/refined grains.[1] Opt for the whole-grain version of bread, pasta, crackers, rice, and cereals. For example, you can replace white bread with oatmeal and granola at breakfast. You can prepare your favorite sandwich with whole-grain bread. You can switch your white rice for brown rice at dinnertime.

Don't be shy about adding different types of grains to your meals. Try wheat, triticale, faro, millet, quinoa, oatmeal, barley, and rye. If you are intolerant to gluten, then remove wheat, barley, rye, and triticale from your diet. I suggest you visit your health food store for gluten-free products. You will be surprised by the variety of available products including cereals, crackers, bread, and even pizza!

Dairy Products – Milk products are rich in proteins and contribute to your health by providing many nutrients including calcium, vitamin D (for products fortified with vitamin D), and potassium. The *Dietary Guidelines for Americans* recommends three cups of fat-free or low-fat milk or milk products for people over the age of nine, two and one-half cups for children ages four to eight, and two cups for children ages two to three years.[1]

Dr. Walter Willett, MD, PhD, professor of epidemiology and head of the nutrition department at the Harvard School of Public Health, suggests consuming less than three cups of milk daily. According to Dr. Willett, there is evidence linking milk with an increased risk of fatal prostate cancer, and though the evidence is somewhat mixed, the risk of ovarian cancer is slightly higher for those who drink three or more servings of milk per day.[4]

If you choose to consume dairy products, favor low-fat products to reduce your consumption of saturated fats. You can easily find the low-fat version of milk, yogurt, cheese, and frozen dairy products at the grocery store. If you are lactose intolerant, or you choose to stay away from dairy products, choose other good calcium alternatives. These include leafy green vegetables, beans, fortified orange juice, rice, soy, or almond milk.

Protein Food – Protein is important for your muscles, tendons, cartilage, and bone building. It plays a role in your cell renewal, enzyme and antibodies production, and many other functions in your body. Meat, poultry, eggs, fish, shellfish, dairy, whey, wheat, quinoa, beans, soybeans (tofu, tempeh, soy milk), chickpeas, peas, lentils, nuts, and seeds are all good sources of protein.[1]

While your body can produce 13 of the 22 amino acids that make up proteins, there are nine amino acids that you need to consume, which are known as essentials. These essential amino acids are histidine, leucine, isoleucine, lysine, methionine, phenylalanine, threonine, tryptophan, and valine.

Most meats, poultry, fish, shellfish, poultry, eggs, and dairy products are known to be complete proteins, as they contain all nine essential amino acids in adequate proportion. Plant-based protein sources do not always contain all nine essential amino acids, but soybeans (tofu and soya milk), black beans, and the grain quinoa do.[5]

In addition to being rich in the nine essential amino acids, animal proteins contain some vitamins and minerals, as well as the anti-oxidant carnosine and creatine, a muscle and brain energy builder.[6]

Meat has received some bad publicity in the last few years, with red and processed meats being associated with cancer. In addition, there is controversy about hormones and antibiotics being added to meat and milk. We know that high levels of hormones may cause breast and ovarian cancers. While the debate continues and further studies take place, you may favor unprocessed, hormone-free and lean meats.[7]

Fish and shellfish are rich in Omega-3 fatty acids and low in saturated fat, and are known to keep your heart and brain healthy. Cold water fish like salmon, trout, and tuna are a great source of Omega-3 fatty acids.[1] One downfall is that nearly all fish and shellfish contain traces of mercury. For most people, this should not be a major concern. But children, pregnant women, and nursing mothers should opt for low-mercury fish and shellfish. Swordfish, tilefish, and mackerel have higher levels of mercury, but salmon, trout, and sardines bear lower levels.

Other good low-mercury fish and shellfish include canned light tuna, anchovies, crab, scallops, oysters, shrimp, catfish, haddock (Atlantic), flounder, perch (ocean), sole (Pacific), and tilapia.[8]

Oils – While oils are not a food group, they are part of your daily food plan. This category encompasses all those creamy products that just melt in your mouth and contribute to your eating pleasures. You know what I mean: butter on your potatoes, peanut butter on a slice a bread, cream in your coffee, salad dressing, and gravy or barbecue sauce with your meat.

Fats can be found in both animal and plant food. They are classified in three groups: saturated, polyunsaturated, and monounsaturated, with the latter two being known by the name omegas.[9]

- Saturated fat is naturally found in animal food and high-fat dairy products. While it does bear some benefits, it is not labeled as a healthy fat.
- Omega-3 and Omega-6 fatty acids are two types of polyunsaturated fat. As the body does not produce these fatty acids, they are termed essential fatty acids.
- On the other hand, Omega-9 fatty acids are derived from monounsaturated fats. They are not deemed essential fatty acids because your body can synthetize them from certain food.

Trans fats are part of the unsaturated fat family. There are two main types of trans fats: natural and artificial. Natural and artificial trans fats have different chemical composition. Natural trans fats are found in the fatty parts of meat and dairy products, and they are less harmful than artificial trans fats.

On the other hand, artificial trans fats are derived from a process by which hydrogen is added to liquid vegetable oils to make them more solid, and consumption should be limited, as they act like saturated fats and increase your risk of coronary heart disease.[10]

Below is a table that summarizes the fat groups, their benefits, sources, and a few words of caution when applicable.

Fat Groups			
	Benefits	**Sources**	**Caution**
Saturated	• Helps keep your bones and immune system strong. • Helps improve liver health and nerve signaling. • Helps keep your brains and lungs healthy.	• All meats. • All non-low-fat dairy products. • All nuts. • Palm oil, kernel oil, and cholesterol-free coconut oil.	• A high saturated fat diet has been linked to high cholesterol and increased risk of heart disease and stroke.[9] • Bacon, sausage, pork ribs, ground beef, cheese, ice cream, butter, cashew, pecan, macadamia nuts, and Brazil nuts are known to have higher levels of saturated fats.[9]
Polyunsaturated	• Helps reduce risk of heart disease and cholesterol levels. • Promotes proper brain function and normal body growth and development.	• Omega-3-rich food (salmon, mackerel, sardines, herring, trout, walnut, flaxseed, avocado, dark green leafy vegetables). • Omega-3-rich oil (canola). • Omega-6-rich food (soy nut, tofu, sunflower, pumpkin, pistachio nuts, sesame seeds). • Omega-6-rich oils (corn, safflower, sesame, soybean, sunflower).	• Fish may contain mercury, so it is best to choose low mercury fish, shellfish, or fish oil.[8]

Fat Groups

	Benefits	Sources	Caution
Monounsaturated	• Helps reduce bad cholesterol levels in the blood. • Helps lower the risk of heart disease and stroke.	• Omega-9-rich food (avocado, almond, cashew, peanut, pecan, pistachio, peanut, almond butter). • Omega-9-rich oils (olive, canola, peanut, sunflower, sesame oils).	
Artificial Trans Fat		• French fries, doughnuts, baked goods, pastries, biscuits, and cookies. • Pie crusts, pizza dough, crackers, margarines, and shortenings.	• Trans fats may increase the risk of Alzheimer's disease, cancer, liver dysfunction, obesity, and diabetes. In addition, they increase bad (LDL) cholesterol level and lower good (HDL) cholesterol levels.[10]

One word of caution about oils: when heated above their smoking point, they produce toxic fumes. Read the labels to choose an oil that matches your cooking method. Refined safflower, high oleic canola, palm, and refined avocado oils have a smoking point over 450 degrees Fahrenheit. Refined peanut, extra virgin olive, and refined canola oils are medium-high heat oils (up to 450 degrees). Unrefined coconut, sunflower, and corn oils are medium-heat oils that can be used for sautéing (up to 350 degrees).[11]

With fat being present in so many protein foods like dairy products, nuts, and vegetable sources, it is easy to exceed the recommended ratio of 20–35 percent of your daily caloric intake. While fat is a great source of energy, omegas, and vitamin E, you need to choose fat sources wisely and keep in mind that:

- Less than 10 percent of your daily calories should be from saturated fat sources.[1] This translates to 22 grams of saturated fat (200 calories divided by 9) for a woman on a 2,000-calorie meal plan and to 29 grams for a man consuming 2,600 calories per day (260 calories divided by 9).
- In Western diets, the ratio of Omega-6 to Omega-3 ranges anywhere from 10:1 up to 30:1, while the optimal ratio is 4:1, with 1:1 being even better. Many processed foods are rich in Omega-6, making it very easy to exceed the optimal ratio. The bad news is that high levels of Omega-6 are correlated with arthritis, inflammation, and cancer.[12] Read food labels to help you optimize your Omega-6 to Omega-3 ratio. Take an Omega-3 supplement if needed to better balance your ratio.

As a member of the *Fit and Feeling Fabulous Club*, you now have all the information to make life-affirming food choices for bountiful health. Have fun preparing your meals and enjoy being fit and full of vitality!

Play it Safe

Like too many of us, you may find it difficult to eat the recommended portions of proteins, grains, dairies, fruits, and vegetables for all sorts of reasons:

- You are always on the go and too busy to cook wholesome meals.
- You simply dislike cooking. The microwave is your chef, and heated, processed food is your way of life.
- You loathe meat, vegetables, or cooked grains. You are allergic to dairy products and many grains and legumes.
- You have poor digestion with insufficient stomach acid to eat certain food. You are bloated when you eat beans, milk products, cauliflower, and broccoli.

As a result, your body lacks essential nutrients to perform at its peak. For more energy, you turn to sugary snacks during the day, and you drink your guilt with diet drinks. In addition, you are bombarded with environmental toxins. It's true, much of your foods contain pesticides or are fertilized with only a few good elements. This leaves you with a much higher risk for diseases.

"What can I do to help preserve my health?" you might wonder.

Of course changing your eating habits is your best option, but weaving the following tips into your eating plan will certainly give your body more nutrients.

Take a Supplement of Vitamins and Minerals – If you are not into fruits, vegetables, and dairy products, a daily multi-vitamin with the following essential vitamins and minerals is a good start.

Essential Vitamins and Minerals

Vitamins	Minerals
• Vitamin A	• Calcium
• Vitamin B1 – thiamine	• Magnesium
• Vitamin B2 – riboflavin	• Iron
• Vitamin B3 – niacin	• Zinc
• Vitamin B6 – pantothenic acid	• Iodine
• Vitamin B9 – folic acid	• Chromium
• Vitamin B12 – cobalamin	• Selenium
• Vitamin C	
• Vitamin D	
• Vitamin E	

For example, vitamin A is good for general growth and development, and healthy eyes. Vitamin B-complex formulas are great for adrenal support in times of stress. Vitamins B6 and B12 are important nutrients for nerve cell development, cognitive health, and neuron protection. Vitamins C and E, as well as selenium, protect against free radicals.[13] I strongly recommend you consult your health care provider, naturopath, or nutritionist who is cognizant of your eating habits, physical condition, and current medications to best advise you on dosage and timing.

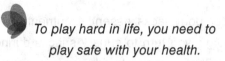

To play hard in life, you need to
play safe with your health.

Eat a More Alkaline Diet – It has been suggested that an alkaline diet may help in the treatment or prevention of cancer, heart disease, and lack of energy. Supporters of this diet explain that one's nutritional program should align with the slightly alkaline pH of the blood. In addition, it has been said that an acid environment may increase the risk of osteoporosis. While there is some scientific evidence in support of such claims, substantiating studies are not significant. It is touted that an 80:20 percent alkaline to acid meal plan is best to improve health, while a 60:40 percent alkaline to acid diet is fine to maintain health.[14]

Alkaline food and beverages contain weak acids that can easily be flushed out by your kidneys. On the other hand, only a certain amount of strong acids contained in acidic food can be removed by your kidneys, with the rest being stored in your body tissues. An acidic environment may be the cause of health problems such as inflammation, bone loss, muscle spasm, skin problems, and fatigue. In addition, cancer prefers an acidic environment.[15]

Not sure which foods are alkaline and which ones are acidic? Whey, almonds, avocados, wheat grass, apples, watermelon, grapes, berries, carrots, green veggies, and the sweetener stevia are good alkaline choices. Acidic food includes animal protein, poultry, fish, eggs, grains, bread, dairy products, alcohol, salted nuts, white sugar, white flour, and saturated fats.

Coffee and black tea are on the list of acidic beverages, and moderation is best. The debate is still out on whether or not green tea and herbal teas are alkaline beverages. They are at times identified on the list of alkaline beverages and at other times attributed to the acidic family.[16]

Add Antioxidants to Your Diet – According to the free radical theory of aging, free radicals may play a role in health issues such as cancer, atherosclerosis, arthritis, and Alzheimer's disease. Proponents of the theory are of the opinion that antioxidant soldiers found in fruits and vegetables—vitamin A, vitamin C, vitamin E (alpha-tocopherol), and beta-carotene—may slow the aging process.

While several studies support the theory, questions remain as to whether or not reducing the amount of oxidants in the body may extend your lifespan. While the debate is still out, you may want to favor a diet rich in fruits, vegetables, legumes, nuts, seeds, red wine, dark chocolate, and green and black tea and coffee that gives you plenty of polyphenols with antioxidant effects.[17]

If you prefer to drink your polyphenols, sip a glass of red wine, but keep in mind the extra 100–125 calories in a four-ounce drink.[17] If your diet lacks antioxidants, consider an antioxidant supplement of polyphenol (resveratrol), Coenzyme Q10, reishi mushroom, or cordyceps mushroom.

Drink Protein Shakes – Multiplying your body weight in kilograms by .8, or weight in pounds by .37, gives you your daily protein requirements. A 125-pound adult woman needs approximately 46 grams of protein per day, while a 180-pound man needs 67 grams. Bodybuilders have increased protein requirements, with a ratio of up to one gram of protein per pound. If you are on the low side in your protein consumption, simply add a protein powder shake that is rich in all nine essential amino acids. Keep in mind that amino acids L-carnosine, N-acetyl cysteine, and L-taurine are known to be antioxidant soldiers against free radicals.

Take a Probiotics Supplement – One way to boost your good gut bacteria is to take a probiotic supplement, especially when you are under antibiotic therapy. Probiotics help maintain your immune system and increase your body's defense against bacteria and other organisms that cause illness. They are touted to improve bowel function and reduce bloating, flatulence, and gastro-intestinal discomfort.[18]

Take Digestive Enzymes – If you have difficulty digesting food and are constantly bloated, you may be subject to poor digestion. You may choose to avoid gas bloating foods. These include beans, broccoli, brussels sprouts, cauliflower, apples, peaches, pears, lettuce, onions, and sugar alcohols (sorbitol, mannitol, xylitol).

Taking digestive enzymes with your meals helps to break down food sources for optimal use of nutrients. Another option is to drink a glass of water 15–20 minutes before a meal for more hydrochloric acid production.[19] Favor peppermint, spearmint, ginger, or chamomile herbal teas that facilitate digestion.

Go Easy on Processed Food – While some people may have no difficulty completely eliminating processed food from their diet, others may really struggle. I strongly recommend that you limit your daily calories from both processed food and food with little nutritional value to no more than 100–150 calories. There are numerous cookbooks and websites filled with great nutritional recipes that will help you stay away from processed food and will please your taste buds.

Sip Organic Coffee or Tea – Coffee contains antioxidant polyphenols shown to prevent cell damage from free radicals.[20] Benefits of drinking a few cups of coffee per day include brain improvement, fat burning, reduction of Parkinson disease symptoms, reduced feelings of depression, increased longevity, slowdown in the progression of Alzheimer's disease, and prevention of type II diabetes and some types of cancer. On the other hand, an excessive dose of coffee can be harmful, with effects such as restlessness, anxiety, stomach upset, irritability, difficulty sleeping, rapid heartbeat, and shaking.[21]

Tea is also a youthfulness drink rich in flavonoids. Drinking a variety of teas provides great health benefits. White tea is touted to strengthen elastin and collagen, thus reducing wrinkle production. Black tea is reported to reduce stress hormones. Green tea is known to boost immunity, lower blood pressure, and help in controlling your weight and protecting your eyes.[22] Steep your tea for a few minutes for higher antioxidant content.

As said, restrain from drinking too much coffee and black tea as they are on the list of acidic beverages. To control your caffeine intake while still pleasing your taste buds, consume decaffeinated teas and coffees, especially in the evening when you are winding down from your busy day. Keep in mind that some tea and coffee brands may contain pesticides and chemical residues. It is best to favor certified organic brands that are free of chemical pesticides.

Limit Diet Drinks – If you like the fuzziness feeling of soft drinks but do not enjoy their calories, you may be a fan of diet drinks. It is best to limit your diet drinks to one a day. Diet sodas have been touted to increase craving for sugary food, thus playing a role in weight gain. While some researchers claim diet drinks disrupt hormones associated with hunger and increase appetite, other experts found they do not.[23] Just keep in mind that moderation is best.

Control Your Sugar Intake – Sugar is found in a number of sources including fruits, honey, milk, sugar cane, beets, vegetables, grains, legumes, barley, and bread. They are categorized as follows:[24]

- Monosaccharides (fructose, glucose, galactose) – referred to as a basic unit.
- Disaccharides (lactose, maltose, sucrose) – consist of two monosaccharides joined together.
- Polysaccharides (starch, glycogen, cellulose, chitin, pectin) – consist of many monosaccharides joined together.
- Oligosaccharides (fructo-oligosaccharides, galactooligosaccharides, mannan oligosaccharides) – at least two monosaccharides joined together but not too many.

While sugar is a great energy source, excessive consumption has been linked to obesity. Claims have been made that sugar may be a cause of Alzheimer's disease, yet the debate continues. Some studies have found a correlation between refined sugar and the onset of diabetes, while other studies conclude otherwise. As supported by some studies, chronic consumption of sugar may lead to cardiovascular dysfunction. There is supporting evidence between the amount and frequency of free sugar consumption (sugar added to food, juices, honey, and syrups) and tooth decay.[25]

It is best to stay away from added sugar found in candies, soft drinks, cookies, and other processed food. Recent draft guidelines proposed by the World Health Organization recommend that sugar intake should not exceed 10 percent of daily calories. The guidelines also suggest health benefits in reducing the intake to just below 5 percent of total calorie intake. The limit applies to added sugar (fructose, glucose, sucrose) and those found in honey, syrups, fruit juices, and fruit concentrates, not to those occurring naturally in fruits.[26]

If you are controlling your weight or blood sugar, favor low-glycemic fruits like raspberries, strawberries, blackberries, papaya, and watermelon over high-sugar fruits such as bananas, raisins, and dates. For example, 100 grams of raspberries contain 4.4 grams of sugar, while 100 grams of bananas adds up to 12 grams of sugar. A good way to add great taste to your recipes without the calories is to use stevia, a plant-based sweetener.

Go Easy When Using Salt – According to the American Heart Association, excess sodium has negative effects on your body, namely high blood pressure, stroke, heart failure, osteoporosis, stomach cancer, kidney disease, kidney stones, enlarged heart muscle, and headaches. It is best to limit salt to 1,500 mg or less per day.[27]

Go easy when you add salt to your salad and meat. Half a teaspoon of salt equals 1,150 mg of sodium. Replace processed food and sodas that are high in sodium with water, tea, grains, and raw fruits and vegetables. Read labels and get your calculator out. You will be happily surprised or shocked by how much sodium you eat in a day.

Listen to Your Body – Joint or other types of inflammation may signal food allergies. Common allergens representing 90 percent of food allergic reactions include: wheat, gluten, eggs, milk, peanut, soy, fish, and shellfish. Widely utilized by traditional medicine, the skin prick test, intradermal skin test, patch testing, and blood testing are common allergy testing methods.[28]

Some complementary and alternative medicine practitioners offer bio-energy testing, which reveals disturbances in energy pathways that may be caused by allergies.[29] I had both skin and bio-energy allergy testing done in the past, with both results being identical. I am a fan of bio-energy testing, as the method is less invasive and done more rapidly.

Turn the Switch Off – Sleep deprivation compromises your immune system and, as a result, it opens the door to various ailments. It also affects your mood and ability to concentrate during the day. One tip to help you fall asleep is to add more relaxation time to your evenings. Simply create a well-being spa for yourself: take a bath, read a book, go for a walk, write in your gratitude journal, do breathing exercises, or listen to relaxing music. Avoid sleeping aids; they may make you feel drowsy and sleepy the next morning. Waking up and going to bed at the same time each day helps in developing a healthy sleep routine. Try a soothing and relaxing herbal tea such as chamomile, passionflower, or valerian. To sum it up, enjoy your lifelong membership to the *Fit and Feeling Fabulous Club* by playing it safe.

Scare Cancer Away

No one wants to hear the words "You have cancer" from their physician's mouth. Only three little words, but so powerful and spine-chilling. They scare the hell out of you and make your heart sink. With medical treatment and a healthy lifestyle, more and more people triumph over cancer. There are numerous extraordinary stories of people who have conquered this debilitating illness by complementing their medical treatment with healthy practices. Let's have a look at healthy choices you can make to scare cancer away.

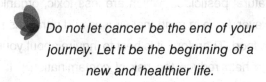

Do not let cancer be the end of your journey. Let it be the beginning of a new and healthier life.

Stop Smoking – Your body has no interest in chemicals and toxins, so crush your cigarette today. According to the American Lung Association, there are approximately 600 ingredients in cigarettes. When burned, they create more than 7,000 chemicals. At least 69 of these chemicals are known to cause cancer, and many are poisonous.[30]

To quit smoking is not an easy task, especially when each puff is a pleasure. If you can't win the smoking battle by using anti-smoking aids, consult a counselor or a neuro-linguistic programming (NLP) practitioner to maximize your success. Some people also report success with hypnosis and self-hypnosis.[31]

Go Easy on Meat – While red meat contains minerals, some B vitamins, and the powerful antioxidant lipoic acid, a 2007 report of the American Institute for Cancer Research and World Cancer Research Fund reveals that red meat and processed meat intake possibly increase the risk of esophageal, lung, pancreatic, stomach, colorectal, endometrial, and prostate cancers. According to the report, there is convincing scientific evidence of an increased risk of colorectal cancer with the consumption of red meat, processed meat, and heavily cooked meat. Carcinogenic compounds have been found in cooked meat.[32]

According to a University of Minnesota study, eating well-done or charred meat regularly may increase your risk of pancreatic cancer by up to 60 percent. If you are a BBQ lover, choose leaner meats, as flames create smoke that leads to the formation of carcinogens.[33] Eggs, fish, shellfish, pasta dishes, legumes, nuts, seeds, soy, grains, dairy, and whey are other protein alternatives to consider. As said, favor low-mercury fish and eat acidic protein food in moderation.

Go Organic – Both organic and non-organic food may contain pesticide residue and harmful bacteria and parasites. As organic farmers are only allowed to use natural pesticides, which are less toxic, organic food is a safer option. However, keep in mind that viruses and parasites may still be present in organic food. Therefore, it is best to inquire about your suppliers' safety practices to help reduce the risk of contamination.[34] It is good to know that the United States Department of Agriculture's National Organic Program's regulations ban the use of synthetic drugs like antibiotics and growth hormones in organic food.[35] In fact, genetic modification/engineering techniques are not allowed in organic food, making them much safer.

Wash Your Veggies – Make sure to buy a fruit and vegetable soap in a health food store. Wash your produce thoroughly under clean water before eating it to remove dust and reduce residual pesticides, viruses, and bacteria. Keep in mind that no washing method will completely eliminate them.

Eat Lots of Fruits and Vegetables – While coping with cancer, you want to bombard your body with nutrients and enzymes. Half of your eating plate should be filled with fruits, vegetables, and grains. In addition, get the juicer and blender out of the cupboard and drink homemade fruit and vegetable juices at least three times a day. Again, wash your produce before juicing or eating it. No time for juicing? Buy green juice powder and mix it with water.

Add Supplements – Each one of us is different. It is best to talk to your health care provider to see if you need to take supplements. You may need a multi-vitamin, probiotics, enzymes, and antioxidants. You want to ensure that your diet plan contains all the nutrients and antioxidants needed to boost your immune system and prevent or fight cancer. If your physician is not vested in nutrition and supplements, add a qualified health professional (nutritionist, naturopath) to your healing team. Make sure all members of your team are well-informed of your nutritional plan, medical treatment, and medications.

Reduce Your Sweets – While there have been reports that sugar feeds cancer cells and makes cancer cells grow faster, these claims have been denied by the Canadian Cancer Society. What research has shown is that being overweight or obese increases your risk of cancer. As explained by the Canadian Cancer Society, obesity may cause changes in hormone levels. Changes to insulin or sex hormones may increase the risk of developing breast, colon, or uterine cancer.[36]

As said, no more than 10 percent of your total daily calories should be from added sugars. Those are found in honey, syrups, fruit juices and concentrates, and exclude those occurring naturally in fruits. Favor fruits with less natural sugar like raspberries, strawberries, blackberries, papaya, green apple, and watermelon. Avoid sodas, candies, cookies, donuts, and pastries with refined sugar.

Eat Low Mercury Fish and Shellfish – Mercury is a poison that damages some body systems and organs, in particular the nervous and endocrine systems and kidneys. Shift to fish and shellfish with much lower mercury content. Consider trying salmon, trout, sardines, canned light tuna, anchovies, crab, oyster, shrimp, catfish, and pollock.

Opt for BPA-Free Containers – If you like to carry water in a plastic bottle, make sure to use bisphenol A (BPA)-free bottles. BPA is being reported as an endocrine disruptor linked to several illnesses, from breast cancer to sexual dysfunction. Likewise, if you are cooking with a microwave, make sure your containers are BPA- and phthalates-free and are labeled as microwave safe.[37]

Use Non-Toxic Cleansing Products – Many household products contain toxic chemicals. To limit exposure to dangerous chemicals that may cause cancer, use home cleaning products that are free of toxic substances. Take time to read household product warning labels; they may provide information as to whether or not the product may cause cancer.

Use a Speaker Phone – As reported by the American Cancer Society, most scientists agree that cell phone antennas or towers are unlikely to cause cancer. Other sources of information report increased evidence that long-term cell phone use may cause brain damage. As we await further studies, play it safe and use a speaker phone or limit your cell phone time. Carry your cell phone in your purse rather than in your pocket.[38]

Add Some Fiber – Essential to a healthy diet is eating plenty of fiberous food, known to prevent colorectal cancer and lower blood sugar and bad cholesterol levels. Fiber is found in whole wheat bread and pasta, oatmeal, barley, legumes, avocados, pears, artichokes, apples, prunes, broccoli, and almonds.[39]

Do a Body Cleanse – Increased energy, glowing skin, and less bloating are some of the benefits reported by those who favor intermittent detoxification programs that cleanse and nourish the body, and may protect against cancer. While not scientifically proven, a body cleansing is touted to eliminate body toxins, heavy metals, bacteria, fungus, and yeast. Detoxification can be achieved through dieting, fasting, colon cleansing, chelation therapy, and the removal of dental fillings.[40]

Detox and cleansing dietary supplements are also available in health food stores and drugstores. You may opt for a one- to two-week cleansing diet supported with detox and cleansing dietary supplements once or twice a year, or you may choose green detox daily supplements.

If you suspect candida in your digestive tract, consider an antifungal supplement that contains oils and herbs such as oregano, olive leaf extract, and garlic. The herb goldenseal takes care of parasites, and milk thistle can aid people with liver problems associated with alcohol.[41] Before starting your detox journey, learn more information on all possible side effects. Speak to your physician who will guide you on nutritious food and nutrients to add to your detox diet. These include high-protein fruits and vegetables, lots of water, B-complex vitamins, vitamin C, magnesium, and selenium.

Clean up Your Emotions – If you are still lingering after negative emotions, now is the time to let them go and live freely, with a joyous heart. As a complement to your medical treatment, explore energy-based healing techniques as further detailed in the section *Harmonize your Energy Fields*. There is no room in a healthy body for suppressed negative emotions. As the *Marvelous You*, activate your *Love Power* app and practice forgiveness for yourself and others. What is done is done, what is said is said. Yesterday is gone. Live the beauty of today and fill your heart with hope for tomorrow.

Wear Sunscreen – While 10 minutes of sun exposure is beneficial to your body, over exposure to the sun is to be avoided. Wear sunscreen when outside, and avoid suntan booths to protect yourself from skin cancer and avoid premature skin aging.

Get Screening Tests – Screening helps detect cancer early, which increases your chance of complete recovery. With a greater understanding of your health concerns and family history, your physician will recommend screening tests that are most appropriate for you. These may include imaging (radiology) tests, tumor markers in blood or urine, a breast biopsy, a mammogram or other breast imaging procedures, and endoscopy procedures, including colonoscopy and sigmoidoscopy.[42]

Calm Your Mind – To harness your incredible mind power, you need to add more relaxation in your life. Activate your *Fun and Play* app and go for a walk, take a nap, do breathing and light body exercises, listen to uplifting music, read a book, write in your gratitude journal, practice visualization, praise God, get a massage, take a hot bath, call a friend, or simply give hugs. Practice relaxation techniques (breathing, guided imagery, progressive muscle relaxation). Use aromatherapy oils, incense sticks, or candles with fragrances that soothe and calm your mind. Clary sage, lavender, mandarin, bergamot, and palmarosa essential oils are all good choices.[43]

Engaging in relaxing activities shifts your mind from high- to low-frequency alpha and theta brainwaves. You will feel calmer and will be at peace while experiencing greater well-being physically and emotionally. Your brain will release powerful immune-boosting chemicals—serotonin, dopamine, relaxin, and endorphin—that will increase your white blood cells and natural killer cells.

Relaxation is touted to improve your creativity, concentration, knowingness, and alertness.[44] Keep in mind that exercise will bring more oxygen to your body, helping in flushing toxins, thus speeding the recovery process. Saunas or steam baths are also good toxin eliminators.[45]

Have a Good Laugh – If you have forgotten to turn on your *Be Happy* app, then it's time to do it. With *Be Happy*, your mind is filled with positive thoughts, and you breathe optimism as you fight your battle with cancer. Laughter lights up your soul. It elevates your mood, releases tension, increases blood flow, and lowers blood pressure. It is touted to improve natural killer cells' activity.[46]

Keeping yourself captive of good-feeling thoughts will help you climb to new heights of well-being. Call uplifting friends who will cheer you up and energize you to continue the good fight. Add some fun movies as part of your recovery program. Read testimonies of cancer survivors; their stories will be a great source of inspiration on your healing journey. Join a support group to develop new friendships and encourage each other through your ups and downs.

Activate Your *Higher Power* App – With your *Higher Power* app activated, your lips are praising God. In unity with Him, your days are filled with hope, and in His arms, you find comfort and warmth. Your heart is filled with gratitude.

Cancer has no right on you. You were born with extraordinary apps and amazing healing systems to keep you healthy physically, emotionally, and spiritually. Fuel and fortify your healing systems and get in the fight today to reclaim your health! You are *Marvelous You*, courageous, and resilient, and victory is in you.

Say No to Dieting

Unhealthy eating habits may have left you with extra pounds that limit you physically or endanger your health. You are dreaming of a more svelte physique, but nothing seems to work. I have the answer for you, and it is not dieting. In fact, you must stop dieting to get leaner and adopt a balanced nutritional plan.

Drastic diets usually don't work on a long-term basis because your mind associates diet with a loss of pleasure and comfort. A nutritional plan with foods that are pleasurable is your greatest ally for a full body transformation. Weave the following tips into your eating plan, and over time you could be at your desired weight.

Opt for a Long-Term Nutritional Plan – If you need to lose weight, women should opt for a 1,200 calorie daily meal plan and men should go for 1,800 calories per day, as illustrated below. This nutritional plan should lead to a one pound per week weight loss and keep you from starving.

Nutritional Plan

	Equivalents to One Portion Size	Woman	Man
Fruits	Small apple or pear (1), banana or grapefruit (½), cherries (10), blueberries, raspberries, or grapes (½ cup), fruit juice (½ cup), dried fruits (⅛ cup) ~ 100 calories	2 portions	2 portions
Vegetables	Salad (5 cups), potato, corn, or carrot (½ cup), other veggies (1 cup) ~ 50 calories	3 portions	4 portions
Grains	Bread (1 slice), muffin or bagel (½), rice, pasta, or cereals (½ cup), crackers (6) ~ 100 calories	2 portions	3 portions
Dairy Products	Low-fat milk or yogurt (1 cup), cheese (1 oz), ice cream (⅓ cup) ~ 100 calories	2 portions	2 portions
Protein Food	Eggs (2), beef (2–2.5 oz), chicken or pork (4 oz), fish or shellfish (5–6 oz), nuts (20), whey protein powder (6 tbsp), sesame or pumpkin seeds (4 tbsp), beans or chickpeas (¾ cup), tofu (2 cups) ~ 200 calories	2 portions	4 portions
Oils	Soft margarine, butter, peanut butter, mayonnaise, cream, or oils (⅓ tbsp), salad dressing (1 tbsp), gravy (6 tbsp), barbecue sauce (2 tbsp) ~ 50 calories	1 portion	2 portions
Total Calories		1,200	1,800

Unless otherwise recommended by your physician, there is no need for more drastic calorie reduction. This eating plan translates into a 50-pound weight loss at the end of the year. It is better to take more time to lose the weight and succeed, than losing weight rapidly and gaining it all back in a matter of weeks.

If you get off the wagon one day, let it be, and get back on the program the next day. You really want a cookie? Then take one. Eating one cookie does not mean you've blown it and need to eat the whole cookie bag.

Eat Small Meals – Eating small meals, five to six times per day keeps you energized and makes you feel full during the day. By choosing nutritious foods that you enjoy, you strengthen your commitment to your nutritional plan. Try to limit your carbohydrate (bread, pasta, oatmeal, cookies) intake at night. You may not have the chance to burn these calories before going to bed, which will lead to the storage of fat.

Leave a Little Something on Your Plate – Listen to your stomach's bell and when it rings, stop eating. When you feel you are not hungry anymore, then put your fork down and leave whatever is left on your plate. There is no need to eat everything that is on your plate. Favor smaller portions to avoid the temptation of overeating.

Don't Worry About the Scale – Monitor your progress by tracking your weight, body fat percentage, and body measurements each week, preferably first thing in the morning before breakfast, and in the buff. Taking pictures and keeping a journal are great monitoring tools. Don't worry about the scale going up when you exercise. Exercise builds muscle, and muscle weighs more than fat. Keep in mind that certain food and hormone fluctuation may cause water retention.

Drink Water – Don't be shy to drink water. Research by German researchers Michael Boschmann, MD, and his colleagues from Berlin's Franz-Volhard Clinical Research Center showed that metabolic rates increase slightly with water.[47]

Get a Fitness Buddy – Body transformation is a big commitment to yourself. Having a fitness coach or trainer helps in keeping your motivation up. Being accountable to someone makes a big difference in sustaining your dedication. I enjoy muscle-building exercises, and I must say that my training intensity is much stronger under the care of a fitness trainer.

Be Inspired by Others – Inspire yourself reading stories of men and women who, like you, made the decision to transform their body and succeeded. Knowing that they, too, struggled and had good and bad days will uplift you and motivate you to stay on track. Another good way to be inspired and support others is to join a support group.

Reward Yourself – When tempted to return to your unhealthy habits, value the long-term outcomes and chase those temptations with a *Flash Mob Thought* and say, "Day after day, my body transformation is taking place. I choose to stay on course. I truly enjoy creating a healthy and fit body." Recapture in your mind the joy of seeing the scale going down week after week. Celebrate each victorious day. Be creative in finding healthy and fun options to reward yourself. Write your progress in a daily journal, read an inspiring book, take a nice, warm bath, get a massage or pedicure, call a friend, or go see a movie.

See food for what it is: nutrients for your body, not for your emotions.

Raise Your Metabolism Slowly – The key to successful weight loss lies in the weeks after you have reached you weight goal. Your body does not handle a rapid calorie increase well, and transforms the extra food into fat. It is crucial that you do not increase your calorie intake by more than 100 calories per day in the first week. Then add another 100 calories per day in the second week, and so on, until you reach your ideal calorie intake. By adding calories moderately, you are letting your body adjust to the new calorie intake.

Remember, you have the power to achieve any weight goal you set for yourself. Get going today and power up your health by reaching and maintaining a healthy weight.

Increase Your Brain Power

Protecting your brain from Alzheimer's and other brain diseases is something you start early in life to reap future benefits. Take a look at my favorite tips to keep your mind sharp and performing at high speed.

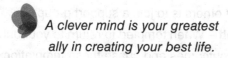

*A clever mind is your greatest
ally in creating your best life.*

Eat Fruits and Vegetables – The Alzheimer's Association recommends a heart-healthy diet that may also have benefits for the brain. Favor protective foods such as prunes, blackberries, blueberries, cherries, strawberries, broccoli, dark green leafy vegetables, brussels sprouts, beets, alfalfa sprouts, almonds, pecans, walnuts, trout, and wild salmon.[48]

Not a veggie eater? Easy solution; just drink your vegetables. Get into juicing, and make sure to add a few dark leafy greens in your drink. Add fruit and ginger for more taste. Don't forget to add a cucumber and a few strawberries as they contain fisetin, an antioxidant known to improve memory. If you are not into juicing either, then take a daily multi-vitamin with essential vitamins and minerals, as well as an antioxidant supplement.

Don't Forget Your Omega-3 – If you don't like fish and shellfish, take a fish-based Omega-3 fatty acid supplement for higher brain performance. Fish and shellfish have been reported as a brain protector. In addition, they are known as cognitive enhancers. Omega-3 fatty acid supplements are touted to reduce inflammation, and may help in cases of fatigue and depression.[49] Inquire on a mercury-free brand with no aftertaste that is generally found in health food stores.

Spice it Up – Add spices to your food for more brain power. Rosemary, sage, onions, and garlic are full of antioxidants and are great to improve memory and cognitive performance. Garlic and sage may help prevent Alzheimer's disease. Onions and sage are known for their memory improvement properties. Research has shown that rosemary aroma plays a role in improving cognitive performance.[50]

Smile – A smile is powerful in relaxing your body and mind. It makes you feel connected to others; it reminds you of the goodness in others. Smile to people on the street or in the elevator. Smile as you do your grocery shopping or run errands. A similar power is behind a good laugh. Nobody to laugh with today? Just think of something you have found funny in the past, and over time, you will have a smile on your face. Remember: smile and laugh.

Take Mini Breaks – Taking a 30-second to one-minute break every hour or so is great to relax your mind. Relaxation helps increase concentration and alertness. Walk around the office, do a few stretches, or simply take a few deep breaths. You will quickly see your shoulders relaxing and you'll feel more energized.

Manage Your Stress – Stress management is critical in increasing your brain performance. Stress can hinder your ability to concentrate and think clearly. Good-feeling thoughts are powerful in calming a racing mind. Do not overlook exercise, and practice relaxation techniques to calm your mind, release tension, and increase your well-being. Faith is a great antidote in the face of stressful situations that come your way during the day.

Eat Dark Chocolate – Dark chocolate is rich in flavonoids, known to improve memory, cognitive abilities, and verbal fluency. Some studies reveal that flavonoids have anti-inflammatory and anti-bacterial effects. It was also found that daily intake of flavonoids may reduce gastric carcinoma in women, and the risk of airway/gastrointestinal tract cancer in smokers. Furthermore, flavonoids are touted to reduce blood pressure and the risk of atherosclerosis.[51]

Keep Your Mind Busy – Make your life fun by keeping your mind active. Life is all about expansion. Learn to dance and cook. Practice a new sport or hobby. Read a book and take a class to hone your skills. Stay informed, and open yourself to new possibilities.

Sleep Well – Sleep is great to regenerate your body and of course, your brain. On average, teens need approximately 8–10 hours of sleep each day, while an adult should be fine with 7–9 hours. As everyone is different, see what works best for you. As said, avoid sleeping pills, as it may take a few hours the next morning for your mind to become fully awake.

Go Easy on Alcohol – Alcohol has an effect on the brain's communication pathways. Too much alcohol makes you feel sluggish the next morning. It is therefore not a good idea to hold an important meeting after a night out drinking. Your mood will not be at its best, nor will your mind. You will be functioning in slow motion—simply not as sharp. In addition, alcohol is on the list of acidic beverages to consume in moderation.

Drink Water – Your body is approximately 50 to 65 percent water. Being dehydrated is often the cause of headaches, fatigue, a lack of concentration, and dry skin. Dividing your weight in pounds by two gives you the amount of water in ounces to drink each day. A 110-pound woman needs 55 ounces of water, or seven large glasses of water daily.[52]

To sum it up, brain power with long-lasting memory and increased cognitive abilities is yours with just a few changes in your lifestyle. On your mark, get set, go!

Become a Fitness Lover

As a member of the *Fit and Feeling Fabulous Club*, exercise plays a role as important as sensible eating in developing a strong immune system and living a healthy life. Exercise increases circulation throughout the body and helps flush toxins. It makes your immune system stronger and more resistant to diseases. It helps build your muscles and contribute to more flexibility, leaving you less prone to back and neck pain.

 Fitness is a fit mind in a fit body.

When it comes to keeping your body strong and your mind fit, four to five sessions of exercise per week make all the difference in keeping your energy level up and making you feel invincible. Thirty minutes of exercise is all you need for your mind to bathe in endorphins, those good-feeling hormones that scare away depression, laziness, and fatigue.

If four sessions per week is too much for you, then commit to a minimum of 10–15 minutes per day with your fitness program, combining some stretches, a few strength-training exercises, a brief walk, or a bicycle ride. It is best to mix up your workouts with three types of exercises: flexibility, strength training, and cardiovascular conditioning. Not only do you want to improve your balance and flexibility, but you want to build strength and increase your blood flow.

Flexibility – Flexibility exercises are touted to decrease the risk of injuries, enhance posture, increase blood flow to muscles and cartilage, and help relieve conditions such as arthritis and lower back pain.[53] They rejuvenate your body and alleviate tension build-up. They also elongate muscle fibers that translate into more muscle mass for those trying to build muscles. Stretching, Qi Gong, and Pilates are relatively easy to do, and they are known to increase flexibility, circulation, and blood flow to muscles. Several people give yoga high praise as a flexibility and strength enhancer.

I like stretches, as they can be done anywhere and at any time of the day. They are certainly part of my daily routine. I wake up and go to bed with them. Every hour or so, I stretch at my desk. I always complete my workouts with a few stretches to reduce the lactic acid buildup responsible for muscle soreness.

Strength Training – Running and lifting weights build endurance and physical strength. The benefits of lifting weights are just amazing, from increased body mass and osteoporosis prevention to reduction in arthritis and back pain, as well as improved joint function. In addition, intense exercise increases your levels of dopamine, serotonin, and norepinephrine, which in turn elevate your mood.[54] I have been including bodybuilding exercises in my fitness routine for several years now, and I am still in awe as to how good I feel each time I step out of the gym.

Strength training is also good for maintaining a healthy weight. More muscles mean more calorie burning each day. One pound of fat and one pound of muscle have very different energy requirements, with muscles needing more calories than fat.[55] Running is not only good for cardio endurance, but it also builds stamina. Like everything else, practice makes perfect. It takes time to become a fitness machine. Start slowly, but be consistent. It's the best way to increase your endurance.

Cardiovascular Conditioning – Fast walking, kickboxing, cardio exercises, cycling workouts, playing tennis, stair climbing, and running are all great ways to keep your heart pumping and improve blood vessel function. They increase your heart and breathing rates, and of course, your sweat levels. Cardio training expands your blood vessels for more oxygenated blood to be delivered to your muscles. As house cleaning removes dust, cardio training sweeps away unwanted toxins. Running for extended periods is known to enhance endorphin release.[54]

For those who want to lose a few pounds, cardio training is a very good contender as a calorie burner, especially when you want to burn fat located in your hips and thighs. A 35–40 minute run on a treadmill, an elliptical machine, or a stair climber at moderate intensity does wonders for your thighs and cellulite. According to the American Heart Association, it is best to keep your heart rate between 50–85 percent of your maximum heart rate (MHR). Subtract your age from 220 and you will find your MHR. It's as simple as that.[56] No need to reach a higher level, for fear of burning glycogen in your muscles.

"Does sex count as cardio?" you might ask with a smile on your face.

The answer is unfortunately no, sex is not part of the cardiovascular training list. A cardio exercise is one that elevates your heart to 50–85 percent of your MHR and sustains it there for some time. Heavy breathing does not necessarily mean you are in a cardio zone. Sorry!

Having said that, an active sex life brings more vitality into your life. It is touted to reduce stress, release endorphins, and give you a healthy glow and a more toned body. In addition, it lowers your risk of heart disease and increases life expectancy. These are all good reasons to keep the blankets warm.

Taking time to nurture yourself makes you feel wonderful. The hardest part of exercise is to get going. Once you are at the gym or on the tennis court, you soon comprehend that you can't live without exercise. Remember that what you give to your body today, your body will give back tomorrow.

The bottom line is that exercise will keep you healthy and happy, and feeling better about yourself. See you soon at the gym!

Let Go of Addictions

Are you tired of harmful cravings, assaultive compulsions, and destructive behaviors? Are you tired of the guilt and shame? Then read on; there is light for you at the end of the tunnel. As the *Marvelous You*, you are life. Tobacco, eating disorders, excessive shopping, gambling, stealing, compulsive behavior, passive-aggressive behavior, drugs, alcohol, or other types of destructive addictions have no rights on you.

There is much emotional pain, anxiety, and fear behind addictions. I know pain and fear, and I have learned over the years to better master them, and so can you. In my early twenties I was an emotional eater, and food was my *dear friend* and soothing companion. Then one day I chose life, and life revealed itself to me. My heart became filled with trust, confidence, and love for myself. I truly understood that I was precious in the eyes of God. I learned healthy tips to ease pain, fear, and frustration. You, too, can choose life and cause your full potential to flourish.

 Addiction is pain and fear in disguise.

Pain of being unloved and unworthy.

Fear of life and love.

*Fear not, He holds you in His hand and
He will wipe away your tears.*

Perhaps your life experiences have left you deeply disappointed, scared, and lonely. Your heart is shattered, and you don't want to live life, with its good and not-so-good moments. You see human interaction as a lie. You do not see value in yourself and others. All you want is comfort from your *dear friend*.

As the *Marvelous You*, you are not powerless; you are indeed powerful. You can free yourself from substance and behavioral addictions. You are able to transform your life for more goodness and maximum wellness. You are not a victim, you are a conqueror. You have the commitment, self-discipline, and dedication to be all that you can be. All is in you to live a fulfilled life.

Let me remind you again that you are eternally embraced by God. You are connected to a sea of love, and you are not alone in this journey. He is always present with you. Let this truth take root in your heart and give you the will to live. Let God be your source of hope. Let Him lift you up. If His love is not real to you, then activate your *Higher Power* app now and speak to Him daily.

With *Higher Power* activated, your heart sees the invisible. You understand that your life has a purpose of love, and that your actions to make this world a better place do count. With expanded awareness as to who you are, you develop a sense of worthiness.

Through this transformation, you desire to better care for yourself and others. You no longer need to destroy yourself physically, emotionally, and financially. You allow yourself to live to your full potential and thrive. You accept that life is full of surprises. Some of them are not always welcome, but it's all fine. You are strong, and learn new mechanisms to journey through challenges with more ease. You are armed with courage and resilience, and you bounce back easily from adversity.

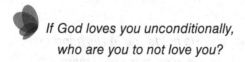

If God loves you unconditionally,
who are you to not love you?

You are more confident about tomorrow because you trust in the orchestrating Power of life. In your heart, you have found a place of safety, security, and inner peace. Trusting in the grander plan of life, setbacks do not scare you. You know that all is well and good. You trust that He will open the way for you and for your life to be a blessing. Your heart smiles at the thought of celebrating another great day.

From this level of consciousness blossoms love for you and for others. No need to be enraged anymore. With *Love Power* activated, your heart is forgiving, free to move on. Not only do you easily forgive those who have wronged you, but you forgive yourself. You are ready for new adventures and the great life you deserve.

To help you in your journey to freedom, join a support group or enroll in a recovery program. Support meetings are great to meet other people who share similar difficulties, and they allow for personal accountability and support, even outside the meetings. Many rehabilitation facilities offer treatment programs that have proven to be very successful. Their teams include physicians, psychologists, addiction counselors, therapists, and nutritionists.

In addition, several people have had amazing results in breaking free of their addictions with techniques used by NLP practitioners aimed at changing behavior. Reprogramming dysfunctional beliefs about yourself and your life makes a difference in your journey towards addiction freedom.

To sum it up, follow the path of love and respect for yourself, and freedom can be yours. By letting love expand and flow through you, there is no more need to struggle and cling to your addictions. You will be free to rise to higher levels of wellness. Your *dear friend* will be replaced with two new ones: pure bliss and well-being. You will boldly say, "I choose love for myself. I have the power to transform my life, and I will become all that I can be."

May your heart be filled with deep joy, hope, and peace while you journey towards healing, freedom, and greater love for yourself and those around you. This is my dearest prayer for you.

Harmonize Your Energy Fields

Oftentimes a poor diet, lack of exercise, environmental toxins, viruses, germs, bacteria, fungi, parasites, excessive sun exposure, and too much stress and anxiety hide behind sickness. You are blessed with an impressive internal healing system that knows how to repair a small cut, get you back on your feet when you have a cold, and flush toxins out of your body.

Good hygiene, proper nutrition, exercise, and rest are keys in keeping your body's natural defense mechanisms in full force. At times, your body needs conventional medicine to nurture itself back to health with drugs, surgery, radiation, or other means.

At other times, energy medicine (energy healing) is an option to explore. As said, proponents of energy healing claim that energy fields permeate, surround, and sustain the body. They suggest that imbalances in the body's energy fields—blockages, distortion, holes, tears, or lack of synchronization between auras, chakras, and the meridian system—may be the cause of illness, and re-balancing the energy fields may help restore health. The energy fields may also be affected by emotional issues, unfelt or unreleased emotions, physical issues, negative thoughts and behavior, drugs, alcohol, and different types of toxins.[57]

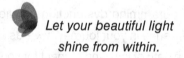

Let your beautiful light
shine from within.

Great benefits are reported from energy healing. These include more vigor, stress reduction, better sleep, decreased pain, emotional freedom, allergy healing, and greater well-being. There are various energy-based healing techniques, namely acupuncture, reiki, Brennan Healing Science, reflexology, polarity therapy, and therapeutic touch.[57]

Take time to learn more about these energy healing techniques and see which ones would be good companions in your healing journey. Keep in mind that the use of these techniques should be a complement, not a replacement, to conventional medicine. Do not stop medical treatment unless recommended by your physician.

Remember you are body, soul, and spirit. Wellness and vitality are experienced when your whole self is in harmony. If you have not been well for a long time and medical treatment has failed to bring relief, explore energy healing. A gentle touch can go a long way!

CHAPTER 8

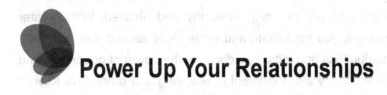

Power Up Your Relationships

True friendships are precious treasures.

Activate Your *Love Power* App

You are the *Marvelous You,* wonderfully gifted with the power to love. Simply by activating your *Love Power* app, you experience more joy and fulfillment from your relationships. As a being endowed with free will, you can shut down your *Love Power* app, which in turn leaves a void in your heart. All sorts of reasons may trigger this choice:

- Being abandoned or abused at a young age led you to believe that love and emotional pain go hand in hand. You feel insecure, and unconsciously you forego any future attachments.
- The loss of a loved one or a break-up is so overwhelming that you can't stop crying, and you fear to love again.
- Moving forward after your spouse's infidelity or a betrayal is not easy. You are filled with anger, hate, and hurt, and you just can't forgive. You wrongly believe that no one is to be trusted again.
- Consumed with the thought of scarcity, you do not have a generous spirit.
- You harbor envy and cannot rejoice in the success of others.

With *Love Power* turned off, your heart is filled with insecurity, grief, anger, distrust, selfishness, lack of forgiveness, or enmity, which may lead you to create human suffering. If you want your heart to sing again, activate your *Love Power* app today. Love will fill your life with a new song.

With *Love Power*, you empower your most important relationship, the one you have with yourself. You heal past wounds and crush the disempowering beliefs of being unworthy and unloved. With greater love for yourself, you appreciate and value those around you, with their unique contributions and gifts. You discover the power of goodness, and experience much joy and fulfillment in receiving and giving love to your family, friends, partners, and the world. With an open heart, you create loving, harmonious, and fulfilling relationships.

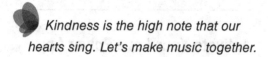 *Kindness is the high note that our hearts sing. Let's make music together.*

You emanate kindness, acceptance, patience, understanding, and compassion. You travel light by forgiving those who have abused or wronged you, understanding that everyone is on a path of learning and growing. You listen with a loving heart, and your speech is kind.

Your heart smiles at the thought of God's desire to bestow kindness to others through you. You are a thoughtful companion, a caring parent, a skilled listener, a compassionate comforter, a patient teacher, a loving guide, a nurturing provider, and an engaged peace activist who uplifts everyone around you.

As a parent or spouse of someone with attachment issues, you are patient and calm. You love unconditionally through kind words and actions that inspire understanding, trust, support, and openness. You make others feel safe, and you respect their personal journey towards healing and wholeness.

You make efforts to live in peace and make this world a better place to live. As a being of love, you embrace diversity and respect different cultures, genders, races, ethnicities, and religions. You embrace the power of differences.

So don't wait any longer; activate your *Love Power* app and get ready to receive and unleash your love. The world needs your rays of sunshine and great beauty.

Let Love In

You are meant to be a channel for the power of love to flow in abundance from your heart to others. For any number of reasons, you may have turned off your *Love Power* app, and your love channel is impeded and the cause of serious attachment issues.

Maybe you have been abandoned and uncared for at a young age, going from one foster home to another, or you were physically abused or raped as a child or teenager. Unconsciously you feel unworthy of love. You rarely express your emotions, and your heart is filled with anger, loneliness, sadness, and self-doubt. Self-repression and self-rejection are your friends. You indulge in substance abuse. You avoid physical and eye contact, or have an aversion to physical contact. You are uncomfortable receiving and giving love and developing relationships.

Perhaps you were a victim of physical or verbal abuse by a parent or spouse, or your spouse cheated on you, and you are going through a difficult split. You live with a smile on your face, but your heart is crying. As self-protection, you are good at developing friendships but avoid closeness, intimacy, and romantic love.

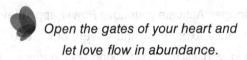

Open the gates of your heart and
let love flow in abundance.

The good news is you can triumph from attachment issues. You can say good-bye to self-repression and self-rejection and dry your tears. You are the *Marvelous You*, and you can be the love channel you are meant to be. Turn on your *Love Power* app today and choose to embark on a courageous healing journey and transform your life with more fulfillment. As you take small steps along the road to recovery with a knowledgeable therapist, unhide and release painful events and emotions to let your wounds heal. If you hit a few bumps here and there, remain positive. Over time, your tears will dry up, and you will make peace with your past.

Through this healing process, forgive those who have abused or wronged you, and let go of past hurts leading to the restoration of your love channel. As you overcome your attachment challenges, you will regain trust in others. Your heart will smile again, and love will gently flow through you and shine out to the world.

Immersed in God's love and healing, you are no longer lost; you are fulfilled. You find in Him a safe refuge and a sturdy foundation, allowing you to be the love you are meant to be. In His love, you find someone who cares deeply for you and will never forsake you. You are no longer afraid to be hurt, knowing that He has the power to heal your broken heart. You love for the simple pleasure of being loving, setting the other person free to love you back—or not. You give freely, and look out for the best interests of others, without expectations. You grasp the concept that reciprocation is not a requirement of love.

With *Love Power*, you now believe that you are lovable and worthy of love. With these new beliefs, you set yourself free from negative emotional bondage and insecure attachments. You find pleasure in being loved. Like a blooming flower, you grow in the greatness of love. In practicing the *Path to Serenity Technique*, you experience closeness and bliss, deeply rooted in God's love.

Don't wait any longer. Activate your *Love Power* app today and let your heart be restored to fully experience the beauty of life and the power of love. By letting love in, you will freely offer kindness, harmony, forgiveness, and joy to those around you.

Beware of the *I8U* Virus

The *I8U* virus, also known as the *I hate you* virus, is presently causing a world-wide pandemic. The virus is not new, but we have seen a recurrence of cases everywhere in the world over the past few years. There is not a day that goes by where appalling cases are not being reported in some countries.

The virus is spreading at an alarming rate and is infecting our kids, families, communities, and leaders. We have seen cases in schools, churches, businesses, militant organizations, and governments. If your life lacks love, forgiveness, respect for human life and values, honesty, or integrity, it means you have caught the *I8U* virus. Viral symptoms include lies, deception, corruption, unlawful behavior, bullying, threats, rape, physical and verbal violence, hatred, constant confrontation, oppression, and terrorism. It is responsible for so much misery and brokenness around the world.

The *I8U* virus causes serious social, ethical, and political issues. It brings a lot of darkness into the world, hiding the beauty of life. Some people spread the virus without any fear of the consequences, thinking they will gain more power, material things, or notoriety.

Some strains of the *I8U* virus are extremely serious, and can be deadly. We are seeing more and more cases of total disregard for human rights. The virus is as powerful as any bomb, enabling people to kill innocent people for no valid reason. It can even drive people over the edge, leading them to commit suicide.

 The most powerful weapon on earth is your mind.

Not used properly, you can destroy your life and the lives of those around you.

To sum it up, when you catch the virus, you move towards the *Powerless You*. The good news is that we know the origin of the *I8U* virus, and we have the antiviral treatment to fight against this madness disease. The source of the virus is a lack of awareness as to who you truly are.

Let me remind you that you are a beautiful human being, connected to the Life Force that sustains the universe. You are here on planet earth to allow your true essence, the *Marvelous You*, to emerge in all its beauty. Your true purpose and greatest accomplishment in life is to learn, grow, and be all that you can be, loving and creating for the betterment of all.

With your *Love Power* app turned on, you fully activate the *I8U* anti-virus. Immense love flows into your heart and mind. You embrace this love and let it grow to disintegrate barriers and bring peace and fulfillment for yourself and those around you. With your thoughts and actions captive in love, unloving thoughts disappear. You make better choices that reflect compassion and forgiveness, which in turn enlighten the world.

"Can *Love Power* change the world?" you might ask.

Yes, the power to create world peace is within each of us. By activating your *Love Power* app, you understand that the Life Power sustaining the universe flows within you and others. You acknowledge that violence, confrontation, and oppression are not from Spirit, who is true love. With expanded awareness, you no longer want to fight or annihilate people of different views or religious foundations, knowing that all human beings are precious children of God.

You are driven to create a new world, where people of all religions and philosophies of life live harmoniously. You see diversity of personalities, ideas, genders, cultures, races, and ethnicities as enrichment, with each person being a source of beauty. You understand that diversity is the basis for expansion.

As intended by God, you do not impose your religious beliefs on others, honoring His desire for people to come to Him out of love and free will, not out of force and compliance. You let Him complete their spiritual transformation as He chooses to.

Tirelessly, you celebrate life and freedom. You cultivate peace and resolve conflicting perspectives with an understanding mind and open dialogue, using peaceful means. You recognize other people's needs and values, and you strive for respect, compassion, and the well-being of all.

As a government leader, you serve in true love for the betterment of your people, not for your personal empowerment and enrichment. You develop laws and policies that support non-violence, promote equal rights for all, respect diversity, eliminate corruption and oppression, and embrace world peace.

Simply put, we each have a responsibility to turn on our *Love Power* app and be a spark of kindness and a light in the physical world. In unity, we will transform the world. Stand up today and get ready to be a peace ambassador, an agent of change for the betterment of all. Fill the world with harmony, peace, righteousness, appreciation, and tolerance. You will be a shining star for eternity.

Keep the Flame Alive

Do you remember the excitement, the thrill, and the butterflies you felt in your stomach when you met your beloved? You were walking above the ground. He was the cutest, the smartest, and the most wonderful. You couldn't stop bragging how your loved one was your soul mate, and your love was meant to be.

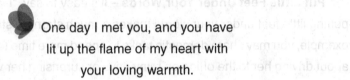

One day I met you, and you have
lit up the flame of my heart with
your loving warmth.

Now a few years later, the butterflies are gone, and you wonder where they went. The excitement has vanished, and your love flame is flickering. Love is like a wood fire. If you constantly throw water on it, you will eventually put it out. You will then need to let the wood dry and carefully stack it up again with a bedding of kindling and paper before relighting it. Every harsh word, lie, deception, blame, unrealistic expectation, or heated argument is more water that diminishes or even extinguishes your love flame.

With your *Love Power* app activated, you can rekindle love and strengthen your emotional connection. You are the *Marvelous You*, the passionate and the lover, remember? By nourishing the relationship with kind words, caring actions, truthfulness, forgiveness, and compassion, you can light up the love flame again for more closeness, intimacy, and well-being.

Weave the followings tips into your love life, and you will soon see beautiful butterflies flying in the garden of your heart:

Become Best Friends – As best friends, you love spending time talking and laughing together. You love freely, without expectations, and for no reason. You call or text just to say hello. If your lovely spouse is scared, you speak reassuring words. If she cries, you dry her tears. If he is tired, you give him space to rest and relax.

Cooperation is in, nagging is out. You create space for both of you to communicate truthfully, without being afraid of being judged or criticized. You listen deeply, without forcing your opinions. With kind words, you stay away from heated argument. Most importantly, you don't wake up old skeletons, and you leave the past buried in the past. No need to get mad if your lover has a different viewpoint. You are both students of life, open and interested in learning from each other.

Put Little Feet Under Your Words – It's easy to say, "I love you," but putting little feet under your words makes a much stronger statement. For example, you may share domestic tasks to spend more time together. How about driving her to the office on rainy days or surprising her with flowers? How about buying him his favorite car magazine? You can send him a quick love note at the office. Or perhaps you can prepare his favorite meal. Send him a sweet selfie or surprise him with a romantic get-together. Loving gestures warm the heart.

Let Your Loved One Be – Supporting each other's dreams makes room for both of you to learn and grow. Give each other freedom to pursue activities and interests you love, even if it means time apart. Be proud, and rejoice in each other's growth. Spending time apart does not necessarily open the door to growing apart. In total freedom, respect, and love, different evolution can be a source of excitement and spark in your relationship. Together, celebrate all of your personal successes, small and grand.

Pursue Common Goals or Activities – Enjoy each other's company and solidify your union with common goals or activities. For example, share ideas and work together in turning your common aspirations into reality. Build great memories of time shared together, whether it's a vacation, a golf or tennis game, a boat ride, a walk in the park, a picnic, a bicycle ride, or a nice meal at her favorite restaurant.

Warm Up the Blankets – Spending some romantic time together warms up a relationship. Start the day with a kiss. Express your love physically with lots of kisses, a gentle body touch, holding hands, a hug, or a massage. Keep the blankets warm. Not only does sex release stress and help you release endorphins, it gives you a healthy glow and a more toned body. For many women, sex starts outside the bedroom. A woman well-treated outside the bedroom will greatly care for her man in the bedroom. Harmony, both in and out of the bedroom, is one of the secrets to great couple relationships.

With *Love Power*, I have no doubt that you will be quite creative and will be coming up with your own ideas on how to keep the flame alive. I can already feel the heat...

Resolve the Solvable

Are you going through a rough patch in your love relationship? Is your friend's attitude driving you nuts? Did you have a fall-out with a colleague? Is someone telling lies about you? Are you sending distress signals to no avail?

Perhaps both of you have been stressed out lately and are impatient. Your comments are tinted with sarcasm. Your tone of voice is on the angry side and you can't communicate without yelling. You speak words that are far from being lovey-dovey and caring. You avoid responding to calls and texts. Simply put, you know that this situation can't go on anymore.

At times, lovers, best friends, and even colleagues do fight, and they can reconcile and resolve the solvable. With *Love Power*, they can power up their relationships and work together at addressing the issues that cause the rift. Passive communication leads nowhere other than to a place of more frustration and resentment.

You were gifted with freedom of speech, and you have the right to express your opinions and views, and be who you want to be. You are not going to resolve any issue if you withdraw and do not talk about what's bothering you. People do not have crystal balls, and can't possibly know what you dislike and how upset you are unless you tell them.

Positive dialogue, openness, genuine compassion, a forgiving heart, and peaceful negotiation are four ingredients for peaceful reconciliation and more harmonious relationships.

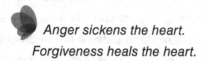

Anger sickens the heart.
Forgiveness heals the heart.

Positive Dialogue – In the heat of a debate, many choose harsh words as their weapon of choice to speak up about their frustrations. Unfortunately, sarcasm, coarse language, and shouting do nothing to calm a storm. Throwing poisonous words that kill love will only keep you in troubled waters. Communicating in a calm and non-threatening manner will lead to a collaborative dialogue and a more fruitful outcome. When ready to leave your anger at the door, find a quiet place with no distractions to hash out the issue.

Openness – Take turns in expressing your individual concerns and feelings. Most importantly, explain why you disagree with what has been said or done, or in the manner it has been said or done. Take time to confirm your understanding and ask questions for further clarification. Avoiding using generalizations and accusing words.

For example, avoid saying: "You are always so rude and impatient." Instead, you might say, "When you yelled at me last night because I was late, it crushed my heart because it's hard for me to associate love with rudeness." Another example is to replace: "You always spend our money on unnecessary things," with "When you bought a new stereo last week, well aware of our limited budget, it made me feel really insecure, and financial security is important to me."

Genuine Compassion – Be honest in sharing your beliefs and feelings. A greater understanding will help in negotiating an arrangement that is agreeable to both of you. Listen attentively, and acknowledge concerns with an open mind and heart. Make an effort to grasp the other person's perspective and show compassion towards their feelings. Summarizing your understanding in a few words is a way to affirm that you truly have captured the issue and care about the resolution.

Forgiving Heart – Oftentimes, people have the best intentions in doing what they do. They don't have a mean intent, and are unaware that their attitude is ruining their relationships. Reflect on your part in the conflict or issue at stake, and how you could have done or said things differently. Don't overlook activating your *Love Power* app. Asking for forgiveness is powerful in mending relationships, especially if you lost your temper and your words were abrasive. Forgiveness automatically breaks barriers, and it opens the door to a loving resolution.

Peaceful Negotiation – With an open heart you are now ready to move into the negotiation phase for a peaceful resolution. Start by communicating your ideas for possible solutions to the issue at stake. Be respectful of the other person's freedom to agree or disagree. There is no room in conflict resolution for controlling or dominating the other person. If one of you disagrees with a proposed option, explain why, and propose an alternative.

In the name of love, work together in identifying an arrangement that is realistic and suitable in meeting both of your needs. Negotiation is about finding a satisfying solution where you both feel respected and will engage in its implementation.

With these tips in mind, you will likely resolve your conflicts and issues in a more collaborative and compassionate manner, and you will build stronger relationships. At times you may face a dead end, with no resolution on the horizon. In such instances, do not hold a grudge, but give the other person time to reflect on the issue and its resolution.

Make Hard Choices

If you are unable to resolve the rift with a loved one, explore the possibility of seeing a counselor. With an independent party working with both of you, it may be easier to stay within the boundaries of positive dialogue and resolve conflicts and concerns.

A support group can be of great help when dealing with issues such as substance abuse, anger management, depression, anxiety, post-traumatic stress disorder, or eating disorders. If you were not able to find a compromise to a persistent issue with counseling and support, peace will be short-lived. In such cases, ask yourself if you can live with the unsolvable. No one is perfect, and it's unrealistic to expect that your partner will behave the way you want at all times. It's up to you to decide what you can and cannot accept.

Ask yourself some hard questions: How much do I want this relationship to work? Am I ready to accept my partner's imperfections? How badly am I affected by the person's attitude? These questions can also be asked with friendships that are emotionally draining. You are the only person who can answer these questions. No one else can give you advice. Listen attentively to your inner voice. Your heart holds all of the answers.

If you suffer from physical and/or verbal abuse, I suggest you take a time of reflection outside your home to avoid further conflicts and emotional traumas. If one of you struggles with substance abuse, consult a therapist or counselor before making your final decision about the future of your relationship.

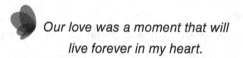

*Our love was a moment that will
live forever in my heart.*

You may love someone dearly, but may not be able to live under the same roof and maintain a healthy relationship. Some relationships are simply not salvageable due to physical or verbal abuse, or incompatible personalities, views, values, and needs. Some let themselves shrink and inhibit their personal growth to let the other person feel secure. Others lose their inner joy with too many differences and demanding compromises. Do you recognize yourself? Be strong, and let go of toxic relationships.

Saying good-bye and moving on is not easy, but it may be the best choice for both of you. Give yourself and your children the gift of uncoupling with respect and love. There is nothing more difficult for a child than being in the middle of a war zone. Harsh words and tears are painful for a child who loves both parents.

If you choose to invest in your relationship, cherish it with all your heart. Make your bond stronger by sharing and supporting each other. With compassion, kindness, and care, you will bring the best of who you are in the relationship and keep the flame of your heart alive.

Give Your Child Wings to Fly

As a parent, you are endowed with the great responsibility of teaching your children how to activate their apps and be all that they can be. One day your children will leave the nest, and you want them to have a great set of wings to fly high.

First things first. Activate your *Love Power* app to let love flow freely from your heart. Below are *Love Power Parenting Techniques* to help your children become the *Marvelous Beings* they are meant to be, full of creativity, autonomy, passion, and love.

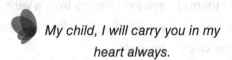

My child, I will carry you in my heart always.

You are my sunshine, my reason to live and love.

Fly high in the sky. You are free to soar and sing your song of greatness.

Encourage Creativity – Each child is imbued with talents and skills. Early on, encourage your children to develop their creativity and imagination with games, coloring books, drawings, LEGO blocks, and craft supplies. Encourage them to take classes to further develop their skills and creativity.

From dance arts to sports classes, they are all great ways to learn, grow, and develop friendships and memories.

Let your children be free to express themselves and allow them to use objects around the house as props. It is so much fun for children to engage in role playing where they can be superheroes, doctors, schoolteachers, or firefighters.

I developed my love of fashion with paper dolls. I would spend hours carefully cutting out all the paper clothes, and then use my imagination to create day and evening events to dress them up for the occasion. I also remember the snow fort my brother used to build every winter. With my dolls warmly dressed up and tucked in the sleigh, I would walk around the house, pretending I was lost in the Arctic. My stories always ended well, finding refuge in the snow fort. I had lots of fun with my dolls, from tea parties to camping, and they were always up for a new game. To this day, I cherish those beautiful memories buried in my treasure chest.

Incite Independence – Provide opportunities for your children to exercise their freedom and autonomy. Teach them color harmony and let them choose their clothes. Ask your children to help you prepare their next day's lunches, and let them choose their snacks from a variety of nutritious foods. Let your children pick a weekend activity for the whole family, with each child taking turns week after week.

Be Passionate – Be excited about life, and your passion will be contagious. If you are telling your children that life is hard all the time, you are simply cutting off their wings. As they grow up, they may have difficulties in seeing the beauty of life, and may be scared and hesitant to get engaged and take action.

Be a Supporter – If your children understand early on that life challenges are opportunities to be more creative, they will view roadblocks as positive experiences. They will be resilient and courageous, and they will see life as an adventure. Your children will bounce back quickly, as they will be well-equipped to face life's storms. As your children face problems, ask for their ideas to resolve the issues. Encourage them to listen to their inner voice. You can guide them with wisdom, giving them options to choose from.

Set Boundaries – Rules and consequences of disobedience need to be explained clearly. Consistency by both parents is key in disciplining children. Children making a mistake or disobeying a rule is not a reason to yell. Stay calm, look them in the eyes, and communicate what they did wrong.

If you feel a punishment is warranted, enforce it. Forego physical punishment. Instead, direct your children to a room or other home area (kitchen corner, stairs) where they can't access their toys. Once the punishment is over, take a few minutes alone with them and ask them to tell you what they did wrong and why they think it's wrong.

This allows your children to better understand what they had been asked to do and the reasons why. Show them how they can make amends if they have wronged someone else. Most importantly, reassure them of your love. I have seen this technique used with great success by a number of parents.

Praise Your Child – Praise your children for their successes, even small ones. Praise reinforces good behavior and confidence. As they succeed in small tasks, they will be moved to take on greater ones. Your children need your help to develop the belief they can do anything they desire if they put their minds to it. If you celebrate one of your children's successes, like winning a race or acing an exam, make sure you also praise your other children for the good things they do. It breaks my heart when I see parents favoring one child over another. You simply reinforce the child's feeling of never being good enough.

Avoid Comparison – Avoid comparing your child to his siblings. In doing so, you may nourish feelings of inadequacy or unworthiness in your child. Let your children develop at their own pace. Children are like flowers as they bloom in different seasons of their lives. Focus on what your children do right, help them develop their skills, and celebrate their progress. In doing so, your children will be on their way to become all that they can be.

Let Them Be – Do not force your dreams on your children. Let them be who they want to be. Stop the yelling and pressure to perform. These approaches won't boost confidence and self-esteem. This means no name calling and yelling in the car if your child did not score in a soccer game or misspelled a word in a spelling contest.

Remember that you can only give what you have and who you are. Yes, it all starts with you. If you do not enjoy life, your child will not be excited about life, either. If you do not practice true love, you will not be a great love teacher. If you are not respectful, your child will not learn respect. Most importantly, remember that raising children is a gift of love, without expecting anything in return other than seeing them fly high.

Teach Your Child to Love

There is nothing more beautiful than seeing your children fly to greatness and become adults grounded in love. As a *Marvelous Parent*, you are embedded with the task to teach your children to love. It is your role to show your children how to activate their *Love Power* app for their love to illuminate the world around them. For your children to be fruitful in love, they first must see love in you. You must exemplify love, kindness, generosity, and compassion in your own life for your children to embrace and walk on the love path. For this to happen, you, too, have to activate your *Love Power* app.

 The moment I held you in my arms, my heart leaped with deep joy.

You are a gift from God, and now it's my time to give you back to the world.

Be fruitful in love, my child, my love.

As a *Marvelous Parent*, do not be afraid to be affectionate and give your children lots of hugs and kisses. Tell each one of them, "I love you so much, you are so precious to me, and I am so proud of you. You bring me so much joy."

Take time to listen to their aspirations and show interest in their daily activities. Be a great listener, interested in their problems and feelings. Have fun playing and spending quality time with them. In doing so, you are building their self-worth.

Impart your children with love, in both actions and words, for their siblings, classmates, and neighbors. Show them the pleasures of simple acts of kindness, like sharing their toys, helping a classmate with homework, or assisting a neighbor in need. Praise them, and celebrate their goodness.

Teach them to be patient, forgiving, and compassionate towards others. As they see your unconditional love in action, their hearts will express the same genuine love. If they've been wronged, they will forgive with more ease, knowing that each one of us is learning and growing.

Communicate the importance of respecting people and their cultures, differences of opinion, and divergent religious beliefs. Instruct them to say please and thank you as a means of appreciation. If they are not behaving well, take private time with them to explain why their attitude is not one of love, and how to make amends and do better in the future.

Having a pet in the house is a great way to instill a sense of responsibility and ignite a nurturing spirit. Boost your children's team spirit by getting them involved in domestic chores or in team sports that align with their age and physical capacity. Each little action counts.

Be excited to show them the beauty of life. Visit a zoo, a museum, or an art gallery, go hiking or fishing, or take a walk in the park, to name just a few activities you can do together.

At family dinner, take turns expressing something you are grateful for. Teaching your children to practice gratefulness will help them get through life's storms with more ease. They will appreciate and take pleasure in the little things of life. Their hearts will be filled with an inner joy for the simple reason of being alive.

Last but not least, activate your own *Higher Power* app. In doing so, you open the door for your children to do the same, and know God's love for them. Encourage your children to speak to God as if they would speak to a friend. Introduce your children to the concept that God co-creates with them. It is very comforting for children to know that they are not alone in life. In His hand, they will feel safe and secure.

In being raised with love, your children will soar high and glide through life with more ease. Setbacks will not impinge their progress in life, and they will rise above adversities.

Fill Your House with Laughter

Laughter, giggles, chuckles, and smiles are sparks that enliven the heart. Do you remember the joy you felt when your baby laughed for the first time, or when your youngster ran around the house as Peter Pan or Superman, giggling and screaming? A child's laugh is all you need for a heavy heart to vanish.

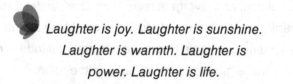

Laughter is joy. Laughter is sunshine.
Laughter is warmth. Laughter is
power. Laughter is life.

Laughter takes the drama and tension out of life. It reminds you that life can be fun amidst unwelcome challenges and changes. It heals a crying heart. It is the sunshine that brightens rainy days. It is the warmth that keeps you warm on colder days. It is the power that keeps you moving forward.

Activate your *Fun and Play* app and let laughter fill your house with joy. Make it your mission to be a *laughmaker* in your house. From little children to big ones, get a huge smile on each face of your family members.

Babies love playing peekaboo. Silly faces and animated puppets surely produce a big grin on their faces. Don't forget funny voices, animal noises, or other hilarious noises. Babies are naturally playful and joyful in a loving environment. They easily respond to your smile and feel your love.

As your children grow up, encourage them to play role-playing games and let them express their joy with laughter and giggles. Run around the house with them and be a child yourself. You will soon forget the hardships of your day. Their world will become your world. You will find yourself in Cinderella's castle or rising high in the sky like Superman. In playfulness, there is no fear and tension, only a feeling of pure enjoyment.

Play family games and get excited at the prospect of winning. Laugh if you win, and laugh if you don't. Make it a fun experience for everyone, with little prizes for all who participated. Show your children that you can still have fun even when you are not winning.

Take the family to an amusement park and get on rides with your children. Laugh, shout, and have fun trying different rides. Buy each child a little souvenir. All these special moments will be buried forever in their treasure chest, along with their smiles, laughs, giggles, and chuckles. On stressful days, encourage your children to read comic books or watch a comedy. Invite their friends for a sleepover, and in no time you will hear the echo of their giggles.

As a parent, don't take life too seriously. Faced with difficulties, look for the best in every situation. Laugh at your mistakes, learn what you have to, and move on. Focus on simple things that bring you pleasure. Laughter is a natural relaxant that evens out stressful moments. Play hide and seek with your children, go for a walk with the dog, call a dear friend, or watch funny videos. Over time, you will notice how laughter brings sunshine back into your life.

There will always be a little child inside of you. You are the *Marvelous You*, playful and joyful. So let your inner child be; set it free.

Reach Out

As the *Marvelous You*, the world is your home and mankind your brethren. With *Love Power* activated, you enjoy reaching out to others to create moments of happiness in your life. You experience a sense of belonging. You discover the great beauty in others. You give and receive love. You share who you are and what you have. You make beautiful music in the lives of those around you. Simply put, reaching out is the experience of openness and of deep connections that enrich your life in so many ways.

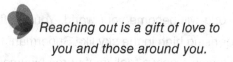 *Reaching out is a gift of love to you and those around you.*

Reaching out starts by inviting people into your home, or taking steps out of your home. Make meeting new people a fun event, a time to learn, grow, and give. Invite coworkers, neighbors, or friends to your home for coffee or dinner. Work the phone while supporting a political party, a telethon, or other social needs. Attend social events, participate in a fundraising activity, become a member in a business network, play in a team sport, take or teach a class, or volunteer in the community.

If you lack confidence in meeting new people, put a smile on your face. Smiling is your best ally to make you and other people more comfortable. Start the conversation by introducing yourself: "We haven't met, my name is … and I work at …."

Then genuinely show interest in the other person's life with open ended questions: I haven't seen you in a long time. What's new? I think we met last month. How've you been? Why do you like coming to these events? Where do you work? What projects are you working on? What are your kids studying?

Be attentive, speak nicely, and smile to make the other person feel at ease. Compliment the person if you like their clothes or hair. Listen and be open to their views. Share your point of view and the reasons why without being obnoxious. You may want to say: "I understand your point, but I see things differently. I find that …"

As you speak, uncross your arms, a body language sign that you are not open to conversation. Pay attention to what the other person is saying. Don't look around as the person talks. If you need to reach for your cell phone, apologize, and explain you are expecting an important call. Don't monopolize the conversation; leave room for others to share their thoughts. Be honest and genuine. People quickly recognize those who are the overbearing type and tend to dissociate from them quickly.

When you feel it's time to move on and talk to someone else, simply say: "It was nice meeting you. If you will excuse me, I would like to go say hello to .... I hope we meet again soon." Give the person your business card, phone number, or e-mail if you wish to do business with them in the near future.

You may discover common areas of interest or similar life experiences with some people. Who knows? Some relationships may result in long-term and solid friendships embedded in mutual love, care, and kindness. In creating a connection, you transcend individual boundaries and awaken to oneness with humanity. You see the good in others and appreciate their gifts and talents. Your life is enriched by the diversity of views and experiences. As you share your positive experiences, you may inspire others to live their best lives.

By volunteering in the community, you become more attuned to other people's needs. You serve using your skills and abilities for the betterment of others. Without knowing it, you may foster hope and courage in those who are facing difficult times.

Reaching out is a source of fulfillment and a blessing for you and others. Embrace these moments of togetherness. Be a light unto someone else's path and let the other person's sunshine brighten your life. Together, both of your glows will outshine darkness.

CHAPTER 9

Power up Your Finances

You were born rich. Believing is the key
that opens the treasure chest.

Activate Your *Financial Tycoon* App

Have you heard the saying, "Money does not grow on trees"? Well, that's right, money does not grow on trees; but it holds the power to grow over time. With your *Financial Tycoon* app activated, you nourish your mind with new beliefs that you are worthy of blessings and goodness, and there is nothing wrong in being rich. You understand that money is a tool to be used to better your life and the lives of those around you.

 Only your mind can stop prosperity
from flourishing in your life.

The *Financial Tycoon* app helps you formulate a financial strategy that best aligns with your vision. From revenue generation to expense reduction, each of your wealth seeds bears the possibility to create more richness in your life. The cost? A change in your money habits. The benefits? More wealth and financial freedom for you to enjoy and share with others in the future.

Financial Tycoon gives you the patience, discipline, and commitment you need to warm your seeds for germination. With empowering beliefs about yourself and money, you are giving your seeds all the nutrients they need to grow. You keep your soil healthy with a positive attitude.

With good-feeling thoughts, you remove negativity weeds and get rid of little bugs like high interest loans and credit card debts that are eroding your saving power. You protect your assets against life's storms with insurance. Most importantly, by adding investment fertilizers, your crop grows faster, and you are on your way to a fruitful money garden.

Activate your *Financial Tycoon* app today and take pleasure in flourishing wealth.

Think and Feel Prosperity

Money is meant to circulate, and it comes to you and flows from you. If scarcity is your daily experience, it means you have lost your money growth momentum. With *Financial Tycoon* turned on, you transform your crop into an abundant harvest for more wealth in your life.

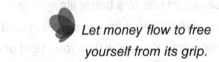

Let money flow to free yourself from its grip.

Nourishing your mind with fertile thoughts will provide a prosperous environment to combat money infertility. With good-feeling thoughts and beliefs about money, you will shift away from poverty mindfulness and move towards prosperity consciousness, and that will inspire you to sow prosperity seeds to enhance your wealth.

Flood your mind with the following positive thoughts, and you will soon be on your way to more abundance. You will be proclaiming, "I feel better about thinking rich. I look forward to planting prosperity seeds. I am a prosperity channel, and I am able to remove any weeds that hinder prosperity from coming into my life." Gather your tools today and get ready for action!

- You are the *Marvelous You*, richly blessed. Wealth is meant to flow with all good things for you to enjoy a better life. Let it be, let it flow by opening your mind and getting engaged. You are gifted to bring more richness into your life. You are deserving of prosperity and a better future.

- Money is a blessing. It is a life enhancer that gives you more options to better care for your needs and those of others. Money does not define your success, but affirming your *Marvelous Nature* does.
- Life is to be seen with eyes of abundance. You are a powerful creator who holds the key to unleashing more wealth into your life. With your thoughts, beliefs, emotions, and actions well-aligned towards prosperity, you hold the power to bring more riches into your life. You alone can change your thought and belief patterns and take action to reap more wealth.
- With more money comes more freedom, freedom to be all that you can be. Freedom to buy what you want, and freedom to help others live a better life.
- More money means more sharing and great joy in helping others achieve their desires and create a better life.
- By activating your *Higher Power* app, you trust in God's power to bestow goodness on you. You know that you are of great value in His eyes. Anchored in His love, you feel worthy of life's blessings. You acknowledge that He co-creates with you and directs you on the prosperity seeds to sow for an abundant crop.

Set a Wealth Action Plan

Not sure where to start to create financial growth? By following this four-step approach to financial success, you will soon see your prosperity seeds grow and attain financial freedom. Keep your *Financial Tycoon* app activated and make sure to turn on your *True Inspiration* and *High Drive* apps to be inspired with winning strategies that will fire you into action.

I encourage couples to map their financial plan together. If you have completely opposite financial goals, where one is a big spender and the other isn't, you will need to resolve the conflict early on and compromise in the interest of love for a secure financial future together.

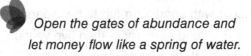

*Open the gates of abundance and
let money flow like a spring of water.*

Step 1: Assess Your Current Financial Situation – Knowing where you stand today and where you want to be tomorrow is a good start to developing a successful financial strategy. Looking at your net worth, investment portfolio, and current budget tells you where your money went, what you've been reaping, and how much you have to create growth. It also gives you a foundation to identify worthy financial goals and develop a strategy to create growth.

Let's start by determining your net worth, which is essentially your total assets minus your total liabilities. To ease the accounting, write down all of your assets, whether they are paid for or not: bank accounts, certificate of deposits, treasury bills, stocks, bonds, exchange-traded funds, mutual funds, retirement funds, education plans, savings plans, accounts receivable, real estate properties, vehicles, furniture, cash surrender value of your insurance policy, valuable art, jewelry, and collectibles.

Continue the net worth exercise by preparing a list of all your liabilities: unpaid bills, credit card debts, notes payable, school loans, mortgage, car loan, boat loan, and unpaid income taxes. Write down the interest rate attached to each liability, which will help in determining which debts to pay off first.

If you have an investment portfolio, prepare a list of all your investments and their rate of return over the past five years. A view of your portfolio is useful to assess if your current investment strategy is still appropriate to meet your investment goals.

Now, it's time to prepare your current monthly budget by listing all your sources of revenue, living expenses, savings, and debt repayments to identify your potential for additional savings and required budget changes. Complete your financial inventory by listing all your insurance policies to ensure you have sufficient and appropriate coverage.

Step 2: Develop Your Financial Goals – With more clarity on your financial situation, you are now ready to reflect on your financial horizon and define a blueprint with short-term (up to two years), mid-term (from three to five years), and long-term (more than five years) goals to move you into action for more richness in your life.

A positive net worth certainly provides more financial freedom and investment power. You have more options to create wealth. A deficit net worth raises a red flag, stressing the need to take action swiftly to return to a surplus position. Don't get discouraged; you can only go up when you are at the bottom of the ladder.

 Abundance is in you and around you.

Let's look at Andrew and Mary's financial situation to see how their financial situation, investment portfolio, and budget have played a role in determining their short-term, mid-term, and long-term goals.

Andrew is in a deficit position, has no investment portfolio, no budget surplus, and high-interest debts. A situation many of us can relate to. His main focus in the short-term and mid-term is to pay off his debts and set an emergency fund to avoid creating new debts.

Budget Surplus: No		High Interest Debts: Yes
N	**Time Horizon**	**Financial Goals**
E	Short-Term	• Buy a home insurance by next month.
G		• Make a payment of $400/month against credit cards to eliminate them by the end of the year.
A	Mid-Term	• Establish an emergency fund by setting aside $200/month once credit cards are paid off.
T	Long-Term	• Once the emergency fund is set, invest $200/month for a down payment on the purchase of a home.
I		• Accumulate $700,000 by retirement age.
V		
E		

On the other hand, Mary has a positive net worth with a good investment portfolio and no debts. She is planning to buy a home with a down payment of $15,000. She has more flexibility when it comes to pursuing her dreams. She has a monthly budget surplus of $600, which she plans to invest to replace her car in two years and become a financial tycoon at retirement.

Budget Surplus: Yes		High-Interest Debts: No
P	**Time Horizon**	**Financial Goals**
O **S** **I** **T**	Short-Term	• Buy a $60,000 accident and life insurance policy next week. • Buy a $150,000 home in six months, with a down payment of $15,000. • Invest an additional $300/month in a retirement savings plan, starting next month.
I	Mid-Term	• Invest $300/month over the next two years to replace her car.
V **E**	Long-Term	• Amass $3 million at retirement with a more aggressive approach of 80 percent stocks and 20 percent bonds.

As you can see, Andrew and Mary's contrasting financial situations and distinctive personal priorities have led both of them to set different goals. A good way to set financial goals that truly matter to you is to use the goal-setting *S.I.M.P.L.E. Criteria*, as further detailed in the section *Move to the Creative Plane*. You want your financial goals to be stretching, inspiring, measurable, purpose-driven, life-changing, and engaging.

Be clear on what you want to accomplish, and don't be afraid to stretch yourself by earning more and reducing your spending to create more growth. Your financial goals should inspire you to create wealth and get you excited for what is to come.

A good way to make your goals measurable is to ask yourself some simple questions: How much? How many? By when? For example, ask yourself: How much more will I save? How many times per month will I stash money in a savings account? By when will my goal be completed?

You want your financial goals to be purpose-driven and life-changing. Ask yourself: Why am I choosing this financial goal? What are the benefits? What will I do with the money? How will it change my life? Your goals need be attainable to engage you in action. You won't commit for a long time to an unrealistic goal.

Now that your list of goals is done, you need to prioritize them to achieve financial success in less time. Not sure how to prioritize your goals? Follow these tips to help you elaborate your financial plan.

- Whether your net worth is in a deficit or surplus position, one of your first short-term goals should be to insure your earning power and your possessions. Many with no home, accident, disability, or life insurance have lost all their precious personal effects and were back to square one when faced by life challenges.

- As the *Marvelous You*, you are empowered to be the master of your finances, not a slave to debt. Your next priority should be to exterminate high-interest debt bugs. By increasing your revenue and cutting on spending, you will free yourself from these little bugs that grind down your saving power.

- With high-interest credit cards paid off, saving for an emergency fund should be your next priority to avoid the temptation to use your credit cards again.

- Next should be saving for a secure retirement. The power behind compound interest is phenomenal. By starting early on this goal, you will secure a comfortable retirement for you and your spouse.

- Now that you have a comfortable emergency fund, you may choose to divert some of your extra dollars from your paychecks to a home fund. Keep in mind that there are pros and cons in buying a home. A home offers more stability and quietness. Yet oftentimes the monthly cost of owning a home far outweighs the cost of renting. In some areas, real estate growth has not been substantial enough to offset the difference in costs. Crunch the numbers and do a cost-benefit analysis before reaching a final decision.

- Now that some high priorities have been dealt with, you are ready to put money aside for other daydreams: a better car, an education fund for your kids, a future business, or trips around the world. You may choose to pay off your mortgage more quickly. If education is non-negotiable goal, the decision to invest in an education fund will come easy.

Your family situation, whether you have children or not, are married or single, envisioning a career change, or plan to retire soon, will influence your financial priorities. I encourage you to reflect on what you and your family want to achieve in the future.

Saving and investing go hand in hand to helping you create more growth. As said, by adding investment fertilizers, you multiply your saved dollars. As further detailed in the section *Invest Wisely*, a number of factors need to be considered in determining your specific investment goals: your risk appetite, capital needs, age, available money, and tax optimization, to name a few.

Step 3: Set up a Strategy – To help you achieve your financial goals, do not overlook gaining more knowledge on financial matters, including budgeting and investment tools. Surround yourself with trusted financial advisors who can guide you in your journey towards financial success.

For each of your goals, prepare a list of actions to move you closer to your financial vision. For example, protecting your assets and income will lead you to contact two or three insurance brokers to compare insurance quotes. To generate more savings to eliminate high-interest debts, you may rent a room in your basement or scale down on your lifestyle by $400/month. You may consolidate your debts at a lower interest rate to save $100/month.

For greater peace of mind, you may stash $200/month in an emergency fund to have a comfortable cushion when life comes around with unwelcome surprises. If you dream of a home or a new car or would like to start a new business in the near future, you may reduce your monthly travel and entertainment spending by $200 for more savings.

You may wish to leverage the power of investing and grow your savings substantially by contributing $200/month to a retirement plan. If your goal is to amass a fortune for retirement, you may opt for an increased portion of high-risk investments in your portfolio that bear a greater rate of return. Your financial advisor and tax professional can help you formulate a strategy and select investment instruments that best align with your investment vision.

Step 4: Revise Your Budget – With your action plan in mind, prepare a revised monthly budget, listing your sources of revenue, expenses, debt repayments, and savings. For successful budget implementation and monitoring, you and your spouse need to track your spending. Keep your bills and total your monthly expenses by type of spending—home spending, daily spending, transport, entertainment, and goodwill—to ease the tracking process. Those numbers will tell you much about your spending personality. A closer look at your spending against your budget will red flag any needed budget adjustments, or perhaps instigate a change in your spending behavior.

Building a secure financial future is an ongoing process. For this reason, chart your progress periodically by reviewing your financial situation and investment portfolio. If your net worth is going up, you are on your way to financial freedom. If your net worth is going down, changes to your financial plan are warranted to pave the way to more wealth. You need to reassess your financial priorities, strategy, and budget for increased growth.

Read on, and you will be empowered with knowledge to navigate with more ease in the fascinating world of finance and investment. From tips to increase your revenue and reduce your debts and expenses, to information on protecting your assets and investments, you will be better equipped to make informed decisions for a fruitful money garden.

Financial scarcity was my reality early on in life, and I have triumphed over the lack of financial resources with discipline, hard work, and the belief that all things are possible to those who are willing to invest time and effort. With action, patience, commitment, and self-discipline, you too can harvest bountifully and create wealth and financial freedom.

Increase Your Revenue Power

Is creating revenue opportunities part of your overall financial strategy? If you've answered yes, then be inspired by the following ideas to sow additional income seeds. If you are in pressing need of cash, here are some good alternatives to earn extra dollars in the next month or so:

- Consider renting a room in your home, your driveway, or storage space in your basement. Simply place a free ad at the grocery store, the gym, the office, or on the Internet. However, be extremely careful who you eventually let into your home. This being said, who knows? This may develop into a new friendship.

- One tip to supplement your daytime Income is to get part-time employment during weekends and evenings. Look for stores that are open during weekends. Inquire at businesses that offer delivery or cleaning services in the evenings. As these options can be physically exhausting, I suggest you don't make them a long-term practice.

- I encourage you to harness your skills to start a part-time home business during evenings and weekends. You're lacking ideas? How about accounting, computer services, translation, proofreading, hairdressing, painting, gardening, day care, pet sitting, dog walking, math tutoring, research, or sewing? Visit your library to find great books on how to start a business at home.

- If you are unemployed, look for employment opportunities in the newspapers and on the Internet. Talk to your contacts and let them know you are looking for employment. In doing so, you are opening yourself to new ideas to come into your life. Keep an open mind and be willing to take a risk and accept a position that is different from your dream job until a better opportunity presents itself.

- If you currently have a business and would like to see it grow, make sure to read Chapter 11. You will find great ideas to take your business to the next level of growth and reap more wealth.

 Increase your revenue power to open
the door to new possibilities.

If increasing your income is more of a long-term goal, then pay attention to the following suggestions:

- Go back to school to learn and develop new skills and abilities. Education is an investment in your future. It generally opens the door to better employment opportunities and a larger paycheck.
- Cultivate your career, learn, and expand your skills through continuous education. Deepen your knowledge in areas of interest by attending seminars and taking courses. Don't be afraid to take on new responsibilities in the workplace. Find a coach or mentor who can guide you in developing your career and profile.
- Leverage your experience by looking around for better employment opportunities that match your skills and abilities.
- Serve your clients well, and build your network of contacts. Oftentimes new and better career opportunities come your way as a result of people appreciating your value.

As you move into action, remember that you are the *Marvelous You*, a powerful creator who is richly blessed. Believe in yourself. There is no challenge you can't conquer.

Spend Wisely

To harvest savings, you must spend wisely and live below your means. This means putting a stop to money being wasted on frivolities. Don't worry, you won't feel deprived. On the contrary, you will feel glee at the thought of creating growth.

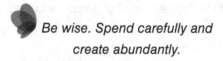

Be wise. Spend carefully and
create abundantly.

Remember to be grateful for all that you have. Smile when you pay your suppliers, and bless them in your heart for their services. Money is a boomerang, and it will come right back to you. Trust me, money is meant to circulate.

By weaving these tips into your life, you will soon be flourishing in wealth.

Home Spending – Having a roommate or renting a room in your basement helps in reducing home costs. Be inspired by the many household saving tips discussed in Chapter 13. You will find many ways to save on utilities, insurance, cable, internet, and phone costs. Have fun finding furnishing and decorating treasures at garage sales. Most people sell items at 20 percent of their original price or less. Challenge your property tax assessment if you feel the value is unreasonable.

Daily Spending – For more savings on groceries and personal supplies, look at sale ads each week. Some families are very successful in saving thousands of dollars each year by using coupons. Don't be shy to step away from your regular brand. You may be pleasantly surprised by both the quality and better prices of other brands. Take advantage of customer reward or loyalty programs that offer discounts, dollars, or points that can be used to purchase items.

Buy in bulk when possible, and shop only for items on your list. Be creative when it comes to meal planning. Choose less expensive ingredients, but still make your meals tasty with spices and sauces. Bring your lunch and coffee to the office. Set a clothing budget for each family member and monitor their budget closely. To save a few dollars on clothing, shop during sale seasons. Wash your clothes rather than sending them to the dry cleaner.

Transport Expenses – Buy a bus pass and commute to work to reduce your gas and car maintenance costs. Take advantage of reduced prices offered by some gas stations on certain days of the week. Buying a demo or used car can save you money. If you go down this route, do your homework.

Remember to verify the past history of the vehicle for accidents, recalls, exposure to flood, and theft. Take a close look at the overall condition of the car and its mileage. Verify outstanding debt and availability of guarantees, as well as the actual value of the vehicle. Do a proper road test, but first and foremost, seriously consider having the vehicle thoroughly verified by a qualified mechanic before putting any money down on this type of purchase. Shop around when buying a new car. In addition to price, pay attention to the warranty, fuel efficiency, and insurance costs, which are important factors in making a final decision.

Fun Spending – By spending less on entertainment, you will find yourself with some extra dollars in your pocket. Watch movies at home rather than going to the theater. Go to the library instead of buying books and magazines. Choose less expensive restaurants. Don't order an appetizer and wine, as they add up quickly on your tab. Consider ordering from take-out restaurants. Invite friends over during weekends and enjoy a nice, home-cooked dinner. Organize a pot luck where everyone brings a delicacy.

If your purse is tight, say good-bye to your massage therapist and hairdresser. Get your spouse to give you a massage. She could even cut your hair, but understand that this suggestion is at your own risk! Cancel your fitness membership and exercise at home. Choose outdoor recreation: take a walk, play tennis, roller skate, or go for a bike ride.

Do not travel during busy seasons when prices are higher. Go camping, or exchange houses through a certified agency if you can't afford hotels. While on vacation, limit your time away from home to one week, and make some family fun around town upon return. If you choose air travel, compare prices for the cheapest fare. Plan your bookings ahead of time, as date and time of departure affect fare prices. Suspend your newspaper subscription while away from home, and consider shutting off the electrical power to your water tank if gone for more than a week.

Goodwill Spending – Even on a tight budget, you can still open your wallet and give with a smile to someone else in need. In doing so, you are affirming your belief that you are a prosperity channel. Of course, you won't be able to give much, but it's the gesture of hope that counts, not the amount. When it comes to family gifts, agree on a gift value that aligns with your budget.

Income Taxes – I encourage you to consult a tax professional to take advantage of all tax measures to help you create wealth. These professionals can help in planning your retirement, mapping a tax-efficient investment strategy, and reducing the burden of education, amongst others.

To sum it up, the whole idea of minimizing your expenses is to amass more wealth. Before spending, ask yourself: Does this expense align with my goals? Is this purchase really urgent? If the answer is no, turn around and run out of the store. With a view of creating growth, frugal living is not as terrible and austere as it seems. On the contrary, it is a positive way of life that will create more pleasant moments and freedom in the future. Enjoy, be creative, and let time do its magic. Soon, your net worth will be going up, up, and up.

Exterminate the Debt Bugs

Many people find themselves tethered to significant debt loads that weigh heavily in their life. From car loan and credit card debts to school loans and mortgages, too many struggle and crumble under debts, stressed out and anxious about their financial future. With your *Financial Tycoon* app activated, you are disciplined and work aggressively at exterminating debt bugs to soon create more wealth. Paying off your debts should be at the top of your financial priorities.

An exception to this rule is if you direct your savings in high-yield investment instruments or an appreciating asset that will earn you more growth than paying off your debt. For example, a low-cost mortgage on a real estate property expected to appreciate in value falls under the exception rule. If you are thinking of borrowing to invest, be wise, get the calculator out, and crunch the numbers.

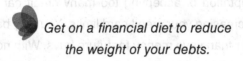

Get on a financial diet to reduce the weight of your debts.

You might ask, "How can I find my way out of debt quickly?"

Scrimping and creating new sources of revenue do speed up the growth of wealth seeds. Reducing spending allows for the transfer of a few more dollars towards monthly credit card payments. Transferring your credit card balances onto a new card with a lower interest rate is another option worth considering. If you are already struggling financially, do not overlook a debt consolidation loan offered by financial institutions at a lower interest rate than the rates of regular loans. Beware of loan sharks who offer debt consolidation at extremely high interest rates. While you may decrease your monthly payments, it will take you months or years to repay your loan in its entirety.

If debt consolidation is not a possible option due to bad credit, then meet with a financial advisor who can work with you in preparing a debt repayment plan. You may be successful in setting a repayment plan over a longer period of time with better interest rates. Your goal should be to avoid bankruptcy, as it negatively affects your credit rating.

Leave your credit cards at home and pay for your expenses with cash unless you are ready to pay your credit cards in full by the due date. While credit cards are convenient to many, they can become a trap for others. Paying cash is the best antidote for impulsive buyers. You withdraw from the bank a set amount of cash each week or month, and there is no going back until the next week or month, as the case may be.

If you have no credit card or little cash on hand, you will likely not walk to the automated teller machine (ATM) to get the additional dollars needed for impulsive buys. The fun is gone by the time you get to the ATM. For those on a cash-based payment system, avoid ATMs that charge high transaction fees, as they can add up quickly. If you do have a credit card, be careful to pay your monthly credit card balance in full by the due date. In doing so, you will not be charged interest from the original purchase date.

Resist the temptation of accepting too many credit cards or line of credit offers and increasing your credit card limits. You may be tempted to use the credit rather than save money for future buys. With no repayment schedules and low interest rates, lines of credit can be enticing; but keep in mind they are debts that you will eventually have to repay. Use them with caution, and get into the habit of paying them in full each month.

Carefully consider inviting payment terms offered by suppliers. No capital and interest payment for a year can be attractive. Look carefully at your budget to ensure payment will not be a burden when the interest-free period ends. If you encounter serious financial difficulties, a good way to repay your debts is to liquidate some of your assets. This means selling jewelry, art, an extra television, or other items you don't really need.

You may consider selling your car to repay your car loan and finance a less expensive car to lower your monthly payments. Oftentimes this option is not feasible because the car value is less than the loan balance. Another option is to refinance your car loan over a longer period. This choice will likely not result in an interest rate reduction, but it will give your budget some breathing room.

When it comes to student debts, you may want to inquire about your eligibility for student loan forgiveness. Some student loan programs may offer loan forgiveness, repayment assistance, or reduced interest rates under certain conditions.

A home is an investment, and you shouldn't let it go unless there is no option on the horizon to help pay off your mortgage. Look into the possibility of refinancing your home at a lower interest rate. Turn your home into a revenue source by renting a room, parking space, or storage space. If you are delinquent on property and school or income taxes, try to work out payment arrangements.

High interest generally accrues on unpaid home taxes. In addition, unpaid taxes can lead to your home or other assets being seized. Not comfortable dealing with such matters? Consult with an expert, lawyer, or other specialist who can help you negotiate a tax debt repayment plan.

A reverse mortgage is generally not a recommended option for retirees in need of cash. The above-market interest rates associated with this type of mortgage can quickly deplete your home equity if you are not making interest and capital payments. Be cautious, and speak to your financial advisor for proper planning. Your age, the mortgage interest rate, your intent to pay the loan interest—all these factors come into play in your decision. To access cash, you may consider selling your home and buying a smaller one, or you may rent a room or the basement.

Most importantly, do not get discouraged when it comes to reducing debts. Resist the temptation to say, "I can't do this. I will never get out of debt." Turn your soul to the *ICAN* radio station and sing, "I am on a path of wealth. I am creating richness. I am financially free." Most importantly, don't forget to act accordingly.

With this approach, you are acknowledging that there is a solution for each problem in life. With your *High Drive* app turned on and the help of experts, you can create a plan to regain financial freedom over time and build more wealth in your life. Stay committed to your plan. Everything is possible for those who believe and work hard at creating their financial success.

Protect Yourself in Times of Rain

You have worked hard to build your wealth, and you certainly do not want life's storms to take it all away. Proper insurance helps you reduce losses resulting from a health crisis, an injury, damages inflicted to others, a natural disaster, fire, or theft. If you do not have access to a publicly funded health care system, then getting a health care plan should be one of your financial priorities. While you may find it hard to set dollars aside for health care insurance, keep in mind that the struggles of not having one outweigh the costs when sickness or disease knocks at your door.

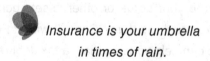

Insurance is your umbrella
in times of rain.

Inquire if pharmaceutical medications, vision costs, and dental costs are covered under your plan. To lower these costs, take advantage of the family health benefit package offered by your workplace. If both you and your husband have employer-based plans, determine the economic benefits of your spouse being covered under your plan. If group coverage through work is not an option, consult an insurance agent to get your own private plan.

Today's health care costs can add up quickly and erode your wealth in no time. You can no longer afford to travel outside the country without appropriate medical insurance. It is crucial that you read your insurance policy and properly answer each question on the application form. Unfortunately, too many people have lost their life savings as a result of their health claims being rejected due to incomplete disclosure of medical information when filling out their application.

In addition, you may consider travel insurance that covers trip cancellation, interruption, or delays, and lost and stolen luggage. Those who travel extensively in motor homes may wish to add a personal effects floater to their home insurance if their personal belongings are not already covered by their home insurance.

To preserve your power to build wealth, consider accident, disability and life insurance to ensure a steady stream of income should hard times strike. Your workplace may offer such insurance at a very reasonable price. A term life insurance policy, purchased for specific periods (5, 10, or 20 years), is the least expensive life insurance option. Once the term expires, further coverage can be obtained under different payment terms and conditions. A permanent life insurance policy (whole life, universal life, variable universal life) guarantees coverage at fixed premiums for the lifetime of the covered individual, and it accrues a cash value.[1]

A permanent life insurance policy is more expensive for two reasons. It offers a tax-privileged savings component, and is designed to pay a death benefit in all cases. On the other hand, term life insurance pays a benefit only when death occurs. The savings feature of permanent life insurance is generally not as efficient as investing your dollars in a tax-advantaged retirement plan, education plan, or savings plan.

For greater peace of mind, get insurance on your home for its replacement value. Don't overlook your car, boat, motorcycle, and personal effects. Pay attention to your policy insurance limit on expensive items. Antiques, artwork, and jewelry may need additional coverage. Don't overlook buying civil liability insurance to cover damages and injuries sustained to others.

As a business owner, protect your property, furniture, machinery, and equipment assets. A good way to protect your business from claims resulting from damage or injury inflicted to others is to carry commercial business/general liability insurance. Someone in agricultural and crop operations is not to overlook insurance for production loss, agricultural products, and livestock.

To help keep your insurance costs down, obtain at least three quotes from different insurance brokers. As you look into your insurance options, take advantage of savings offered by insurers when you bundle your home, car, and other insurance. Remember that the higher your deductible amount is, the lower your insurance premium is. In addition, buying health and life insurance when you are healthy generally translates to reduced premiums.[2]

Taking pictures of your insured assets comes in handy when preparing a claim. A good way to have evidence for a car accident case is to have a police report, gather witnesses at the scene, and use your webcam or your camera to capture the damages. Before making a claim, inquire about the long-term effect on your insurance premiums to see whether you are better off making an insurance claim or paying the damages out of pocket.

If you do make a claim, it is best to keep a file with a summary of your communications. Keep track of the name of the insurance company's representative, phone number, what was said, date, and time. This information is useful should a change of representative or a dispute arise.

In the end, the decision to buy insurance is all about the cost, coverage, risk, financial situation, and ability to live with the loss. Insist on seeing the insurance policy before buying it. "I don't like to read the small print," some might say. I encourage you to wear your eyeglasses and read the small print to fully understand your policy. With these tips in mind, you are now ready to buy or make changes to your insurance umbrella to better protect yourself in times of rain.

Save Today for a Better Tomorrow

As said, there is no magic in creating wealth. The combination of increasing your revenue and reducing your expenses will undoubtedly result in savings. Each and every dollar has the power to multiply, and it is up to you to decide what tomorrow will bring.

Saving is a means to better your life in the future. Well invested, savings can create a steady stream of recurring income, increase your overall wealth, give you peace of mind, and make your dreams come true. Let's look at some savings funds you can set up to fulfill your desires, whether it's acquiring a home or a new car, starting a new business, sending your children to university, or being rocked by gentle waves while enjoying your boat.

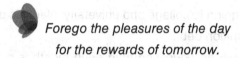

Forego the pleasures of the day
for the rewards of tomorrow.

Emergency Fund – Having an emergency fund means peace of mind when unplanned surprises knock at your door. By stashing a sum of money in an interest-bearing savings account each month, it won't take long for you to stop using your credit cards as your emergency fund.

One word of advice: aim for an emergency fund that covers approximately six months of living expenses. In the event of an employment loss, you should have sufficient cash on hand to cover your mortgage while searching for a new job. It would be a terrible blow to not only lose your job, but be permanently deprived of your home as well. If your current budget does not allow for adequate saving for an emergency fund, I encourage you to earn extra income in your household for that sole purpose.

Asset Replacement Fund – Rather than dipping into your emergency fund, you may prefer to set up an asset replacement fund that serves as a funding source for future repairs and improvements. These could include new shingles for the roof of the house, home renovations, major car repairs, or the purchase of new electrical appliances. You may even use it to fund a new car purchase down the road. Assuming you have a four-year car loan and expect to keep your car for seven years, you have three years to invest monthly an amount equivalent to the current loan payment that you have just paid off.

New Business Fund – Starting a new business needs to be carefully planned. Be careful to have sufficient capital on hand to cover your start-up costs and at least six months of operating costs. Many businesses fail due to lack of capital. Financing between 30 to 50 percent of your business from your own pocket makes your business more attractive for investors and lenders. Being strangled financially is the last thing you want when you start a new venture.

Education Fund – Even with the high costs of education, it has been proven, time and again, that educated workers have a greater earning potential. Education is the best insurance policy in life. As a parent, if you dream of your child going to college and university, plan this day ahead to spare them of high tuition debt.

Stashing dollars in an education fund each month is a solid way to invest in your child's future. It makes sense to take advantage of education funds and savings accounts that offer tax benefits. For great savings, you may wish to inquire about the availability of prepaid tuition plans that lock in education fees at educational institutions.

As a student, get involved in your dream of education. A part-time job and summer employment will help you save some extra dollars. You may also qualify for a student loan to cover some education fees.

Real Estate Fund – Real estate generally appreciates in value over time. For many, investing in real estate—home, cottage, or rental property—has been a great way to build personal wealth. If you dream of owning real estate, then one of the surest ways to come up with a down-payment is to save money on an ongoing basis.

Most lenders have a criteria of 5 to 20 percent down payment to qualify for a mortgage. Well invested, you will see your saved dollars bearing fruit, and soon you will be living in your dream house. Inquire about government programs that give access to a mortgage with zero down or a low down-payment.

Keep in mind that managing a rental property has its challenges, especially when you face bad tenants who do not pay or damage your property. If you desire to own a rental property but are not interested in daily management, invest in a real estate investment group in which a company buys or builds rental properties and subsequently sells them to investors as rental properties. The company manages the units, including collecting rent from tenants and caring for property maintenance, in return for a management fee taken from your monthly rent proceeds.

Retirement Fund – Creating wealth is a life-long commitment, but the benefits of financial freedom far outweigh the discipline and self-control you must cultivate. Aim for savings of at least 8–10 times your salary at retirement. A popular saying is that you need 70 percent of your pre-retirement income to maintain your lifestyle at retirement. With reduced spending and no mortgage loans and debts, you may do just fine with 60 percent. Your lifestyle choices are key drivers as to your retirement needs.

But why live with less when you can amass a fortune by starting today? By funneling money in a retirement plan early in life, you benefit from the amazing power of compound interest. For example, a 25-year-old who invests $80/month at a 7 percent rate of return will amass approximately $210,000 by age 65. If he invests $100/month, he will accumulate $262,480. If he invests $400/month, he will be a member of the millionaire club, with $1,049,925. Taking advantage of an employer pension plan with matching contributions will double these amounts.

Consult a financial advisor and tax professional to plan a tax-efficient retirement. Tax-advantaged retirement plans and savings plans are great tools to let your money grow. In addition, contributions to some retirement plans may be tax deductible.

"How about buying a deferred annuity for investment tax savings?" you might ask.

A deferred annuity is a financial contract issued by an insurance company. In the United States, the growth in a deferred annuity investment is tax-deferred until funds are withdrawn. On the flip side, when funds are withdrawn or inherited, the interest/gains are immediately taxed as ordinary income. As tax measures and types of annuities vary from one country to another, consult your financial and tax advisors for additional information.[3]

With an appropriate strategy, you will find yourself with more money in your pocket at retirement. Keep in mind that you may be subject to a penalty or pension reduction for withdrawing funds from a pension or annuity plan before the age set by the plan.

With proper planning, you will be on your way to more wealth and financial independence to make life more enjoyable for yourself and those around you. Start today, and save your precious dollars for more growth!

Water Your Wealth Seeds

Positivity and faith are the water and sunshine your wealth seeds need to grow to full maturity. As you wait for growth, keep your focus on abundance, not on lack. Worrying and focusing on lack of money moves you towards the *Powerless You*. Anxiety and negativity are weeds that have no place in your money garden.

I know how discouragement and fear are hard to master when you have little left in your bank account. I have experienced financial scarcity in my life, and I know how it feels when you have little or no money in your pocket. Turn on your *Financial Tycoon* app and say with confidence, "My wealth seeds are flourishing abundantly, time is working its magic." Pull out all your negative weeds, and with good-feeling thoughts, stand firm and rejoice for what is yet to come. If your crop is not as fruitful as expected, don't give up. Take your seed bag and vigorously sow wealth seeds again.

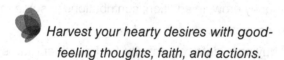

Harvest your hearty desires with good-feeling thoughts, faith, and actions.

With your *Be Happy* app turned on, embrace a positive attitude, and let perseverance and patience be your allies. Read positive affirmations about your true nature, the *Marvelous You*. Empower your wants by practicing visualization. Envision each of your wealth seeds at maturity. Let you heart be filled with joy for all the blessings coming your way.

Activate your *Higher Power* app and trust in the power of God. He co-creates with you and will pave the way. He is All-That-Is, Infinite Consciousness, and the Source of life and blessings. In His hand you find comfort, knowing that He hears your heartfelt gratitude and prayers. Listen to the small voice of your heart for His guidance and creative ideas. Sow more wealth seeds if you are inspired to do so. He will make them grow in His time. Be strong in faith, as a faithful heart is pleasing to God.

Do not be afraid to ask for help. Asking for support with appreciation will enrich your life. God answers prayers through family, friends, colleagues, and even strangers. You will be amazed at the goodness, compassion, and generosity of people. At times, a spark of support is all you need to keep pressing on.

There is no need to envy the accomplishments of others. You, too, hold the power to create the desires of your heart. Rejoice in the success of others and learn from them. Be inspired by their skills and practice what they do. You will soon see your seeds grow and be a success.

Be grateful for the present moment. Gratefulness fills your heart with appreciation and inspires you to let your life flourish. Thank life for who you are, what you have, and where you are going. Celebrate each of your financial successes, small and grand. With faith and good-feeling thoughts, water your wealth seeds daily. Persevere, be patient, and stay focused. Soon you will see your money garden being fruitful. And most importantly, be grateful for your money crop.

Get Ready to Invest

Many have become successful investors by truly embracing four investment essentials: 1) education on investment instruments and portfolio optimization, 2) a team of trusted advisors, 3) a solid investment strategy that aligns with their goals, and 4) ongoing monitoring to reassess the appropriateness of their strategy. Surrounded by trusted investment professionals, you have the power to create capital growth just like these investors. Activate your *Financial Tycoon* app and get ready to create financial growth.

Learn the Basics – No one will care more about your money than you. For this reason, learning the basics of investing will serve you well. With a greater understanding of investment alternatives, you will gain more clarity on your investment strategy. You will have more interesting discussions with your advisors when the time comes to determine your investment mix. In addition, you will be in a better position to personally monitor your investments. You can take classes and workshops offered by education facilities, financial institutions, and other organizations. Classes are also available online, and several websites are rich with valuable information, namely those of financial institutions, investment companies and firms, and business, economic, and financial regulating organizations.

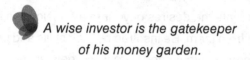
A wise investor is the gatekeeper
of his money garden.

Choose Trusted Advisors – Whether you are a novice in the investment world or an avid investor, I encourage you to surround yourself with trusted advisors who can help you achieve your investment goals. Let's look at how these professionals can best guide you:

- Financial planners are individuals who review your financial situation and help you set an appropriate plan to meet your financial goals. They are well-vested in financial matters, namely personal budgeting, cash flow management, insurance, income taxes, investments, retirement, and estate and business succession planning.
- Investment brokers are licensed agents authorized to buy and sell securities. Full-service brokers offer investment advice while discount brokers do not.
- Broker-dealers are licensed agents who act as brokers when trading on behalf of clients. Broker-dealers can also act as dealers when trading on their own account using their own funds.
- Derivative brokers are licensed agents who provide advice on how to buy, trade, and sell derivatives.
- Investment advisors provide investment advice to clients, and they may or may not be licensed to buy and sell securities. Investment

brokers who provide investment advice are also known as investment advisors. In order to avoid any confusion, confirm the services being offered by the advisor.

- Mutual fund sales representatives are licensed to sell mutual funds, and they are well apprised of the mutual fund products offered by the investment firms, mutual fund companies, banks, or insurance companies they represent.

- Banks have teams of professionals who are well apprised of investment products being offered. These well-informed professionals include financial planners, financial advisors, and mutual fund representatives and agents.

- Tax professionals provide information on tax matters relating to investments, retirement, and estate planning, amongst others.

Develop an Investment Strategy – Financial success starts with a vision and becomes reality with a solid investment strategy. A number of factors need to be examined by a wise investor in developing a success plan, namely risk appetite, capital needs, age, funding available, and tax optimization.

Read the section *Discover your Investment Options* to learn how to navigate the investment world with more ease and map a winning strategy that best aligns with your goals. You will become proficient in money market and capital market instruments and their related risks. The information provided in the section *Invest Wisely* will help you set an investment strategy that best aligns with your investment vision.

Prepare for Monitoring – Monitoring your investments is critical in creating wealth. You need to read your investment statements and monitor the increase in value of your portfolio on an ongoing basis to determine if changes are warranted.

Stock market indices provide a measure of the level of stock prices, allowing you to monitor market changes. Indices vary in terms of components and weighting approach. Some indices have multiple versions resulting from different component weighting and how dividends are accounted for.

For example, the S&P/TSX Composite Index contains about 250 large Canadian companies listed on the Toronto Stock Exchange, and the index is computed by a weighted average of the companies' market capitalization (number of shares times price of shares). The Dow Jones Industrial Average contains 30 of the largest companies in the Unites States and weighs companies by their share price. Also computed based on weighted market capitalization, the S&P 500 Index contains 500 large companies listed on the New York Stock Exchange and NASDAQ. This index has three versions: the price return, the total return, and the net total return.[4]

If your portfolio is not performing as you had expected, speak with your investment advisor to discuss the current market fluctuations. Discuss the need to make any changes to better align your investments with your financial goals and needs. If you are not satisfied with the services provided by your advisor, don't hesitate to consult someone else for a second opinion.

Discover Your Investment Options

The financial market offers numerous investment options in response to different financing strategies of governments, municipalities, corporations, and financial institutions. The money market provides a means for short-term financing, while the capital market is a channel for medium- to long-term financing. Financing is done either through the issuance of stocks or through debt financing.

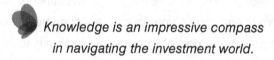

*Knowledge is an impressive compass
in navigating the investment world.*

Stocks signify ownership and pay out dividends to investors. Debt investments are essentially loans made by investors to debt issuers in return of interest. Investment wealth is created from the increase in value of your investments and their related earnings. Interested in knowing the approximate time it takes to double your capital invested at a fixed rate compounded annually? Simply divide 72 by the interest rate. For example, capital invested at a 6 percent interest rate will take 12 years to double. Be cautious, as the formula does not work for significant rates of return.

With so many alternatives being offered, navigating the investment world can be overwhelming to a novice. While you may never buy some of the offered investments, knowing their existence makes you a well-informed investor. With the help of your trusted advisors and a greater understanding of your investment choices, you will be able to better align your investment decisions with your financial vision.

The money market instruments encompass deposits, certificates of deposit, treasury bills, commercial paper, bankers' acceptances, negotiable instruments, Eurodollars, and repurchase agreements (repo).[5]

There is no such thing as a risk-free investment. However, money market instruments carry a low investment risk.

Deposits – Deposits encompass sums of money deposited in a savings account, checking account, or other type of account with a bank, credit union, or other financial institution.

Certificate of deposit – A certificate of deposit is a promissory note issued by a bank, credit union, or other financial institution. Essentially, the issuer promises to reimburse a sum of money to the payee at a fixed future date or on demand, under certain terms. Its maturity date varies from three months to up to five years.

Treasury Bills – Treasury bills are short-term debt obligations of the government that mature in less than a year. This security is available through a financial institution, an investment broker, a dealer, or it can be bought online.

Commercial Paper – A commercial paper is a short-term unsecured debt issued by a corporation to finance receivables, inventories, and short-term payables. The average maturity of commercial paper is one to two months, but it can extend to up to nine months. Interested? Contact your investment broker or broker-dealer who takes care of these transactions.

Banker's Acceptance – A banker's acceptance is a short-term debt issued by a non-financial firm and guaranteed by the bank. It is used to finance imports, exports, and other goods transactions. Generally sold in multiples of $100,000, a banker's acceptance is traded on the stock exchange.

Negotiable Instrument – A negotiable instrument is a written document that promises the payment of a specific amount to a named payee, either on demand or at a set time; the payer is also named on the document. Checks and certain promissory notes are examples of negotiable instruments that can be exchanged for cash at financial institutions. Keep in mind that the term negotiable instrument may have different meanings depending on what country it is being used in and what laws are being applied.

Eurodollars – Eurodollars are U.S. dollar-denominated bank deposits at foreign banks or foreign branches of American banks. Eurodollar banking takes its name from the funds being mostly held in Europe. There is no relation whatsoever with the euro currency. Deposits have a maturity of less than six months.

Repurchase Agreement – Under a repurchase agreement, a dealer or holder of a government security (usually a T-bill) sells a security and buys it back at a later date at a higher price. A reverse repo is the opposite. Maturities of repos are normally less than 30 days, but term repos have longer maturity dates.

The capital market, also known as the securities market, consists of company stocks, bonds, debentures, and derivatives.[6] Stocks are generally riskier than bonds. Generally the higher the risk, the higher the rate of return.

Stock – Corporations issue two types of stock: common shares and preferred shares. Preferred shares do not automatically assign voting rights to shareholders, and they are generally entitled to a dividend that must be paid out before any dividends to common shareholders.

On the other hand, common stocks have voting rights, and dividends are paid out as set by the board of directors. A public corporation is one that has issued its shares to the general public through a stock exchange. The first step to buy and sell publicly traded stocks is to open a brokerage account, either through a full-service or discount investment broker, a broker-dealer, or an online brokerage.

Bond – A bond is a medium- to long-term debt issued by a corporation, government, or municipality to fund their activities. Most corporate bonds are traded over the counter via a full-service or discount investment broker, a broker-dealer, or an online brokerage. Most federal and municipal bonds can be purchased through brokerage firms and some financial institutions. In some countries it may be possible to buy them directly from government agencies.

There is an impressive variety of bonds with different interest rates and maturity dates, namely fixed-rate, floating-rate, zero-coupon, high-yield, convertible, exchangeable, inflation-indexed, asset-backed securities, subordinated, covered, perpetual, bearer, registered, government, municipal, book-entry, lottery, war, serial, revenue, climate, retail, social impact, and the Build America Bond. A stripped bond is one that has its coupon detached from the principal portion of a bond, therefore creating two separate products.[7]

Debenture – A debenture is a medium- to long-term unsecured debt documented by an indenture agreement. They are issued by large corporations with excellent bond rating reputations. Like bonds, they are traded over the counter via a security dealer network, with some being traded at stock exchanges.

Derivative – Used to mitigate market volatility, a derivative is a financial contract between two parties with a value that is derived from the expected future value of the underlying assets, which may be stocks, bonds, commodities, currencies, interest rates, and market indexes. The nature of the derivative drives where it is being traded, either on an exchange or over the counter in a dealer market.

The most common types of derivatives are futures, forward contracts, options, and swaps.[8] Exotic derivatives are more complex products offered by banks and large financial institutions to meet the special needs of their clients.

- A futures contract is a contractual obligation under which a buyer is obliged to purchase an asset (or the seller to sell an asset) at a determined future price and date. Contracts are standardized to facilitate trading.

- A forward contract has the same characteristic as a future except it is traded over the counter, allowing for contract customization.
- An option contract offers, but does not oblige, a buyer to buy an asset at a determined price during a time period or at a certain date. If not used, the option can be sold to another party.
- A swap is the exchange of one security or stream of cash for another.

In addition to the above money market and capital instruments, the financial market offers a number of investment funds which are essentially pooled funds from investors used to buy stocks, bonds, and other securities.

Mutual Funds – Mutual funds are large pools of funds that provide a means for portfolio diversification to someone with limited funds to invest. Generally actively managed by experts, they may be the answer to someone who has neither the time nor the interest to get highly involved in managing their investments.

Mutual funds are purchased from banks, insurance companies, investment firms, mutual fund dealers, and mutual fund companies. Normally classified by their principal investments, you will have no trouble finding the right funds to meet your investment strategy. For example, the market offers money market funds, bond funds, stock or equity funds, hybrid funds that invest in both stocks and bonds, and index funds that seek to match the performance of a market index, such as the S&P 500 Index.[9]

Being managed by experts, they have higher management and operating expenses than exchange-traded funds (ETFs). Their management expense ratios (MERs) generally range from 1 to 3 percent. Calculated annually, the MER is the percentage of a fund's management fees and operating expenses over the average value of its managed assets. This measure is required by the Securities and Exchange Commission (SEC) to be disclosed to investors. Mutual funds are traded only at the end of the day.

Exchange-Traded Funds – Relatively new, an ETF is an investment fund traded on the stock exchange through an investment broker or broker-dealer. Generally passively managed, their MERs are lower than those of mutual funds and range from 0.1 to 1 percent.

Just like mutual funds, ETFs offer investors a number of choices, namely index ETFs, stock ETFs, bond ETFs, commodity ETFs (also known as exchange traded contracts, or ETCs), currency ETFs or ETCs, actively managed ETCs, exchange-traded grantor trusts, inverse ETFs, and leveraged ETFs.[10]

Unlike mutual funds, ETFs can be traded at any time of day. Both mutual funds and ETFs pass their income to investors by paying out dividends and capital gains. Fund losses are not passed through to investors, but kept to reduce future years' fund income. ETFs' tax efficiency makes them attractive. As less trading is generally involved, they generate less capital gains. In addition, the tax efficiency is enhanced by the fact that they do not have to sell their securities to be able to meet investors' redemption.[10]

Private Equity Funds – These funds are not offered to the general public. A private equity fund is a limited partnership of organizations that pool large amounts of money to buy securities, real property, and other investment assets. Their MERs range from 1 to 2 percent during the commitment phase to decrease during the termination phase at 0.5 to 1 percent.[11]

Hedge Funds – Just like private equity funds, hedge funds are not available to the general public. Hedge funds are structured in limited partnerships or limited liability companies, and they pool large sums of money from investors for investment in diverse securities.[12]

Actively managed by experts, hedge funds are being charged performance fees and management fees. The performance fee is typically 20 percent management of the year's profit, with the range being from 10 to 50 percent. The management fee ranges from 1 to 4 percent, with 2 percent being the standard.

Investment Club – An investment club is essentially a group of less than 100 people who meet for the purpose of pooling funds together for the purpose of investing. Organized in partnerships, the group decides on investments through a voting process, and income or losses are passed to the partners.[13]

Knowledge is precious, and paves the way to a successful investment journey. Keep this information in mind, and you will make better informed decisions when it comes to selecting investment options that best suit your financial goals.

Invest Wisely

Risk tolerance, age, capital needs, fees, available funding, and tax considerations all play a role in crafting the most efficient strategy to meet your financial goals and create growth.

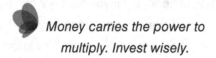

Money carries the power to
multiply. Invest wisely.

Determine Your Risk Tolerance – Every day is a new day full of surprises when it comes to the investment world. One day the market is up, the next day it's down, just like a roller coaster. The investment world can be a risky place, and knowing your risk profile is critical in determining your investment strategy.

Generally, the higher the risk, the higher the return. A very conservative investor typically deposits money in a savings account, or invests in low-risk financial instruments such as certificates of deposit, treasury bills, and government bonds. For greater peace of mind, the conservative investor keeps an amount that is less than the deposit insurance in an insured bank. However, the return of liquid investments barely beats the rate of inflation.

A diversified portfolio is the answer for a moderate investor interested in capital growth but concerned with capital protection. To help mitigate financial risks and build their wealth, many opt for a mix of 60 percent stocks and 40 percent bonds, or buy balanced funds that hold similar weightings of stocks and bonds. Generally when the stock market falls, bond value rises, and vice versa. This helps to mitigate financial risks.

Some choose foreign investments for currency diversification. Others use a more diversified strategy by adding commodities (gold, silver, oil, gas, beef, grains, etc.) to their stocks and bonds portfolio. Commodities protect your portfolio against inflation. When inflation rises, commodity prices tend to go up. A floating-rate bond that pays a variable interest rate is another good measure against inflation. When inflation goes up, the government generally responds with a monetary policy that raises interest rates to keep inflation down.

A moderately aggressive investor focused on growth generally opts for a 70 percent weighting of stocks. An even more aggressive investor has eyes for a portfolio with a higher proportion of stocks, say 80 percent or more. Generally focused on the long-term capital growth, the aggressive investor is willing to take the risk of market fluctuations in return for higher returns.

Not interested in buying individual stocks and bonds? Then explore stock and bond ETFs or mutual funds to keep investing simple. Some stock funds manage risk through a mix of growth stocks and value stocks. Expected to grow at an above-average rate, growth stocks generally have high price-to-earnings ratios. With their lower price-to-earnings ratios, value stocks are bought in anticipation of a future increase in price when the market recognizes their value.

A good start to set your investment allocation is to have an open and honest discussion with your financial advisor. This expert will help you gain more clarity on your risk profile to better develop your investment strategy, which should be reviewed each year.

 Some flowers bloom in the spring of their life, some in the summer and others in the fall. It's never too late to bloom financially.

Consider Your Age – Your age is a determining factor in your investment strategy. An old rule of thumb to determine stock allocation has been to subtract your age from 100. For example, a 40-year-old man would aim for 60 percent stocks and 40 percent bonds. A 60-year-old woman would aim for 40 percent stocks and 60 percent bonds. The whole idea is that your age drives your bond portion. With increased longevity, some financial planners now recommend that younger people aim for a higher percentage of stocks than those resulting from this calculation.

The reasoning behind this? They have time as their ally to recover from an economic downturn. On the other hand, someone close to retirement does not have the luxury of time and may not have the chance to ride out a stock market crash.

Yet some late bloomers with little retirement plans and savings have targeted high stock weighting to create more capital growth. If a moderate strategy is in order, then mix your portfolio with low- and medium-risk investment instruments such as certificates of deposit, treasury bills, and government bonds. This approach leads to a lower rate of returns, but it will let you sleep better at night.

Clarify Your Capital Needs – Your capital needs have a direct impact on your investment strategy. Short-term investing for less than a year is best served with more liquid investments. Savings accounts, treasury bills, certificates of deposit, and money market funds are all good options, but bear in mind they do not generate high yields.

Keep only what you need in those instruments, like your emergency fund and other liquidities you may need in the near future. Remember that withdrawing a certificate of deposit before maturity may lead to a withdrawal penalty, and there may be a fee for cashing treasury bills or other savings bonds. Banker's acceptance and public stocks can be sold at any time, subject to a trading commission.

When it comes to mid-term goals of less than 10 years, like buying a home or replacing a car, your risk appetite will likely influence your strategy. Not only should capital growth be at the forefront of your strategy, but capital protection as well. A good way to help ensure capital protection is to hold a diversified portfolio of certificates of deposit, bonds, and stocks, as a moderate investor would do. Balanced funds with a mix of stocks and bonds are other options to consider. While bonds and certificates of deposit have modest yields, the higher rate of returns of stocks should give you an overall return that is closer to your desires.

A long-term investment strategy is generally more aggressive, with your portfolio bearing a higher weighting of stocks and a smattering of bonds. Buying stocks directly and indirectly through stock mutual funds or stock ETFs are good alternatives. Your young age plays in your favor when it comes to surviving a stock market crash. Individual and employer-based retirement plans with income tax shields will likely be at the top of your list. Buying real estate may be of interest to accrue wealth over time.

Say No When It Is Too Good to Be True – Be wise in selecting your investments. There are predators in the investment world patiently waiting to devour their prey. Many who are not well-vested in business and investments are the target of reprehensible scoundrels who make a fortune with fraudulent techniques. Don't be intimidated by these angels of darkness who have more than one glitzy trick in their bags to steal your dollars.

As the saying goes, "If an investment seems too good to be true, it likely is." Like the famous fictional character Inspector Clouseau, take charge and investigate before investing. Inquire as to the financial advisor's qualifications and licenses. Evaluate the reputation of the offering company through references from friends and colleagues. A free service allowing you to check disciplinary history of investment brokers and advisors is provided by the SEC and the Financial Industry Regulatory Authority (FINRA).

Demand to see audited financial statements of companies. While the past does not necessarily predict the future, past performance may give an investor some reassurance. No financial statements? Raise the red flag. Frequent change in auditors? Another red flag. New company? Be cautious, as startups are generally riskier. Make sure to read all documents requiring your signature. Ask for clarification if you do not understand their complex terms. If you suspect fraud, contact the SEC or FINRA. They will investigate.

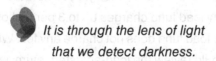

It is through the lens of light
that we detect darkness.

Take Advantage of Other's Pessimism – When faced with economic uncertainty, many investors react out of fear and sell their higher-risk stocks to take refuge in much lower-risk investments. You can take advantage of this reaction that draws down the price of stocks or stock-based funds. A word of caution: not all stocks that go down rise again. If you have some extra dollars and are eyeing free-falling stocks, consult your financial advisor before opening your wallet. Consider factors such as current price, past growth, length of time price has been declining, company reputation, restructuring plan, and new products.

Take Into Account Commission Fees – To start investing on stock exchanges, you need to set up a brokerage account. You have the choice of three categories of brokerage: full-service brokerage, discount brokerage, and online brokerage.

Full-service brokerage offers, above all else, investment advice. Commissions vary on the type of trade, ranging from $30 to $300 per trade, with $120 being the average. The discount brokerage comes with narrower services. They tend to not provide investment advice, and generally charge $5 to $15 per trade, but the price can increase to $30 if they provide advice. Most investment discount brokers now offer an online brokerage service, with much cheaper commissions, generally varying from $5 to $10 per trade, with some as low as $1. Online brokerage is a good start for self-directed investors.

Buying mutual funds generally comes at a cost. You may pay sales charges also known as loads. Funds may be offered with a front or back-end load, low load, or no load. In some instances, they may charge other transaction fees, like an account fee or an exchange fee when you transfer funds to another fund within the same group.

Here's how mutual fund load works. A front-end load fee is deducted from your investment amount at the time of acquisition, and the fee varies from 2.5 to 5.75 percent. A back-end load fund charges up to 6 percent when you sell your units or shares. The longer you hold the units or shares, the less you pay. A low load fund charges up to 3 percent on your buy and sell transactions. A no load fund does not charge any fee. When comparing mutual funds, you should review the load-adjusted return, which is the rate of return adjusted downward to reflect the sale charges.

Compare Management Expense Ratio – A low load or no load mutual fund does not necessarily mean a better rate of return. Just like an ETF, a mutual fund's rate of return is highly influenced by the fund's MER. As said, the MER is a measure of the fund's management fees and operating expenses.

Management fees are essentially the direct costs of the portfolio manager and other experts assisting in the investments' management. The management fee varies based on the complexity and size of the fund. The operating expenses include bookkeeping, administration, marketing, audit, legal, and other costs that may be needed to operate the fund. All these expenses affect the fund's rate of return. When analyzing your investment options, pay attention to the MER, but most importantly, direct your eyes on the rate of return net of all expenses.

Do Not Overlook Income Taxes – For tax-efficient investing, empower yourself with knowledge on how investments are taxed. Tax efficiency should be at the forefront of your investment strategy to maximize your after-tax return. It is best to speak to your investment advisor and tax specialist for more information on tax-efficient investment instruments. Some investment instruments are deemed to be less tax-efficient, and the rule is to hold them in a tax-deferred account or tax-exempt account. In addition, your tax professional can assist you in calculating the after-tax rate of return of investment options. In the end, what counts is what is left in your pocket after income taxes are paid.

Consider Available Funds – By not keeping all your eggs in the same basket, you protect yourself from market volatility and reduce your risk of losses. If you have little funds to invest, investing in a mutual fund or an ETF are good alternatives to easily achieve portfolio diversification. These funds hold a variety of securities that you wouldn't be able to acquire with limited money, considering the commission fees associated with each investment transaction on the stock exchange.

When buying an ETF or a mutual fund, you are acquiring shares or units of the funds that hold a variety of investments, thus giving you easy access to diversity at low cost. In your decision as to whether you should buy an ETF or a mutual fund, consider factors such as the MER, the transaction cost, tax efficiency, and most importantly, past and current rates of return.

With investing now being demystified, you should be able to navigate safely the investment world. Surround yourself with wise and trusted advisors, and you will reap greatly.

Be a Prosperity Channel

There are moments in life when, despite our best efforts, we experience a difficult year financially. Sickness, job loss, physical disability, mental illness, tornados, floods, earthquake, economic crisis, war, and persecution are just a few examples of life events that can prevent us from financial success. Those of us who have achieved greatly are called to let money circulate and multiply for the betterment of all.

When your neighbor prospers, your community prospers, your country prospers, and the world's economy prospers. In sharing, you are the spark that lights up the chain. Not only does it better your life, but it grants you the ability to help make positive changes in the world.

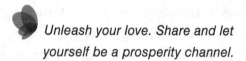
Unleash your love. Share and let
yourself be a prosperity channel.

Giving money carries a double blessing. It gives joy to the receiver and giver. For the receiver, it gives the courage to move on. It fills the heart with hope that there will be a better tomorrow. For the giver, it brings purpose to life. It warms the heart to see a thank-you smile.

In sharing, you are allowing abundance to flow and bear fruit in other people's lives. By opening your hand, you bridge individuality to experience oneness with other human beings. You learn the true meaning of love.

I have experienced both the joy of giving and receiving in my life. My life has not always been easy, and I have walked in dark tunnels a number of times. To this day, I still remember the appreciation and recognition that filled my heart when wonderful people took my hand and walked with me. They lit my path and gave me hope and courage to keep walking until I was able to see the light at the end of the tunnel.

As a parent, teach your children to become a prosperity channel. Show them the importance of sharing with those in need, whether by volunteering on a community project, getting involved in a fundraising event, or by giving away a few dollars. In learning at a young age to sow seeds of compassion and generosity, your child will harvest love and prosperity in his life.

The lesson in all of this? You are the *Marvelous You*, connected to Infinite Abundance. In being a prosperity channel, God will entrust you with more to create a better world for all. With a humble heart, you will serve and create blessings in other people's lives. Simply put, in giving more, you will reap more. Activate your *Financial Tycoon* app and light up the prosperity chain!

CHAPTER 10

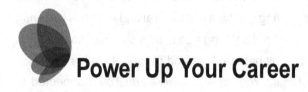

Power Up Your Career

*The ingredients to mastery and excellence
are passion and commitment.*

Activate Your *Go Getter* App

Are you looking to create a great career for yourself? If your answer is yes, then activate your *Go Getter* app today. Career greatness means different things to different people. For some, it means climbing the corporate ladder. For others, it means an inspiring environment where they use their skills to the best of their abilities.

Whatever greatness means to you, *Go Getter* will help you reach your career goals. This app helps you define your strengths and weaknesses for the purpose of developing an *Up You Go* career plan that will move you into action each day.

Surrounded by an inspirational and powerful team, including your performance manager, coach, and mentors who care about your success, you journey with clarity, accountability, and inspiration. Your passion in what you do translates in enthusiasm and commitment. You review progress and celebrate successes, small and grand. You welcome feedback and change course as needed to achieve your goals with more ease and in less time.

Being the *Marvelous You*, you face challenges and setbacks with a positive attitude. With your *True Inspiration* app activated, you look within yourself for inspiration, intuition, and creativity for well-thought-out solutions. Hardworking, you keep marching on, with your eyes focused on success. With *Go Getter,* you live excellence. You are committed to giving your best in what you do. You are brilliant in coming up with performance improvement ideas.

Using your skills and talents, you participate with all that you are in achieving your employer's vision, mission, and goals. You care deeply for your colleagues, and help them achieve their personal goals. As a great communicator, you inspire trust and respect. To sum it up, with *Go Getter* you walk the talk and bring the best of who you are at work.

Find Purpose, Find Passion

Passion is the magic that moves you to your destination of success with more ease. Nothing lights up passion faster than gaining clarity on your life vision of success, mission, and purpose. With greater clarity, you empower your life with an inspired direction that moves you into action with greater satisfaction.

As the *Marvelous You*, you are gifted with talents, skills, and capacities. When you gain precision on how and where you can best use your abilities and capacities, you create harmony within yourself, allowing the seeds of greatness that are planted in you to flourish. You don't struggle trying to be someone you are not meant to be.

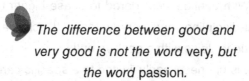

The difference between good and
very good is not the word very, *but*
the word passion.

Aligning your career path with your life purpose is powerful in bringing work fulfillment and satisfaction. Not only does it allow you to live your values and passions on a daily basis, but it enables you to contribute with your own greatness to the betterment of your family and society. Many people find it difficult to find their life purpose, making it hard to align their career with who they truly are and the values they believe in.

"How can I easily discover my life purpose?" you might wonder.

As said earlier, there are many ways to discover your life purpose. Activate your *True Inspiration* app for greater inspiration and intuition. Look at your natural abilities, and tasks or hobbies you enjoy. Identify books you take pleasure in reading. Participate in a career orientation program to learn more about career choices. Talk to your friends, family, and colleagues for their input on the greatness they see in you. Listen to the little voice of your heart. Consult a good life coach and find mentors who can help you gain clarity. Take action; your eyes may open to your life purpose.

As said, it is through my community involvement that I found my life purpose. I realized that my heart was jumping with joy when I was surrounded with people, helping them create their best life. Captured by the breath of my life purpose, my life turned around. It filled my heart with so much glee and passion, with each moment filled with gratefulness and hopefulness.

I was then able to embed my life purpose in all my undertakings, making each day more interesting and valuable. It gave me direction and passion in all my doings, both at work and in the community. While I enjoyed my work as a CPA, my work became even more meaningful. There was a purpose behind my services that translated in pleasure, excellence, and greater satisfaction in assisting my clients and those on my path.

Finding my life purpose led me to fly high like an arrow in the sky. It moved me to put little feet under my career dreams with vigor, passion, and excitement. With confidence, I dared to chase bigger dreams. With commitment, self-discipline, and perseverance, I achieved my career goals, and continue to do so with a positive outlook.

A life purpose is not necessarily limited to a specific career. You may find fulfillment in different careers that align with your life purpose. There are many ways that enable you to live your life purpose and become all that you can be. If you are looking for great fulfillment and satisfaction in your career and haven't found it yet, don't give up. Look within and out of yourself to find your passions.

With a greater understanding of your natural abilities and personality traits, what you like and don't like in life, the work environment you enjoy, and pros and cons of different careers, you will find your ideal career. Once you have found it, have the courage to pursue it. Too many people stay in jobs they do not like out of fear. With no passion in their work, they sadly live each day of the week for the next day off. Don't be one of them. Dare to live your best life.

I have said many times to team members who were questioning their career choice, "You may not enjoy your work at all times, but if you do find pleasure in your work 80 percent of the time, then stay where you are. If the scale turns around, and you enjoy your work only 20 percent of the time, do yourself a favor and look for another job that will be more satisfying. You owe it to yourself." You are meant to realize your *Marvelous Nature*. Be daring, and live the life you want. You deserve to be all that you can be and live with purpose and passion.

Craft an *Up You Go* Career Plan

Some people are not the success they are meant to be by reason of forgetting, or not being aware of their *Marvelous Nature*. They do not believe they can create career success. As a being of pure creativity, endowed with freedom and gifted with talents and skills, you can pursue the career path you deeply desire and reach new heights of success. Success is in you, and you hold full responsibility to bring it to light.

Whether you are a young or seasoned professional, nothing will provide more momentum in your life than having an inspired and well-thought-out career plan to transform your passions into actions and bring about the very best of who you are with your talents and skills. You deserve a pleasurable and engaging work life that allows you to maximize your potential. Actualizing your own uniqueness, increasing performance, cultivating work-life harmony, striving for excellence, becoming the best that you can be, continuing your personal growth, and empowering your team are sturdy pillars of a fulfilling and exciting career.

"There are so many career choices and so much competition in the workplace. How do I get started?" you might ask.

Start by activating your *Go Getter* app and reflect on the questions below to gain more clarity on your strengths and weaknesses. This reflection will help you craft your five-year *Up You Go* career plan to move to your destination of success. With your *True Inspiration* app activated, reflect on each question. Then write down your inspiring career goals against each of the seven *Up You Go* career pillars.

Up You Go **Career Pillars**		
U	**Uniqueness**	- What is my life purpose? In what ways am I unique? - What are my interests and motivations? What fires me up? - What are my natural abilities? What am I comfortable doing? What can I learn to make a unique difference?
P	**Performance**	- What tools can I use or create to improve my performance? - How can I improve team performance? - How can I be a better performance manager or mentor?
Y	**Youthfulness**	- How can I cultivate work-life harmony?
O	**Outstanding**	- How can I better live excellence at work? - How I can create a culture of excellence in my team? - How can I become a true leader? - What training should I take to become a guru in my field?
U	**Uppermost**	- What does success look like to me? What new responsibilities can I assume? - What are my career options and their pros and cons? - Where will I best contribute to the organization? - How can I manifest high values and ethical standards?
G	**Growth**	- How can I stretch myself? - What new skills can I develop?
O	**Outgoing**	- How can I better advance the organization's cause? - Who can I reach out to? - How can I improve my relationships with my peers? - How can I better serve my current clients? - What can I do to better market the enterprise's product or services? - How can I develop new client relationships?

Consider the goal-setting *S.I.M.P.L.E. Criteria* explained in the section *Move to the Creative Plane* to set career goals that are stretching, inspiring, measurable, purpose-driven, life-changing, and engaging. Look at your availability to help ensure that your goals are reasonable and achievable.

Be honest when you assess your strengths and weaknesses to identify skills you need to develop to achieve your specific career goals. Chapter 11 provides a number of secrets of great entrepreneurs and leaders who have mastered sought-after success skills. You will be inspired by their search for excellence and their *Up You Go* attitude.

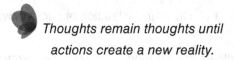

Thoughts remain thoughts until
actions create a new reality.

With more clarity on your goals, it is now time to complete your five-year action plan with inspiring and engaging steps that will engage you to action. Don't forget to turn on your *High Drive* app. For each of your goals, determine activities to be completed and their frequency, time frame, and needed resources. With the identification of a timeline for each career goal, you will be able to identify in which year these goals will be in your sight, as influenced by your availability and other commitments. Break down long-term goals that span over a number of years into smaller goals.

Your next step is to work down from your five-year career plan and develop a career plan for the year to come. For each of the seven pillars, select one goal on which you will focus your efforts in the next year. A total of seven goals is sufficient to keep you engaged in action. Too many goals may discourage you. Define one or two activities that you will undertake to achieve each goal, their frequency, needed resources, and time frame.

With an inspired career plan and the commitment to engage in action, you will become the greatness you are meant to be and find more enjoyment in what you do. My advice to you is simple: whatever you do, do it well, and do it with your heart and passion. With an *Up You Go* career plan, you will live your own uniqueness and excellence, and you will learn and grow to be the success you are meant to be in whatever career you choose.

Share Your Career Goals

Many organizations have adopted a structured performance process with goal setting and regular performance discussions to increase both employee career satisfaction and performance. Performance management is truly a continuous and constructive process to help you achieve your full potential and move you to your destination of success with more ease and in less time.

The process allows for sharing with your performance manager the results of your reflection on the *Up You Go* questions. It enables a discussion of your intended career goals for a better alignment with the organization's vision and goals before mapping out your detailed action plan. It also serves as a monitoring tool to assess your progress against your goals.

An unbiased performance manager will do you good in being truly honest about your strengths, and on gaps between your current skills and what is needed to meet your career goals. As a senior leader with a broad perspective of the organization, your performance manager can best inform you of in-house career opportunities, required expertise, and skills.

In addition to providing ongoing career direction and insightful feedback, a formal performance management process helps in your career development in many other ways:

- Gain clarity on work expectations for more efficiency.
- Increase your confidence by being informed of what you are doing right.
- Clarify issues and setbacks as they arise and propose changes to your action plan as needed.
- Share constructive ideas for improved efficiency and effectiveness.
- Lean about new tools and techniques to increase your performance.
- Be informed of new initiatives and projects where your contribution in their development would be valuable.
- Discuss alternative paths to actualize your goals, and their pros and cons.

In addition to sharing your goals with your performance manager, I encourage you to discuss them with colleagues who hold positions to which you aspire. You will learn more about their role, responsibilities, working conditions, challenges, qualifications, abilities, and pay benefits.

Often, people dream of a job only to find out after further inquiry that the associated requirements do not align with who they are or want to be. In addition, some people are simply not suited physically, emotionally, mentally, or socially for some professions or employment positions.

You are gifted with your own abilities and competencies, and you can certainly stretch yourself and learn new skills. This is all part of becoming the best that you can be. However, I have one word of caution for you: do not try to be someone you are not meant to be. It will drain your energies and leave you unproductive, stressed, and unhealthy. Learn to accept your own uniqueness and love yourself with your personal beauty. In my career, I have seen many rising stars fall from the sky.

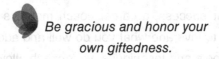 *Be gracious and honor your own giftedness.*

While it is important for you to listen to your inner voice, welcome insights provided by your performance manager and colleagues who can help you discover a career path that will provide fulfilment and happiness in your life.

As said, writing goals and accountability is powerful in goal achievement. Sharing your *Up You Go* career plan acts as a catalyst to do what you said you'd do. There is no greater way to achieve career success than by creating accountability. You can craft the greatest career plan, but success comes when you put little feet under your goals. Informing your colleagues, business acquaintances, and friends of your career plan has the powerful effect of irreversibly engaging you to take action.

To sum it up, in sharing your career goals, you will gain valuable insights, encouragement, better understanding of your options, and greater clarity to confirm your course of action.

Get a Coach and Mentor

The seeds of success are in you, and for them to flourish, you need to water them with action, commitment, and faith in who you truly are, the *Marvelous You*. Being surrounded by an inspiring coach and mentors you respect plays an important role in becoming the success you are meant to be.

Great career coaches see the beauty that resides in their clients, and they take pleasure in helping them live a fruitful life and be accountable to themselves. Skilled in career planning, they help in gaining clarity on vision and goals, natural abilities and skills, and career pillars in need of development.

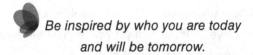 *Be inspired by who you are today*
and will be tomorrow.

Focused on your success, a career coach monitors your progress and shows you how to leverage what you do well and address areas for improvement. With tools and techniques, your coach allows you to open up with confidence about your struggles and challenges, guiding you to find solutions that are right for you and will spur you to action.

Mentors, on the other hand, play a different role in your career advancement. They are sources of inspiration who can help you define and implement your career plan, but not in a way that involves a continuous performance management relationship. They have embraced success and are willing to share their knowledge, perspectives, and positivity for you to become all that you can be.

Interested in your success, mentors ask questions and listen attentively to your career goals, action plan, ideas, perspectives, and concerns. In a respectful manner, they provide you with guidance and feedback on how to implement your career plan with more ease and in less time.

They also share insights and advice on how to improve your attitude and skills needed to actualize your goals. To sum it up, they bring value to your career life in a number of ways:

- Help you gain clarity on your career vision and goals.
- Give guidance on how to best implement your career plan by reviewing your goals for each of the seven career pillars and related action plans.
- Teach you how to better organize your work and increase team performance.
- Provide advice on how to stay positive in a negative environment and handle difficult coworkers.
- Provide suggestions on people or resources that may help you achieve your career plan.
- Encourage you to develop skills and deepen your expertise.
- Motivate you as you journey on you career path and provide feedback on matters that you bring to their attention.

Mentoring is about learning and constructive feedback. If you choose to embark in a mentoring relationship, take your time to find someone you are comfortable with and whom you greatly esteem for their skills, expertise, knowledge, sound judgment, and personal values. If the element of trust and respect is not there, you will not engage in meaningful conversations and learn from your mentor. It makes sense to have more than one mentor if one does not have all the skills you are looking for.

Reflect on your expectations and propose to your mentor a number of topics to be discussed during your meetings for greater focus. Be open to learn, accept feedback in a positive manner, and appreciate the gifts your mentor freely shares with you.

Surrounded by a supportive performance manager, an engaged coach, and inspiring mentors, you are setting yourself up for success. Be inspired by their insights and giftedness, but most importantly, be inspired by yourself, your values, your unique contribution, and the greatness you are creating.

Get Into Action

For many, crafting an *Up You Go* career plan is an easy thing, but getting into action with passion and determination is certainly the hardest. With your *Go Getter* app turned on, you actually do what you said you would do.

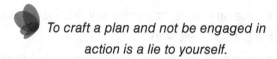

*To craft a plan and not be engaged in
action is a lie to yourself.*

Theologian and philosopher Augustine of Hippo, also known as Saint Augustine, said: "You aspire to do great things? Begin with little ones." Too often, our willingness to achieve our aspirations is crushed by either *Time Stealers* or requests from everyone else. We do little, thus moving at a very slow pace on our career path.

If your deepest intention it to move at a faster pace on your career path, then you need to place a higher priority on activities that involve your personal career growth. With a better allocation of your time and greater focus, you will manifest your true desires in less time.

Weekly and daily planning will help you stay on course. Review your *Up You Go* career plan and write down in your weekly activity planner the activities for the week ahead. For each day of the week, ask yourself this question: What are the two things that I will do on this day to help me achieve my career goals?

Now that you have served yourself first, it's time to add seminars, workshops, and meetings with colleagues, clients, suppliers, and collaborators that must be addressed as part of your work. Next, review your vision of success action plan and make an effort to achieve work-life harmony by allocating time to pursue other personal goals. Schedule time for personal care, family, community events, and other activities of interest. Don't overlook booking time for unexpected events to allow for some flexibility in your schedule.

Working down from your weekly activity planner, prioritize your activities to decide what today, tomorrow, and the next days will be.

Prioritization is essential for effective time and conflict management. Once your prioritization is complete, record in your electronic or paper-based day planner the timing and estimated time of your prioritized activities.

In taking steps each day to move in the direction of your career aspirations, you will get great momentum. You will learn to say no to opportunities that do not truly align with the direction you are heading. You will remain consistent and persevere in your journey.

Taking classes at university or college to develop a competency or accepting additional responsibilities for an upcoming promotion at work may limit your leisure time. In sharing your goals with colleagues, family, and friends, they will have a greater understanding of your aspirations and be much more understanding if you are unable to spend as much time as you would like with them.

Pay attention to *Time Stealers* that can easily take you off course during the day: browsing the Internet, sending messages on social media, and chatting with friends and colleagues. It is essential that you develop strong organizational skills to help you manage your work and personal life with more efficiency.

Seeing the fruits of your efforts each day and how you are getting closer to your destination of success will ignite excitement, enthusiasm, and perseverance. With commitment, dedication, appropriate competencies, and proper feedback, I have no doubt you will achieve your career vision.

Grow from Feedback

Have the courage to ask for feedback to help you move in the right direction. Feedback is meant to be a tool to become all that you can be. It should be welcomed with an open mind to help you unlock your full potential. Be confident enough to accept the comments with a positive attitude. A negative comment does not mean you are a failure, it means you are the *Marvelous You*, someone who is learning, growing, and aiming for excellence.

Clients are a great source of feedback for those of you who interact directly with them. From the quality and timing of the services you provide to your ability to understand their needs, be proactive and look out for their best interest. Client surveys are excellent information tools to nudge you towards excellence.

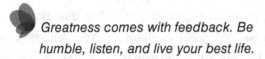

Greatness comes with feedback. Be humble, listen, and live your best life.

Feedback from subordinates is generally tainted unless it is obtained in a confidential manner that ensures anonymity. With a promotion in mind or simply for fear of creating conflicts, your staff may not want to offend you and may not tell the truth, the whole truth, and nothing but the truth.

When possible, ask for further clarification on comments that are leaving you perplexed. A comment that appears to be unique to someone should be dealt with in a personal manner. For example, if all except one person agree that you are doing very well in delegating and monitoring subordinates, you may wish to change your approach with this particular individual, if you can identify him.

If the feedback surveys do not allow for easy identification of commenters, consider using my *Do and Don't Feedback Questions* for a more personalized approach in interacting with your colleagues and clients. For feedback to be a positive and enriching experience, refresh your mind with the 10 positive feedback rules that are also provided in the section *Let Feedback Be your Friend* of Chapter 3.

I encourage you to seek feedback from your performance manager every second month or so to act as an incentive for action, sustain your motivation, help you monitor progress, and change course swiftly as may be needed. Your performance manager can provide great insights on your organizational skills, ability to solve problems, teamwork, and skills to develop.

Each year, complete a full assessment of your progress against both your annual and five-year career plans. Take time to identify what worked and what didn't, lessons learned, and any changes required to your action plan. Adjust your five-year career plan to reflect any needed changes, and then move to plan the year ahead. Of course, don't forget to celebrate your successes, small and grand.

Be flexible when it comes to the achievement of your career vision. Keep in mind what I told you about desires with the *W. D. Factor.* Your professional desire is to create a fulfilling and inspiring career. With the *W. D. Factor,* you are open to different avenues to achieve your desires.

If one plan fails, simply craft another one. A setback is not always a sign to quit. It can be an opportunity for growth and creativity. Be wise, use your judgment, speak with colleagues you trust, and listen to your heart; you will find the path that will lead you to a satisfying career. Welcome feedback discussions as opportunities to learn and be inspired with insights to move with more ease to you destination of success.

Walk the Talk

With *Go Getter* activated, you live an *Up You Go* attitude that translates into skills development, strong organizational skills, work-life harmony, work excellence, valuable contributions, personal growth, and team collaboration.

Skills Development – Investing in your own uniqueness allows for your seeds of greatness to grow to their full maturity. By improving your natural skills, abilities, and talents, you strengthen yourself to move to your next level of success. You fully realize who you are meant to be. Taking classes in an educational facility, attending skill development workshops, accepting new responsibilities, volunteering, learning from peers, working with a coach, being inspired by mentors, and finding a job better aligned with your skills are all good ways that lead to self-development and improvement.

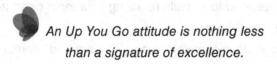

An Up You Go attitude is nothing less
than a signature of excellence.

Strong Organizational Skills – In being well-organized, you will contribute greatly to team performance and excellence. I encourage you to weave the following tips into your work life for greater performance.

- Plan the week ahead and promptly update your day planner with new action items as they arise.
- Set up a system of references and archive working papers. Use a scanner to go paperless when possible. Keep all business contacts, including their street and e-mail addresses, in a contact database.
- Lead outcome-oriented meetings for better time management. Ensure that a nominee takes minutes of meetings summarizing the discussion. Take notes during the meeting to remember relevant action items you will be accountable for.
- If you hold a management position, develop a plan and weekly schedules for clear direction and effective delegation. Aim for the best person to do the right thing, at the appropriate moment, and in the right amount of time.
- Provide clear instructions on expectations and deadlines to avoid misunderstanding and minimize time-wasting. Coordinate and monitor progress on an ongoing basis and develop a contingency plan as needed to meet expectations of clients, suppliers, or other stakeholders.
- Resolve conflicts as they arise for greater teamwork and productivity.
- Master internal e-mails with a priority system where team members are asked to identify the urgency of an e-mail request with a letter placed in the e-mail subject: H (high), M (medium), and L (low). Respond to priority e-mails swiftly and leave other e-mails for later in the day.
- Always respond to e-mails requiring your input or an action item within 24 to 48 hours.
- Set time aside to complete important tasks and inform colleagues accordingly to minimize interruptions and reduce drop-in visitors.

Work-Life Harmony – Passionate achievers easily get lost in their work, to the point that they forget to go outside to smell the roses. As the *Marvelous You,* you want to live life to the fullest at all levels. You want to experience the joys of a healthy lifestyle, spiritual connection, great relationships, and community contribution. You need to make an effort to achieve work-life harmony and enjoy all that life has to offer. There are unique moments of happiness outside of work, and finding them brings you a sense of reverence and awe for all the beauty that life has to offer. You will feel refreshed and energized when you come back to work.

Work Excellence – For those who aspire to a senior leadership position, your commitment to excellence is critical, as there are few senior leadership positions available within an organization. The true reality is that many aspire, but few are chosen. Excellence is a key differentiator in promotion decisions. Whether you are looking for a promotion or not, your signature should always be one of excellence. Are you not the *Marvelous You*? There is great satisfaction to be found in knowing you completed the task at hand to the best of your talents and skills. Doing your best at all times is an important factor in being a great team player.

Valuable Contribution – With your own gifts and abilities, aim to contribute to the success of the organization and your colleagues. Be a person of influence who is competent, enthusiastic, focused, generous, caring, and of high integrity. Do not shy away from responsibilities. Be eager to engage in new activities, initiatives, and projects. For some, their contribution may translate into the development of a career plan to climb the corporate ladder. For others, it may mean supporting the climbers and senior leaders. Whatever you choose to do, invest all that you are in achieving your goal.

As someone who strives for excellence, be genuine. Be yourself, and don't try to be someone you are not. In acting with true honesty and integrity, you will attract respect and trust. Being known for your high values and ethical standards is a great accomplishment in life.

Personal Growth – Personal growth is all about breaking barriers, crushing unfounded beliefs, and shutting down the lousy voice in your mind that says: *I can't do this. I don't have this talent. I am simply not good enough. I can't learn this. This is way too hard. What is the point of learning this?* By learning and developing new skills and abilities, you allow yourself to live up to your full potential. With classes and lots of practice, you can learn new skills. You may even discover natural abilities you didn't know were in you. As you develop your career plan, reflect on the *Up You Go* career pillars. Consider ways to develop competencies, expertise, knowledge, and improve performance and relationships.

Team Collaboration – As a team player, you are reliable, committed, ready to help, flexible, and respectful. You are a solution seeker, always looking out for the best interests of all. As a team player, you do not throw the ball around at the last minute; and of course, you do not take credit for something you did not do. This wouldn't be too gracious from someone who is the *Marvelous You*.

With an *Up You Go* attitude, your light will shine, and I have no doubt you will be known as a person of excellence and positive influence.

See Through the Mud

Someone who sees through the mud is one who has an ability to identify issues and who is skilled at crafting well-thought-out solutions. Below are the *Hurdle Free* steps to help you identify and resolve issues swiftly.

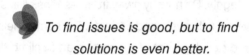 *To find issues is good, but to find solutions is even better.*

Be a problem-solver, not only a problem-finder.

Identifying issues gets easier when you listen to those around you, exercise skepticism, pay attention to details, tune in to your intuition, and use your analytical and evaluative abilities.

- Listen to what your colleagues are telling you, especially in informal meetings where everyone is more at ease. You may uncover problems you were not aware existed within the organization.
- Carefully read comments provided in client surveys. You may find issues in client service and product quality.

- Look for non-verbal communication and read between the lines. You do not need psychic skills to do this. Look at eyes, change in facial color, and body movement of your coworkers. They may tell you that somebody has an unresolved problem and is deeply upset about it.

- Pay attention to poor quality of work and delays by personnel in submitting agreed-upon deliverables. This may indicate that quality processes are not in place, and that commitment and excellence are lacking.

- Analyze data for consistency with your expectations. Large variances in financial and performance reports may be indicative of financial irregularities, performance issues, inappropriate marketing, or fundraising strategies that need to be addressed.

- Pay attention to details such as inconsistencies in reports or databases that are interrelated. They may indicate incomplete or double entries.

Next comes resolving issues with greater efficiency, creativity, ingenuity, and teamwork. Activate your *True Inspiration* app and weave the following tips into your working practices to facilitate the problem solving process:

- Meet with relevant parties to share your thoughts and perceptions of potential problems. You may discover one of four things: there are no issues, issues are as understood, issues are even worse, or not as bad.

- If there are issues to be addressed, deal with them, don't sweep them under the rug. Eventually you won't be able to walk on the carpet, and you will stumble hard.

- Take time to understand the nature of the issues and their root causes. Discuss with your colleagues all possible options, together with their pros and cons. Examine costs associated with each option.

- As a team, identify the solution that appears to be in the best interest of all. Some problems need drastic changes to be resolved.

These could be termination of employment, changes in processes, and greater controls.

- Communicate changes in a timely manner and provide supporting reasons. Understanding the why behind decisions helps engage your colleagues in the change. Providing tools and written instructions also facilitates change implementation.
- Monitor change implementation to help ensure that the adopted solution resolved the issue. If not, go back to the drawing board and try the next best available option.

I do believe there is a solution to each problem. With intuition, analysis, evaluation, creativity, ingenuity, and teamwork, you will become skillful at finding issues, identifying problems, and resolving them swiftly. In addressing the root cause of the problem, not only will you put a bandage on the wound to stop the bleeding, but you will see that the wound heals.

Excel in Team Communication

One of the qualities of great leaders is their ability to communicate effectively with their teams. Team communication is key in increasing performance and creating a culture of excellence. Communication can take different forms: e-mails, memos, newsletters, manuals, written tools and methodologies, internal blogs, performance and team meetings, and informal discussions, like a quick chat with colleagues. You may wish to consider the following tips to empower your team communication:

- To share strategic changes in the organization, it is best to invite all team members to a meeting to communicate the new vision, direction, changes involved, and expectations. Be clear on what you want to say and how you are going to say it. Take time to prepare a convincing and inspiring message to engage your team in the change movement.
- To facilitate the endorsement of changes, explain with clarity and enthusiasm the future benefits for the team and organization. Ask

for comments and suggestions. Listen to critics with calm and interest. Let the best ideas win.

- Do not lead out of fear and with negative and demotivating words. You want greatness in your enterprise? Speak words of greatness. Focus on the strengths of each of your team members. Be inspiring, and engage your team in sharing their ideas.

- Be known as someone who invests time in helping others create success. In your communication with team members, provide insightful feedback to help them reach their vision.

- There is no need to communicate severely to all team members when the message should be addressed to just a few slackers. Get rid of the bad apples when all options to have them embrace a more positive attitude have failed.

- Resolve conflicts as they appear, and harness your emotional intelligence to resolve them. Avoiding conflicts will not make them disappear. If you feel tension, be open and mature enough to say: "I sense something is wrong. Am I right?" You may realize you are totally wrong. You may find out there are no major issues, just a simple misunderstanding.

  If there are issues to solve, tune in to what the other party has to say for a better understanding of the problem. A good approach is to say, "What do you think would be a good solution? Is there anything I can do to resolve this matter?" Walking on a path of resolution builds strong teams and promotes greater harmonization.

- If you disagree on a specific matter in face-to-face meetings, agree to disagree. This means there is no need to get into lengthy debates and argue vehemently. Some people need reflection time before changing their mind. Give them that time and space for further consideration.

  I love a gracious attitude with words that say, "I understand your point and respect it. Is there any additional information I can provide to help you better understand my position?" Or you may say, "Let's agree that we disagree. I am open to a mutual compromise. Is there another option that we could both consider and agree on?" With these open questions, you will likely move the discussion to the identification of fruitful and mutually engaging solutions.

- To confirm proper understanding of work instructions, invite the person to summarize key elements that have been agreed upon, either verbally or in writing. Take notes of agreed terms for future reference and monitoring.

- Seek opinions of your team members. Ask for feedback on tools and methodologies to help ensure accuracy and completeness.

- Use memos and newsletters to announce promotions, minor changes, and upcoming events.

- Use an internal e-mail management system where team members are asked to identify the urgency of an e-mail request with a letter placed in the e-mail subject.

- Take time to read your e-mails prior to sending them and add a complete signature—position, name of the business, street address, phone number, fax number, website Universal Resource Locator (URL), and e-mail address—to facilitate communication.

- As said, respond to e-mails requesting your input or an action item within 24 to 48 hours. Not responding to e-mails is simply rude, and sends a message that you are uncooperative. If you are unable to answer swiftly, be polite, acknowledge receiving the e-mail, and provide a time when you will reply with the required information.

- Keep your door open to encourage informal communication. This type of communication is the best channel to know what is really going on in the organization and what people truly think. People tend to open up more with one-on-one communication. They feel less threatened by how others might respond to their opinions and ideas.

If you are unable to engage in the conversation due to other commitments, simply say, "I have to finish this task, but I would love to chat with you. How about I call you in the next hour, and we can then chat." Most importantly, don't forget to call, and give the person your full attention. If you are waiting for an urgent call or e-mail, let the other person know about it in advance as a matter of courtesy.

In your interactions with your team members, look for non-verbal communication and read between the lines. Look at their eyes, face, and body. Watch for their tone of voice, emotional reactions, the way they look around the room, and play with their pen or their hair. What does it say? Are they annoyed? Bored? Do they want to get out of your office? Keep your eyes open and hear what is not being said.

By developing your communication skills, you will become not only an effective communicator, but a great leader.

Plan Effective Meetings

To encourage communication, many leaders have opted for weekly and monthly team meetings. While they offer great benefits, meetings can truly become a routine exercise that kills productivity. To talk for the sake of talking is a complete waste of everyone's time. If you do not wish to waste precious time in never-ending meetings, then consider these six elements to transform your meetings into fruitful collaborative efforts:

- Clearly identify the purpose of the meeting and expected outcomes with an agenda. If your team understands the meeting objectives and decisions to be made, the meeting will be more productive. Your team will be active and engaged in focusing on the expected outputs.
- Take time to determine who should attend the meeting and who should not. Just like money, time should not be wasted. Some people may be invited to participate in the discussion of a few agenda items, while others may be asked to attend the full meeting. In addition, identify a meeting facilitator. It may be you, someone from your team, or an external facilitator.
- Set a time for the meeting, with a timeline for each agenda item. In doing so, you can easily interrupt those who can't stop talking and

derail the conversation. You may simply say, "Thank you, Joe, for your input, but for the sake of time, we will let other team members express their ideas."

- Start the meeting on time, and ask for cell phones to be on vibration mode. Most importantly, the meeting facilitator should stick to the agenda and encourage the decision-making process.
- Run shorter meetings. Long meetings are generally more exhausting and not as productive. Teams do not seem to have the same level of energy and creativity when meetings last for hours, unless you schedule breaks every hour or so.
- Send meeting minutes to all participants, summarizing the discussions of each agenda item. In addition, send a reminder e-mail with action items resulting from the meeting, the accountable staff member, and deadlines.

By following these guidelines, you will run meaningful meetings that will heighten the participation of your colleagues and produce the sought-after outcomes.

Show Me the Leader in You

Leadership development seems to be the new kid in town. With more and more leadership programs, workshops, university classes, books, tools, websites, and magazine articles, leadership development is on the rise and in the crosshairs of senior management.

Why so much interest? Many believe that with leadership comes positive changes. Others understand that leadership contributes to business success. For others, leadership is a skill that transforms good leaders into great ones. So what exactly is leadership? It's a 10-letter word that truly signifies inspiration, wisdom, passion, integrity, positivity, courage, determination, flexibility, openness, communication, service, humility, self-efficacy, and commitment to excellence. How do you develop leadership? Turn on your *Go Getter* app and read on.

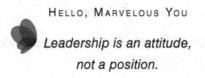

Leadership is an attitude,
not a position.

People in leadership positions who embrace the very nature of leadership truly have the following competencies:

- With their *True Inspiration* and *High Drive* apps activated, they set an inspiring vision and direction to lead the organization to success.
- They are strategic thinkers with an ability to think outside the box and see the big picture. They are skilled in anticipating shifts, trends, and risks, and they are proactive in identifying needed changes.
- Not only do they have high values and ethical standards, but they fully embrace an *Up You Go* attitude. They create a culture of honesty, integrity, respect, and service. They are influencers who walk the talk.
- With *Be Happy*, everything about their management style is positive: their thoughts, words, behavior, habits, actions, and values. Passionate and inspiring, they enrich their teams with enthusiasm and confidence.
- They see challenges as opportunities for growth. Courageous and determined, they work closely with their teams to identify winning strategies and change course as needed.
- With a great understanding of the power of a vision with the *W. D. Factor*, they are flexible on the *hows,* well aware that there is more than one way to their destination. They lead out of creativity, not out of fear.
- They are skilled at both listening and communicating. They enable the sharing of ideas for new initiatives, projects, and programs that may improve performance and growth.
- As influencers, they inspire and empower their team members to become all that they can be. They provide valuable feedback to

help them reach their goals. They sincerely provide encouragement and support.

- They are humble, knowing that success is the fruit of everyone's effort. They praise their teams and celebrate successes.
- Well organized, they are focused and committed to excellence. They know when to delegate and to whom, providing clear guidance and proper oversight for greater efficiency.
- They lead with a serving heart for the well-being of all. They invest time in developing a leadership attitude in their teams.
- To sum it up, their *Marvelous Nature* is in full bloom.

Leadership is a way of life. You do not need a management position or title to confirm your leadership skills. As the *Marvelous You*, you have all the seeds of a great leader in you. When everyone in the organization lives leadership, the impact is both positive changes and success. By embracing the qualities that make a great leader, you will be a true role model at work, at home, and in the community.

CHAPTER 11

Power Up Your Business

Suffocation comes from hiding your head in the sand.
Success comes from keeping your head up, no matter what.

Activate Your *Fly High* App

Are you overwhelmed at the thought of starting a new business? Have you been in business for a number of years, but each day is a struggle to keep your head above water? If you've answered yes to either of these two questions, it's time to turn on your *Fly High* app and swim in the business sea like a flying fish.

With your *Fly High* app activated, you are a strategic thinker, creative, and intuitive. Inspired with great ideas, your whole strategic planning exercise is better focused. With innovative thinking, you jump to success by aligning your business direction with your vision. Well-supported by your team, you are focused, growing your business at high speed by doing the right thing, and investing the proper resources at the right time.

With a strong marketing strategy, you reach great heights. Like a torpedo, you get into action, steadily aiming to remain on course. You keep your eyes on the bottom line and cash flows, and you welcome change to drive growth and increase performance for more profitability.

Communication has no secrets for you, and you have the ability to motivate your team and leverage their skills. You celebrate their successes and inspire each one of them to be their very best. As a true leader, you walk the talk.

You protect yourself from predators with sufficient cash flow to propel yourself in new ventures. With flying wings, you easily glide through economic downturns with leadership, strategic thinking, teamwork, effective monitoring, optimism, and great communication. You triumph with inspired ideas, innovation, and creative strategies. Simply put, with *Fly High*, you have all that it takes to break the surface of success.

Become a Strategic Thinker

"I have worked hard in building my business, but lately my competitors are flying by me. I am no longer at the top of my game." This is a comment I hear frequently from concerned entrepreneurs. Strategic thinking is what you need to move your enterprise from second to first place. It allows management to look at market changes, emerging opportunities, barriers, and influential factors. It enables a better understanding of what works and what doesn't, and what triggers an analysis of available options. It involves team effort, inquisitive minds, intuition, inspiration, and analysis.

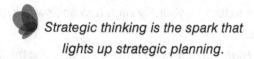

Strategic thinking is the spark that
lights up strategic planning.

With greater clarity on what tomorrow will be, management is in a much stronger position to shape its vision, mission, and purpose. Strategic thinking imbues the strategic planning exercise with creativity, imagination, and innovation, where well-thought-out plans are developed to operationalize the vision with greater success. In a challenging and rapidly changing world, strategic thinking is your ally of choice. Many businesses have found themselves failing because of a lack of strategic thinking. Unfortunately, too many leaders and managers consider strategic thinking as a boring and time wasting exercise. Why's that? Simple. They don't understand the game of winning.

Their annual strategic exercise doesn't ask the real questions about their external and internal environments. They ignore creativity and intuitiveness, and they fail to evolve and react promptly. Management simply hopes the wind will turn in their favor. This approach is called pathetic planning and will lead their enterprise to failure. It will leave their teams totally demotivated.

I encourage you to activate your *Fly High* app and use the following three-step approach—inquire, analyze, and strategize—as part of your strategy-making process for a successful journey. Ideally, senior management should start the process with their management teams six to eight months prior to the start of a new fiscal year.

Step 1 is all about being inquisitive and intuitive. This step revolves around capturing external information to gain valuable insights on clients and target needs, market shifts and trends, and external risks and barriers. These inquiries help in the identification of new product and service offerings. They are also beneficial to determine external factors that may influence the success of the business.

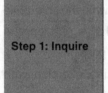

Step 1: Inquire

- Understand the needs of clients, targets, and stakeholders.
- Look at attractive adjacent markets and emerging opportunities.
- Inquire about economic and community changes.
- Anticipate shifts, trends, risks, threats, and emerging barriers.
- Look at what competitors are doing.
- Listen to your team.

Step 2 involves looking at the enterprise's internal environment to gain more clarity on its current situation. It helps identify strengths and weaknesses, analyze what works and doesn't, pinpoint competencies to develop, and reflect on possible investments and changes to processes and operations for greater efficiency.

Step 2: Analyze

- Assess current resources (material, financial, human).
- Review internal structure and accountability framework.
- Review current operations, processes, and technology.
- Review product and service offerings, and current pricing strategy.
- Review marketing strategy.
- Summarize collected information (strengths and weaknesses, critical factors, strategy options).

Step 3 is all about developing strategies, and involves inspiration and intuition to better respond to a dynamic environment and position the enterprise for the future. For this reason, I encourage you to ask your teams to activate their *True Inspiration* and *High Drive* apps as you undertake this step. With just simple questions, you initiate a reflection with your management team:

- **Vision** – As an organization, what do we aspire to achieve?
- **Mission** – What do we do, and for whom? What experiences do we want to create?
- **Core Purpose** – Why does it matter?
- **Values** – What do we stand for?

With more clarity, management synthesizes the collected information to articulate the enterprise's vision, mission, and core purpose statements in a few lines that are inspirational, clear, directing, and moving. Focused on excellence, management defines the enterprise's values to give life to what the enterprise stands for on a daily basis. These powerful statements instill drive, passion, and momentum to move teams into action with inspiration and passion.

Strategic thinking empowers the strategic planning exercise with more creativity, imagination, and innovation in the development of a successful direction. With inspiration, management defines five or six strategic outcome-oriented goals that align with the vision. Then comes the development of mid-term strategic objectives, which are essentially intermediate goals necessary to achieve the strategic goals. The strategic planning exercise continues with a reflection on winning strategies and tactical plans, often referred to as action plans or operational plans, meant to provide stellar momentum to realize the mid-term strategic objectives.

Step 3: Strategize	- Set inspiring vision, mission, purpose, and values. - Identify long-term, strategic, outcome-oriented goals to achieve the vision. - Determine mid-term strategic objectives to achieve long-term strategic goals. - Identify strategies and tactical plans to achieve mid-term strategic objectives.

Strategic thinking enables management to look at things from all angles. It provides a foundation for change, new ideas, and responsiveness. Lingering problems are resolved, and new life is imparted to strategies that no longer produce results. Management considers all winning strategies, such as offering new products or services for more growth, adapting prices to market game changers, positioning players to play their best game, developing new competencies, doing things differently for increased performance, changing compensation to reflect new realities, investing in state-of-the-art technology, and developing partnerships for greater expansion.

To sum it up, strategic thinking is at the heart of a successful business, fueling management with an inspired vision, innovative ideas, and creativity to develop winning strategies and action plans. Day in and day out, successful entrepreneurs breathe strategic thinking, always looking for new opportunities and innovations to grow their business. If you are not already at the top of your game, get ready to give a fresh start to your business. Become a strategic thinker who inquires, analyzes, and strategizes. Your whole organization will be fired up for action, and together you will move to first place.

Plot Your Journey to Success

It is critical for a new business to start its journey towards success by designing an inspired start-up business plan. As a new entrepreneur, activate your *Fly High* and *High Drive* apps and define what the business is all about, what it has accomplished to date, where it is heading, and how it will reach its destination.

 Behind business success you find inspiration,
creativity, strategy, action, discipline,
commitment, teamwork, and monitoring.

As summarized below, a start-up business plan has no more than 20 pages and provides a clear view of the enterprise: business structure, industry specialization, product or service offerings, operational environment, distribution channels, growth opportunities, strategic direction, and pro-forma financials. Derived from the strategies and tactical plans, a one-page summary of planned investments helps investors understand the purpose of capital requirements. An overview of the marketing strategies summarizes the go-to-market approach for success. The plan is complemented with other valuable information to help investors make well-informed decisions. Take into consideration expected rate of return, collateral, risks and mitigating measures, and planned monitoring practices.

	Start-Up Business Plan
1.	Executive summary
2.	Vision, mission, purpose, and values
3.	Business name and background, business structure (corporation, partnership, sole proprietor), business location, and product location (online, physical store)
4.	Industry, product or service offerings, operational environment (retail, wholesale, service, manufacturing, seasonal), and regulations
5.	Organizational structure (divisions, units, departments), owners, roles, and responsibilities of key players and their skills
6.	Distribution channels (direct salesforce, retailer, wholesaler, equipment manufacturer), and salesforce (salespeople, distributors, representatives, brokers, direct mail)
7.	Growth opportunities, market share, pricing, competitors, and competitive advantages
8.	Accomplishments to date, market analysis, patents, prototypes, facilities, equipment, go-to-market approach, sales, and current clients and suppliers
9.	Strategic outcome-oriented goals, mid-term strategic objectives, strategies, and tactical plans
10.	One-page summary of planned investments (human resources, marketing, inventory, technology, facility, equipment, product development) and enhancement impacts
11.	Current capital structure, financing requirements, and expected rate of return
12.	One-page summary of marketing and sales approach (promotion and advertising)
13.	Pro-forma financial statements, cash flow statements, and assumptions
14.	Risks and mitigating measures
15.	Performance indicators

With this information in mind, you are now ready to craft a winning start-up business plan. Be confident and say, "I am a strategic thinker, and with a clear vision, a thoughtful strategy, and ongoing monitoring, I am on my way to success."

Navigate Safely

Do you know the real secret behind business longevity and success? I can already hear your answers: "Intuition. Innovation. Creativity. Commitment. Hard work. Flair. A good business sense."

These are all good answers, but there's one you shouldn't forget: having both a clear map to take action, and a compass to monitor progress. Many businesses have failed because they were unable to operationalize their vision and strategies due to a lack of monitoring skills.

Every three to five years, a successful enterprise initiates a strategic thinking exercise for the purpose of confirming or redefining the enterprise's vision and strategic plan, which generally includes the elements noted in the table below.

Strategic Plan	
1.	Executive summary
2.	Business: background, product or service offerings, organizational structure, distribution channels, and operational environment
3.	Market: trends, past growth, competitors, and new opportunities
4.	Strengths and weaknesses
5.	Vision, mission, purpose, and values
6.	Strategic, outcome-oriented goals, mid-term strategic objectives, strategies, and tactical plans with timelines
7.	Financial plan (budget, cash flow statement, investments, financing requirements)
8.	One-page summary of marketing and sales approach
9.	Risks and mitigating measures
10.	Performance indicators

*A strategic plan builds a bridge
between today and tomorrow.*

Working down from the strategic plan, management develops its annual business plan. Well-aligned with the strategic, outcome-oriented goals, the annual business plan sets the strategic objectives and action plans for the year to come. It provides a brief discussion of risks and mitigation measures. It also presents financial information, investments, and financing requirements. A one-page summary of the marketing plan is included in the annual business plan.

Many businesses engage their operational units to complete their respective annual business plan in alignment with the strategic objectives. The information is then consolidated for review, prioritization, and final allocation of resources by senior leadership. This exercise leads to the completion of the annual business plan of the enterprise and each operational unit.

Annual Business Plan	
1.	Executive summary
2.	Business: background, product or service offerings, changes to organizational structure, distribution channels, and operational environment
3.	Market: trends, past growth, competitors, and new opportunities
4.	Vision, mission, purpose, and values
5.	Strategic, outcome-oriented goals
6.	Progress-to-date (successes and challenges)
7.	Strategic objectives and tactical plans
8.	Financial plan (budget, cash flows, investment, financing requirements)
9.	One-page summary of marketing and sales approach
10.	Risks and mitigating measures

For further monitoring, management may wish to elaborate specific plans derived from the annual business plan, mainly a human resources plan, an investment plan, a financing plan, and a comprehensive marketing plan.

A well-communicated annual business plan promotes effective and accountable teams that are well aware of strategies and expectations. By setting personal goals aligned with the annual business plan, the teams are more engaged and focused, which leads to better performance. Monitoring is the compass that gives an enterprise an accurate reading of its progress towards the achievement of its vision. Timely communication of results helps in the identification of changes to the planned course of action.

Get ready to craft your plans, and do not forget to read your compass. Well equipped, you and your teams will navigate with more ease towards your magnetic destination of success.

Drive Growth

As said, the universe is expansion, life is expansion, you are expansion, and so is your enterprise. Driving business growth is key to creating more wealth for yourself, your team, your community, your country, and the world. Successful entrepreneurs drive and live on growth. They are attuned to growth, and many make success look simple to achieve.

With their *Fly High* app activated, growth is an expression of all that they are: strategic thinkers, strategists, innovators, developers, supervisors, team players, networkers, and marketers. Their pure creativity, wit, intuition, inspiration, passion, and commitment shine and attract our attention.

With reflection on winning practices of successful entrepreneurs, you will soon accelerate growth and be on your way to new heights of success.

Understand Your Market – A changing economy means a changing market. And with a changing market comes different needs. Successful entrepreneurs are strategic thinkers. They inquire and reassess the needs of their clients and targets. Their success is highly dependent on their capacity to adapt and meet those needs. To be more productive, follow the path of successful entrepreneurs, and pay attention to economic changes. Anticipate shifts, and look for new trends. Focus on your clients and engage in honest conversations with them to understand their current and future needs, price expectations, views on product or service quality, and ideas for service improvements.

Your key questions should be: Where is the market going? What do clients want? At what price? What changes do we need to make?

Create an Experience – In a highly competitive environment, successful entrepreneurs truly understand what makes them unique. They are strategists who capitalize on their competitive advantages. Good is not in their language. Great is. To move towards success, you need to create an experience that your clients will remember and ask for again and again. Understand what people want, and dare to be different by giving more. There is more in greatness, care, personalized service, satisfaction, and improvement. Clients will always remember those who went the extra mile for them.

Your key questions should be: What makes our business unique? What are my competitive advantages? How can we make our clients' experience memorable? How can we give more?

Target New Markets – Successful entrepreneurs are comfortable in the uncomfortable. They look at emerging and new markets with eyes of hope and great possibilities. They look for complementary acquisitions, and they consider partnerships and alliances to expand their operations and activities. They leverage globalization that opens the door to new opportunities and knowledge sharing, thus creating more growth. To help in the identification of new markets, I encourage you to conduct market research. Reflect on collaborative partnerships and alliances that may benefit you and your stakeholders. Consider investments in marketing, human resources, and technology that may open new doors.

Your key questions should be: Where could our products or services have great market potential? Are we ready for international markets? What investments are needed?

Develop New Products – There is comfort in doing what we know best. However, there is no growth in comfort. Successful entrepreneurs think outside the box. They are innovators and developers. Product development and innovation are at the core of their success.

You want more success? Don't just look at what your competitors are doing. Look at what they are *not* doing, and how you could bring value to people's lives. By creating new needs, you will be marching at the front of the parade. Creating social growth will in turn create business growth. Activate your *True Inspiration* app and let intuition and inspiration flow freely.

Your key questions should be: How can we do better for our clients? What would help our clients create growth? What new products can we develop? What investments are needed?

> *Successful entrepreneurs believe in their greatness, thus they create greatness.*

Build a Stellar Salesforce – Successful entrepreneurs are skilled at putting their products in the hands of customers. They have a strong and productive salesforce who proudly create brand awareness. They attract the right salespeople and sales managers to grow and respond to market needs. They empower their salesforce with goals, support, and a smart compensation package. Through performance management, they guide their salesforce to success.

To drive growth, you must build a strong salesforce with proper sales expertise, training, and people skills. As you evaluate the strengths and weaknesses of your sales team, look for their skills in making a connection with people, and their ability to share the unique experience your products or services offer. In building your salesforce, aim for an appropriate compensation package, fair sales quota, sales manager leadership, and proper response to market needs.

Your key questions should be: Do we have the right resources? In the right number? With the right training? With the right compensation package? And the right sales quota?

Position Your Team to Play Their Best Game – Successful entrepreneurs work in harmony with their teams, and they understand their strengths and weaknesses. They position their teams to play their best game and attract new resources as needed to grow and respond to market needs.

Many service enterprises have eroded their success by asking their professionals to excel in both driving growth and delivering quality technical expertise. In doing so, many employees have found themselves performing sales-related tasks that do not align with their natural abilities. This has caused many employees to be demotivated and not perform at their highest level. While this strategy allows employees to develop new skills, it may kill their passion and lead to precious talents and abilities not being used to their full potential.

If you want to win in the business game, communicate with your team to know more about their passion, and how they can help grow the business. Some may be skilled in sales and marketing. Others may be technical gurus with abilities to create ingenious tools and methodologies. Some others may be the best in research and product development. By positioning your team members to play their best game, you will drive more growth from their passion being directed to areas of interest.

Your key questions should be: What are the strengths of my team? How does my team wish to be involved to help grow the business? What training do they need to excel? What skills do we lack as a team?

Set a Winning Go-to-Market Strategy – Successful entrepreneurs stand out with a well-thought-out marketing plan that presents an executive summary, the product or service offerings, brand name, target market, competitors, competitive advantages, pricing, product location, distribution channels, marketing budget and strategy, risks and mitigating measures, and financial projections.

No entrepreneurs fly high without a strategic plan. Take time to work with your team in developing a winning marketing plan. With more in-depth strategy behind your marketing approach, you position your enterprise for greater success. Encourage your teams to activate their *True Inspiration* and *High Drive* apps and work together in finding innovative marketing strategies.

Your key questions should be: Who are our target clients? What message is important to them? How can we best reach them? Do we have the right sales team in place?

Assess Your Growth Actions – Successful entrepreneurs supervise and monitor progress towards the achievement of their strategic growth objectives. They assess what works and what doesn't, and they are not afraid to change course as needed. Faced with roadblocks, they do not lead out of fear but out of creativity, purpose, innovation, team effort, and great communication. They stand strong and try new ideas.

Let monitoring be your compass as you journey towards success. Monitoring is essential to assess if your strategies are fruitful. It allows you to better assess if changes to your operational environment, marketing approach, team structure, distribution channels, and product or service quality are needed to create more growth.

Your key questions should be: Are we meeting our growth objectives? If not, why? What can we do about it?

Sharpen your Marketing Strategy

Even with the most brilliant ideas, if you have neither words nor a design that move target customers, you are not going to gain much attention and drive growth. Developing a winning marketing strategy starts by defining your product or service brand, which becomes the foundation on which you will build your marketing activities and material.

Who are we? What makes us great? What makes us different? What is our vision? What do we stand for? What is our target market? Where do we find our prospects? What do they really want? What should our target audience know about us? These are questions senior management needs to ask to define their brand image.

A successful brand is one that tells your target public the story of your own uniqueness in bringing value to their lives. What you want is for your target market to know what makes you great, and different from all of your competitors. For this, you need to observe trends, find out who and where your target market is, what their needs and wants are, and what your competitors are doing. Market research certainly helps in gaining such clarity. With greater understanding, you can create a more personalized message to gain the attention of your audience.

A well-defined brand clearly communicates with an image or just a few words the enterprise's personality and competencies. It defines what people will experience when they do business with you. With an experience come emotions. By creating an emotional connection with your prospects, you move and motivate your target market to trust you and your offerings.

> *Sell an experience, not a product or service, and your revenue will hit the roof.*

With your target market, value proposition, and brand image clearly defined, you are now ready to go to market to create brand awareness. Your branding image should transpire in your marketing activities, tools, messages, website, social media channels, business cards, e-mail address, and even in your voice mail message.

Your brand image is not static. Just as market conditions change, you may feel the need to re-face your brand with new product and service offerings, or solidify your connection with your target audience. Your budget, who your prospects are, and where to best find them are key drivers in your choice of marketing channels to best maximize your results. These channels may include traditional marketing, Internet communications, joint venture partnerships, events, public relations, or a combination of these approaches.

Traditional marketing includes radio and television ads, magazine and newspaper print advertising, product catalogues, outdoor advertising, service brochures, newsletters, coupons, telemarketing, direct mail, event networking, and person-to-person selling. While there are generally costs associated with traditional marketing, these techniques may produce great results if your target audience spends little time on the Internet.

The younger generations breathe and live off Internet and social media, and we are seeing more and more baby boomers moving in that direction as they discover the richness of Internet information. If your target market includes younger generations, low-cost Internet communications are certainly marketing options to consider.

A responsive contact list is critical to those who wish to establish a successful online business. Design an e-mail sign-up form on your website. Offer a free newsletter, video, or a special report as an incentive for people to give you their e-mail address. Writing blogs and e-articles, providing a free newsletter, offering vlogs, sending press releases, using online ads, taking advantage of co-registration, sending cell phone texts, having profiles on social media, hosting or participating in discussion groups on social media, and providing conferences are all great ways to drive traffic to your website and help you build your contact list.

For a better sense of where and how you should be active on social media channels, spend some time browsing. Have a look at how similar businesses are using these communication mediums. Read their social media posts and what appears to trigger great responses from the public. You will quickly learn what works and what doesn't, and what information target prospects are looking for.

Create a social media channel plan and reflect on types of messages you want to deliver to your target market. For example, you may use Facebook to create brand awareness and publicize product or service features and upcoming events or promotions. Twitter may be your tool for a last reminder of upcoming events or short customer service messages. Google+ and YouTube may be your platforms for more in-depth informative messages. You may use Instagram to share pictures of community events your enterprise is supporting. Participation in online forums may drive traffic to your website.

When it comes to marketing your products and services online, craft messages that are short, clear, and highlight your value and differentiators. Pay attention to your website tags, structure, and content to optimize search engine results for more organic (unpaid) website traffic. It is best to work with a well-informed webmaster who can assist you with search engine optimization.

Other options to increase brand awareness include online ads, press releases, viral marketing, inviting video clips, powerful text messages, e-mail marketing, speaking engagements, and affiliate programs. Under the latter, Internet joint ventures or affiliate partners inform their contact lists of your products in exchange for a commission on the sale proceeds. A special partner-tracking software installed on your website allows for the identification of sales transactions relating to each partner.

There are a variety of online ads to choose from: Google Search, AdWords, Bing, Facebook, Twitter, Tumblr, Pinterest, Instagram, Reddit, YouTube, a pay-per-click[1] model, retargeting ads, mobile ads, in-game ads, banner ads, video ads, and e-mail ads.

To get new customers' attention or attract repeat customers, consider offering regular discounts or other benefits. These may include first-time order discounts, discount on next product, discount on product bundle, exclusive rewards, free shipping over a certain amount, and an incentive product with all purchases for a limited time.

To sum it up, for a stellar marketing strategy, clearly identify who and where your audience is, and what your target prospects want. Create a winning brand and heartfelt messages around them. With your budget in mind, select an appropriate mix of marketing channels for large market coverage. Don't overlook asking your customers where they heard about you. Lastly, tracking performance will help you identify what marketing techniques work best.

Empower Your Team for High Performance

Often, entrepreneurs see driving growth and performance as two different spheres, while in fact performance is frequently a key driver of growth. With your *Fly High* app activated, you empower your team for greater performance, and you set the stage for stellar achievements, more growth, and long-term profitability.

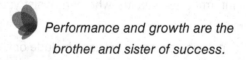

*Performance and growth are the
brother and sister of success.*

As a great ader, your role is to inspire, give momentum, and create more leaders, as well as better employees within your business. "How can this be done?" you might ask with interest. As said, strong organizational skills play a pivotal role in improving performance. Many other aspects, as further discussed below, come into play in accelerating performance and success.

Positive Communication – Leading out of fear does not create team performance, but team annihilation. Great leaders clearly communicate the vision, direction, and team expectations with enthusiasm. They are creative, intuitive, and inspiring to their teams. They lead out of hope, confidence, and a positive attitude. With words of encouragement and appreciation, their teams are motivated to implement the success strategies.

Proper Tools – Ingenious leaders increase performance by providing their teams with the right tools, methodologies, equipment, and technology. They do not overlook consulting with their teams and suppliers on innovative solutions that could deliver greater performance and bring value to the enterprise and its customers.

Motivating Career Plan – The power of great leaders lies in their ability to help their team members achieve their inspiring career vision. They encourage their teams to reflect on the *Up You Go* questions to gain greater clarity on their career goals. As supportive leaders, they assist their team members in the development of their action plan.

Focused Training – True leaders empower their teams with knowledge and training to enable their success and the achievement of their goals. They understand that leadership is an attitude, not a position. For this reason, they encourage their teams to strive to be leaders. In supporting personal leadership, they create improved performance and greatness everywhere within their organization.

Clear Accountability – Success is on the horizon of effective leaders who engage their team members to contribute to the best of their abilities. Accountability is key in performance improvement. It can be communicated through career goals, monitored with performance monitoring, and encouraged through coaching, mentoring, promotion, awards, and compensation incentives.

Pure Creativity – Creativity increases performance in many different ways, with original ideas, renewed tools, product development, new methodologies, and improved systems. Creative leaders encourage creativity enablers: teamwork, lunch and learn sessions, brainstorming, communication, new ideas contests, research, product development, and analysis of strengths and weaknesses. In doing so, they help their reveal their *Marvelous Nature.*

Inspiring Environment – The ability to be creative is a strong driver in performance and employment satisfaction. Inspiring leaders aim to design a workspace that is conducive to inspiration, innovation, performance, and productivity.

Fair Compensation – Fair compensation is also critical in performance. While pay is not the only driver behind productivity, employees who believe they are poorly paid are generally not motivated to go the extra mile. Fair leaders align compensation with the market and the required level of effort. They provide monetary rewards for over-and-above performance.

Ongoing Support – In their quest to create leaders, supportive leaders offer a coaching and mentoring program to their teams to help them gain clarity on their career vision and build their confidence as they move into action. They do not overlook inviting inspiring guest speakers to help their teams develop their leadership skills.

Performance Monitoring – Great leaders understand the power of performance monitoring. They make it a positive exercise where they let employees share what they did well and not so well, and where and how they could improve. As they listen with an open mind, they empower the reflection with positive and constructive ideas to help the employees achieve their career goals. They remain positive even in the face of disappointing results. They engage their teams in finding solutions to create greater performance. They use challenges as opportunities for greater teamwork, creativity, and innovation to rise.

Appreciation – Kind leaders are appreciative of team efforts. They know that a compliment and a thank you note can go a long way in increasing performance. They understand the power of praising words in building confidence and are not shy to say, "I believe in your greatness, and I will help you become the best that you can be." They understand the message of belongingness and care that comes with spending time with employees. They celebrate team successes, small and grand, and they encourage initiative and creativity.

Get Rid of Bad Apples – Wise leaders recommend coaching, mentoring, and training to build up their teams' competencies and desired behavior. At times, to avoid undermining their teams, they may have no other alternative than to terminate an employee who is simply not suited for the work at hand.

To sum up, empowering your team for high performance is truly a winning strategy for greater success.

Aim for Excellence

Aiming for excellence is success in the making. Excellence is expressed with continuous and sustainable improvements in strategic management, organizational structure, values and standards, business functions, processes and controls, technology and equipment, and client satisfaction.

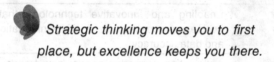

Strategic thinking moves you to first place, but excellence keeps you there.

To create a culture of excellence, I encourage you to activate your *Fly High* app and review all areas of your enterprise to assess if excellence is at the core of your day-to-day operations.

To facilitate the internal review, consider running brainstorming sessions and focus groups with your team, engage in process mapping and analysis, and perform client interviews and surveys. You may complement the review with workshops held by relevant outside consultants who can bring their expertise and skills to the whole process.

With open communication, allow your team to freely identify strengths, constraints, and areas for improvement. For a true transformation, encourage creativity, collaboration, and innovation in the design of constructive changes, new initiatives and investments, system and product development, and other ingenious solutions. All of the following characteristics should be part of your *business signature of excellence.*

Business Signature of Excellence	
Strategic Management	Strategic thinking, a clear vision, mission and purpose, winning strategies and tactical plans, an effective risk management process, continuous monitoring and improvement, and proactive management
Organizational	True leadership, clear structure, roles and accountabilities, winning team positioning, engaging values, ethical standards, teamwork, open and positive communication, information sharing, and management appreciation
People	People excellence (right people with the right skills), engaging career goals, focused learning and development, inspiring coaching and mentoring, motivating compensation and benefits, inspiring performance monitoring, change champion, employee satisfaction, and high personnel retention
Operation	Efficient and effective core business processes and controls, quality control of raw materials, state-of-the-art operating systems, performance metrics, process and control monitoring, results-based monitoring, and appropriate facility
Information Technology	Enabling and innovative technology that supports business processes, user friendly information systems, and data accuracy
Product Development	Anticipation of market needs, new trends and shifts, identification of new markets, proactive response, client focus, and innovative offerings (products, services, tools)
Sales and Marketing	Proper distribution channels, winning sales team, strategic marketing plan, and result monitoring
Customer Satisfaction	Innovative products and services, high quality standards, quality monitoring, client surveys, and complaints follow-up
Financial management	Monthly budget and cash-flow monitoring, variance analysis, accurate projections, and proper capital and financing structure

By integrating excellence in your enterprise planning, execution, and monitoring, your business signature will be nothing less than remarkable. It will be excellence in its full essence, with more growth, productivity, performance, strategy, innovation, collaboration, employee retention, and client satisfaction.

Become a Change Implementation Champion

Developing change champions is part of creating a culture of excellence. Just as leadership should be embraced by team members from all levels, becoming a change implementation champion should be the aim of all employees striving for excellence.

While some team members may be more involved in initiating, planning, and facilitating change, all team members should be engaged in change implementation. By using the *Five Cs Change Implementation Model* below, not only will you facilitate change, but you will ensure success in achieving the desired results.

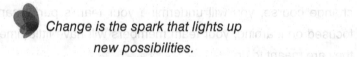

Change is the spark that lights up
new possibilities.

Commitment – Even with the greatest ideas in the world, changes will not come to light if you do not have strategies and tactical plans to operationalize them. Strategic planning is critical to identify who is going to do what, when, how many times, and where. Most importantly, as a leader, you need to build commitment to change and engage your team in action. With strategy and action, change becomes reality.

Communication – Communication is key when it comes to creating change implementation champions. With positive words, you can influence the change process to reduce resistance and open up your team's mind to new possibilities. Change translates into exciting and inspiring opportunities for the betterment of the enterprise and everyone's work life. Communication provides your team with a better understanding of the issues at stake and the nature of the changes. It gives your team clarity on the vision, a clear understanding of what is to come, the new direction, and the implementation milestones and time frame.

Change Preparedness – There is no effective and efficient transformation without proper preparedness to facilitate change implementation. This means preparing an implementation plan, testing, and correcting course prior to training team members. To ease change implementation, I encourage you to set up a facilitation team whose responsibility will be to test the changes, make adjustments before training takes place, prepare the required learning tools, methodologies, and guides, and oversee the training phase.

Coaching – Training and coaching greatly facilitate change implementation. It empowers your team with confidence to move into change with more ease. Well-planned training and a support team enable a better understanding of the nature of the changes and their benefits, and they ease the transition with constant support and coaching.

Consistency – Changes take time and effort from everyone. Let time do its marvelous transformation. If you lead out of panic and constantly change course, you will undermine your team's performance. Always focused on learning, your team members will have little time to do what they are meant to do.

As you implement change, it is best to monitor progress for greater success. Make the experience positive by welcoming feedback and encouraging lessons-learned sharing. Take action swiftly to address needed corrections. Don't forget to show appreciation for all team efforts in the implementation process. In using the *Five Cs Change Implementation Model*, you will create a positive culture of change within your organization and build champions who are committed and engaged in creating an enterprise of excellence.

Keep Your Eyes Wide Open

Let's do a quick exercise. Close your eyes for a few seconds. Tell me, what do you see? That's right, you see total darkness. This is exactly what happens when you keep your eyes shut as you manage a business. You see lots of darkness, and no light at the end of the tunnel.

Many businesses have failed as a result of not keeping their eyes on the bottom line and cash flows, ignoring messages of troubling performance, and not paying attention to lack of processes and controls.

The end result has been the darkness of a very thin or inexistent profit, leaving the enterprise vulnerable and with little space to grow or make appropriate changes.

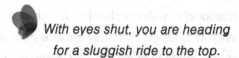

With eyes shut, you are heading
for a sluggish ride to the top.

Successful entrepreneurs keep their eyes wide open and focused on the bottom line. They ask their financial team to perform budget monitoring, with analysis and explanations of budget variances for an assessment of the overall financial situation. With revised financial projections, they see the financial horizon and better manage revenue and costs. They swiftly make necessary changes, cutting unnecessary expenses, or adopting different marketing strategies to push profits up. Cash flows and the accounts receivable aging schedule are also in sight.

To generate revenue is good, but to turn your receivables into cash is even better. Many businesses have faced the unprecedented darkness of bankruptcy as a result of insolvent clients. When it comes to receivables, you have the choice between two strategies: you can avoid them or learn to better manage them by establishing and enforcing a credit and collection policy. If the latter is your option of choice, be firm on your credit terms. Your clients need to understand that you are an entrepreneur, not a bank in the business of offering lines of credit.

When possible, ask for payment prior to delivery of products. This can easily be set up with an online product store. However, if you are a service provider, you may opt for installment payments on delivery of milestones or monthly invoicing. You may consider not activating new orders or providing additional services until all outstanding invoices have been paid in full.

I strongly recommend you include credit terms on your invoices. For example, you may offer a 2 percent discount for invoices paid within 10 days. You may indicate that a 10 percent interest charge will be added to invoices not paid within 30 days.

With eyes on your cash flow, you can better manage your cash-related risks and spend more wisely. In addition, it allows for a more efficient use of available credit tools (overdraft, credit cards, lines of credit) for additional money in your pocket.

Having a good relationship with your banker is a great asset. You have someone who believes in what you do, can provide advice to save you fees, and may assist with credit in times of need. Keep your eyes on your financial structure for a more effective use of your money. For example, if you intend to acquire long-term assets, like equipment or a building, it makes sense to look for long-term financing to avoid dipping into your short-term cash flows. Short-term cash flows should generally be used to finance inventory and pay for day-to-day operating and administrative expenses.

Remember that by keeping your *Fly High* activated, your eyes are wide open, and you are heading for an amazing ride to success. Keeping your head in the sand is not going to make any business issues disappear. Be mature enough to say, "For each problem, there is a solution. I will address problems as they arise, and plan for an effective resolution." Remember, your ultimate goal is to bring the best out of your organization and to create a culture of excellence in all that you do.

Learn the Secrets of Business Communication

Why learn the secrets of business communication? Simple. Communication means interaction, understanding, innovation, ideas, discovery, guidance, productivity, performance, collaboration, sharing, relationships, excellence, and greatness. Communication is the cornerstone to moving your business towards success.

Not only do you interact with your team, but you communicate with your clients, suppliers, collaborators, and prospects. Now that you are a master in team communication, let's look at other secrets of business communication to revive your current business relationships and help you develop new ones with much more ease.

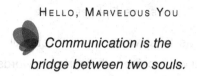

*Communication is the
bridge between two souls.*

Client Communication – If you want clients for life, you need to communicate with them on an ongoing basis. Creating a relationship is easy, but maintaining a long-term one is an investment in time and energy. As part of your efforts to create a culture of excellence, send satisfaction surveys to your clients. If you sell products, ask questions on product quality, reasons for dissatisfaction, price appropriateness, and customer service.

Service enterprises should ensure that their questions are relevant to all clients, or use different survey templates for new clients and long-term clients. For example, asking new clients if they have developed deep relationships with your team or if your enterprise is a contributing factor to their success may not be pertinent questions.

Don't overlook asking for reasons for dissatisfaction to identify areas for improvement. Accept criticism with an open mind and make sure to actively address issues to the satisfaction of the client. Ask for clarification as needed. As a service enterprise that aims for excellence, ask for feedback during progress calls to help ensure that expectations are met. Clients will appreciate your concerns. Take time to meet with your clients to discuss the survey results and their new projects and needs. These discussions empower your strategic thinking and develop closer relationships based on mutual respect and trust.

Supplier and Collaborator Communication – Just as you want your clients to be open with you on their needs, I encourage you to clearly share your wants with your suppliers and collaborators. I come from the premise that, just like you, suppliers and collaborators wish to establish a long-term business relationship with their clients built on honest communication.

Remember that there is no need to yell your dissatisfaction to suppliers or collaborators. Stay calm, and with clear words explain the issue at hand and your expectations. Bring constructive solutions, not simply complaints. Listen to what they have to say. Don't interrupt; they may have good explanations and ideas to solve the issue. You will be amazed at the positive response you will receive with courteous words.

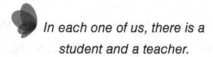

In each one of us, there is a student and a teacher.

Prospect Communication – If you want to be successful in attracting new clients to your business, think of their needs, not yours. In giving more, you will receive more. People are bright and intuitive, and they know if you are genuine or not. When they meet you, they can easily see if you are interested in them, or simply in their money. When you attend networking events, make the conversation not only about you, but about them.

To easily introduce yourself, craft a brief personal pitch ahead of time that defines who you are, your profession, employer, and product or service offering. There is no need to arm yourself, as some do, with an elevator pitch. Let the other person discover the great beauty and talents that are in you.

If the person wants to know more about you, don't worry; questions will come. Ask for their business card, acknowledge the card as a gesture of courtesy, and try to memorize their name. Not good at remembering names? Repeat the person's name silently a few times. Later on, if you want to remember their name, say it out loud for the next few days.

Take pleasure in meeting new people, even if they do not become clients. Having worked in the business world and been involved in the community for many years, I can tell you that each acquaintance has been a source of inspiration either from their kindness, generosity, compassion, and innovative spirit, to their commitment and passion for what they do.

As said earlier in the section *Sharpen your Marketing Strategy,* use proper marketing techniques to communicate clearly your value message and your unique offering. Be responsive to questions asked by prospects through social media channels.

Don't worry if you feel you are not yet an effective communicator. Communication is a skill that can be learned. Above all, my best advice to you is to speak from the heart and interact with care. A person with a genuine heart does not need many words to say, *I listen, I care, and I want to develop a meaningful relationship.*

Successful communication is not only about words, it's also about caring actions that speak louder than words and say you've heard the other person's message. Let your signature be a caring heart!

Triumph Over Tough Times

In today's challenging times, great captains must embrace unique characteristics to navigate their sailboat safely to its destination. As strategic thinkers and intuitive visionaries, they watch the clouds and see the storm coming. With their chief mate, they chart the best strategic course to avoid the storm. Empowered with knowledge, their mates fear not.

Unable to avoid the storm? Great captains employ creative strategies and tactics to avoid capsizing their boat. As wise leaders, they trim the sails for safe navigation. They remain calm and strategic as the waves beat into their ship with force. Committed and combative, great captains give the command to switch to storm sails for more stability. They communicate trust, and their words are impregnated with optimism as the wind furiously blows into the sails. They navigate tirelessly until their ship is safe, heading towards the clear horizon.

> *There is little light on the path of negativity. A bright future awaits those who embrace optimism and walk on the path of new possibilities.*

You are the captain of your enterprise, and you must embrace a number of unique leadership characteristics to triumph over tough economic times that may render the future very bleak. Let's look at some differentiators between captains whose boat capsizes, and those who are true leaders able to navigate safely through storms.

Decisiveness – In difficult times, great leaders keep their *Fly High* app activated at all times. They stand steady and strong at the helm. They show wisdom in their decision making and leadership in all areas of the business, from strategic planning, team structure and management, growth initiatives, and process reengineering, to financial management and communication.

Strategic Thinker – As strategic thinkers, leaders listen to the market to identify shifts, new trends, threats, barriers, and their causes. They look for growth opportunities beyond their current markets. They consider low-cost product development and additional distribution channels. They review current resources, organizational structure, tasks, and internal processes for changes that may increase productivity. With sharp eyes, they scrutinize the operating budget, and with good judgment they cut expenses where needed.

Resourcefulness – Leaders are greatly intuitive and resourceful, focused on new ideas to drive growth, with products and prices to better respond to market needs and remain ahead of the competition. They look for new ways of doing things for greater efficiency and a positive impact on the bottom line.

Team Player – Leaders enable group decisions and support cross-functional cooperation. Jointly with their teams, they wisely analyze risks and financial impacts associated with all options. They then confirm the proper course of action with strategies and tactical plans that align with the new vision. Working down from the strategic plan, business units develop their annual business plans, which are then consolidated for review, prioritization, and final allocation of resources.

Empowerment – Leaders try hard not to downsize the workforce to be ready for the next economic upturn. They position their teams to play their best game. Desired behaviors and staff competencies are reinforced with knowledge, training, tools, methodologies, communication, performance monitoring, awards, and pay incentives.

Continuous Monitoring – Leaders delegate and monitor progress effectively with senior management. Each month, they review each element of the business units' plans and provide quick feedback on progress-to-date and next steps. With eyes wide open, they closely monitor operational cash flow, accounts receivable, and budgets.

Combative Spirit – Leaders do not let a setback discourage them. On the contrary, they are fiercely combative. Their creativity is at its best when challenges appear on the horizon. They encourage discussions and brainstorming sessions with their teams to generate winning solutions.

Commitment – Leaders put action in their passions and keep marching on with confidence. They lead by example, and are committed to the success of the enterprise and their teams. Financial scarcity does not stop them; they continue the promotion of their brand with inexpensive marketing strategies. They support their teams as they work hard in implementing the action plans. They are committed to the culture of excellence they have created.

Great Communicator – Leaders share the new direction openly with all team members for greater clarity. They answer all questions in true honesty and put to rest all rumors. They are good listeners, flexible to new ideas to increase profit. With confidence, they contact suppliers to make more appropriate payment arrangements as may be needed. They leverage their client relationships and business contacts to learn more and build growth.

Optimism – Leaders encourage their teams with kind words. They say no to stress, doubt, and fear. They know they are winners, and challenges are not stopping them. They lead with optimism, celebrate progress, and praise their teams for their efforts. Their positivity and enthusiasm are contagious.

Now well-apprised of the secrets of great captains, no recession or economic downturn will prevent you from navigating ahead safely. Striving for profitable longevity, not survival, will be your signature of success. Be bold and say, "I will not let a storm stop me. I will triumph over tough times. I have a *Marvelous Business*." Remember that a ship has many mates but only one captain, and you are the captain now.

CHAPTER 12

Power Up Your Leisure Time

Play, learn, grow, and transform the world!

Activate Your *Fun and Play* App

More and more people suffer from the *Go, Go, Go Syndrome* caused by our fast-paced lifestyle and never-ending professional and family commitments. Juggling professional and personal life has become a real struggle. For many, life is filled with less and less leisure time, leaving their body and mind surcharged and feeling totally depleted. Our bodies are not meant to constantly be in action. We need time to relax, replenish, and enjoy life's pleasures.

Are you feeling exhausted, out of balance, or bored right now? Are you tired of waking up with no energy each and every day? If you have answered these questions in the affirmative, it probably means you forgot to activate your *Fun and Play* app.

Turn it on, and over time you will see stress and tension disappear. With *Fun and Play*, your mind, body, and soul refresh, and your life is filled with youthfulness and playfulness.

The *Fun and Play* app is specifically designed to say good-bye to your hectic schedule and say hello to more playtime, exercise, fun learning, relaxation, and quietness to energize your body, ease your mind, and promote more well-being. That's right; with *Fun and Play* you bring more leisure time into your life to nurture your whole self in three ways:

1. With less mind and body stress, your body becomes stronger, your mind is more alert, and you experience good-feeling emotions.

2. You learn and grow mentally, emotionally, and spiritually while enjoying more well-being and inner peace.
3. You deepen your connection with yourself, other human beings, and God, which in turn allows you to appreciate life in all its beauty.

> *The path to wellness is simple:*
> *nurture your body, refresh your soul,*
> *and heighten your spirit.*

Remember that you cannot create an enriched professional life with a depleted personal life. An investment in yourself goes a long way in creating your best life. Being in harmony simply allows your spark to light up your life. As said, I have seen a number of rising stars who ignored their physical and emotional limits, and their light faded quickly.

You are the *Marvelous You*, and you have the power to create an enriched personal life. No one else can fill your life with alertness, passion, and excitement. For this reason, you need to activate your *Fun and Play* app to remain positive and full of energy to tackle your professional and family commitments. I am one of those who truly enjoys work and easily forgets to turn on my *Fun and Play* app. While work may feel like fun and play, it is not what *Fun and Play* will bring into your life. You really need to step aside from your busyness to allow for more relaxation time.

Me time is not an act of selfishness, but an act of love towards yourself that allows you to better love others. Be a flying star that will light up the sky for a long time. Stop feeling guilty when taking leisure time, and invest in your happiness and well-being today.

Play to Stay Young

Have you said to yourself lately, "There is always so much to do that at the end of the day, I am just so exhausted and don't feel like doing anything?" To do more with greater energy, you need to play more. "Really?" you may shout. Really, is my answer!

Playtime is indeed one of the best anti-aging formulas. Not only does it refresh your body, but it rejuvenates your soul. Staying young is a lifestyle that involves taking care of yourself, having an open mind, being curious about life, and having a positive outlook. If you are looking for more youthfulness in your life, then add some more playtime to your schedule.

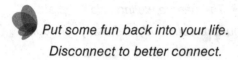

Put some fun back into your life.
Disconnect to better connect.

As a member of the *Fit and Feeling Fabulous Club*, exercise is in your sight. It keeps your body and mind young and healthy. The benefits of a few sessions per week of flexibility exercises, strength training, and cardio conditioning are immense. Exercise releases stress and triggers feel-good hormones in your body. Your immune system becomes stronger. You gain more muscle mass, agility, and flexibility.

With *Be Happy,* laughter keeps your soul young and elevates you to new heights of well-being. It releases tension and stress, increases blood flow, and lowers blood pressure. Not much laughter in your life? Then watch comedy shows and movies, remind yourself of funny moments, laugh at yourself when you are clumsy, go out with friends, play with your pets, and laugh at life's small annoyances. Over time, these moments will raise your positive vibrations.

Connecting through the Internet certainly serves a purpose, but it does not replace the good feelings associated with meaningful human interaction. We all have a deep longing to love and feel loved.

Turn on your *Love Power* app for more social interactions. They work wonders for your body and mind. Practice a sport, have a lunch date with a friend, or become a member of a sports or art club. These are excellent ideas to create moments of happiness and connect with people you enjoy, deepening your relationships and developing new ones.

Mini-vacations are also great to replenish your body and mind. They can be as short as going to the spa for a few hours, to a two-day weekend getaway. Make sure to plan them and care for urgencies ahead of time to limit any guilt from being away from the office. If you are anxious at the thought of some time off, see the experience as time well invested to refresh your soul.

Live each day with a sense of playfulness. Be excited for tomorrow. Focus on the positive and pleasant aspects of life. Don't take life so seriously. Change what can be changed, and let go of what cannot be changed. Such an attitude will keep your soul from discouragement and give you energy to face life's challenges.

With more playtime in your life, you will be more efficient and productive in your work, with greater creativity and inspiration. You will be a better parent, with more patience and understanding. You will be a *Go Getter* with a more youthful spirit both at home and at work.

Learn Something New

People with a youthful spirit never cease to learn and be creative. They enjoy life and have the capacity to see the beauty in both the small and grand things of life. They love to meet new people, be involved in the community, explore new horizons, and be informed of public interests. Their lives are not just centered on themselves but on others as well. They never stop being curious and creative in different ways. They do not lack ideas to refresh their body and mind.

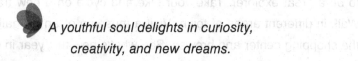

A youthful soul delights in curiosity,
creativity, and new dreams.

Activate your *Fun and Play* app and take time away from your couch or computer for more energy and happiness. Weave these tips into your life, and you will maintain a youthful spirit and age beautifully and gracefully:

Learn Something New – Each year, find something new to learn. You can learn how to paint or play an instrument, take cooking or language classes, learn to play bridge or chess, or take on something more physically challenging, like golf or tennis. Not only will new learning keep your brain sharp, but it will promote a sense of accomplishment and healthy pride in your life.

Give Your Brain a Daily Workout – Each and every day, keep your brain fit and young. Read a book, the newspaper, or magazines. Do crossword puzzles or learn embroidery. Play Scrabble or other interactive games.

Do Something Creative – Make time for creative fun. Compose a song, write a book or poetry, keep a journal, do woodworking projects, start a home garden, take pictures, or do an art piece like a painting, pottery, or ceramics. Engaging your mind and body in non-stressful and distracting activities is much more relaxing than sitting around and doing nothing. Rejuvenating your life with more creativity makes you feel alive. It allows you to discover all that you are.

Learn a Song and Dance – Learn a new song to hum in the shower, in your car, or at home. Sing wherever you want, but sing a song. Dance along if you want (but not in the shower). Singing keeps your soul smiling, relieves anxiety, and maintains a youthful spirit.

Watch Educational Programs – Watch TV shows that provide a wealth of information on educational topics. These include geography, history, travel, nature, culture, healthy living, cooking, cars, religion, and home building. They are great to keep your mind in a continuous learning mode.

Become a Great Explorer – You don't need to travel around the world to be a great explorer. Take your bike and cycle on a new trail in town. Walk in different areas of town. Visit a museum or an art gallery. Go to the shopping center and browse. See what's new this year in clothing or furniture stores. Try a new restaurant and choose something different on the menu. Visit a town nearby and see new sights. Just have fun exploring and finding new treasures.

Be Daring – Don't be afraid to stretch your limits. You may be pleasantly surprised to discover some hidden skills. I am not telling you to jump out of a plane, but if you've thought of it, then do it (with a parachute, of course). Today is the time to do what you've always wanted to do and pursue what you deeply desire.

With your *Fun and Play* app activated, you have the means to keep your mind and brain young and healthy. Have fun, and make it a daily adventure. Your life will soon be filled with more moments of creativity, happiness, and deep joy. The world around you will become much more interesting. Your confidence, excitement, and dedication will be contagious. Over time, you will inspire others to create their best lives.

Unwind Your Brain

With our fast-paced lives, our brains are constantly bombarded by stimulants that ignite a flow of non-stop thoughts. Give yourself the gift of quietness once in a while. When you do so you are proclaiming, "I love myself, and I care for my well-being." With silence comes replenishment, creativity, enhanced mental abilities, and serenity.

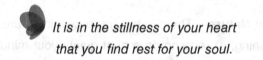

*It is in the stillness of your heart
that you find rest for your soul.*

Silence your brain by activating *Fun and Play* and weaving these tips into your life:

Take Mini Breathing Breaks – Take mini breathing breaks every hour or so and consciously stop your thoughts. There is magic in the practice of deep breathing where you just sit comfortably and observe your breathing. Just a few deep breaths, and your body and mind instantly feel more relaxed and peaceful. Your shoulders are less tense. You are mindful of the present moment, and more in control of your thoughts. This technique avoids stress build-up in your muscles over time, especially if you work at a computer station for an extended period.

Quiet Your Mind – Many people praise the power of 10-15 minutes of meditation to quiet their mind and achieve a profound state of relaxation. Just as a body massage relaxes their whole body, they see meditation as a mind massage that calms their mind.

If meditation does not resonate with you, I encourage you to try my *Path to Serenity* technique. In a state of inner peace and silence, you feel God's unconditional love embracing you and filling your heart. In these moments of quietness and receptiveness, inspiration, intuition, and guidance abound.

Become an Early Bird – Wake up early in the morning and enjoy the sunrise and the stillness in your house. There is much pleasure to be found in the morning quietness of your nest. I am an early bird, and can't get enough of this peaceful feeling that engulfs me when I look outside the window. For me, morning silence is a blissful time, with no phones ringing, no printer running, and no voices to be heard.

Get a Massage – A massage is simply divine to slow down the pace of your thoughts and quiet your mind. While on the massage table, simply focus on the present moment. Listen to the light music in the background, and feel the touch of those healing fingers on your muscles. Let your mind and body relax.

Say Hello to Nature – There is healing power in nature. Walking in nature, going fishing, or relaxing on a boat quiets your mind. Stop near a waterfall and listen to the cascades of water crashing down. Watch a sunrise or sunset. A breath of fresh air just seems to go a long way in calming and restoring your mind and body.

Take a Warm Bath – Add some lavender scent to a warm bath and close your eyes. Within a few minutes, you will be enveloped by the calming effect of the warm water on your muscles. Focus on this pleasing moment and do not give in to thinking about your to-do list. As thoughts come to your mind, let them go, like air you exhale when you breathe.

Take a Power Snooze – Close your eyes and take a 15- to 20-minute midday snooze to reverse fatigue and recharge. A power snooze gives both your mind and body a rest, and it boosts your energy to tackle the rest of the day.[1] Set an alarm clock, because napping for more than 25 minutes may affect your nighttime sleep cycle.

There is no reason to feel guilty for taking a few moments of quietness in the day. In fact, having a date with yourself refreshes your body, uplifts your soul, and allows Spirit to speak to your heart. Simply remember that it is in quietness that you prepare yourself for powerful action. There is no right or wrong way to quiet your mind. Explore the different techniques and see what works best for you.

Make Time for Family Fun

Get all members of your family to activate their *Fun and Play* app and create moments of happiness and love together. Family time gets you to forget for a few moments your projects and tasks, causing your body and mind to relax and feel invigorated.

For some, family time is a movie or game night, a nice dinner, a visit to the museum, a bike ride, or a picnic. For others, it can be reading a book, playing a video game, or having an ice cream cone.

Still others may prefer to be involved in a community project where all family members participate. A few hours at the food bank, a bike ride for cancer, or a community garage sale are great ways to instill a sense of togetherness and contribution. These activities help to develop new friendships, and they open your heart to the needs of others.

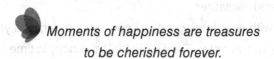

Moments of happiness are treasures
to be cherished forever.

Whatever activity you choose to do as a family, just remember to make it a time of closeness, love, and happiness to be remembered. Family time shouldn't be torture. To make it fun, choose activities that everyone wants to be involved with. If you try something new or an intrepid activity like whitewater rafting or skydiving, encourage each other's adventurous spirit.

Family fun means being present, not feeling stressed out by your to-do list. Schedule family fun ahead of time to really enjoy the moment. Without proper planning, you may get caught in saying yes to new work expectations at the last minute.

Spending quality time with your loved ones is precious. What a spouse and child remember are you being fully present, genuinely interested in their lives, listening to what they have to say, and giving them attention. Ask questions that show your interest in what they do, and what they like and dislike. Get to know them better by asking them to tell you about their aspirations. Engage with them, and simply enjoy who they are.

Make togetherness a fun experience. Play with your children, tease them, and laugh together. Compliment your spouse and show affection by holding hands. Fill your mind with memorable moments of love and togetherness.

Game playing that involves only one winner should be made positive by praising the importance of participation. Teaching your children that effort is what counts will raise their self-esteem. As said earlier, there is no need to constantly emphasize the skills of a particular child over another. Children are treasures who grow in their own time.

My treasure chest is filled with great memories of adventures and special moments with family and friends. Anytime and anywhere, I can simply open my treasure chest and find special moments that make me smile. These memories warm my heart and let me appreciate life with all its small and grand pleasures.

Share time with your family, get to know each other, and your life will be filled with fun and laughter. Time off in their company is time on the path of love and happiness. Not only does it strengthen your family ties, but you are rewarded with their smiling faces that make it all worthwhile.

Explore New Horizons

With your *Fun and Play* app activated, you are ready to explore this beautiful world. Travel is the greatest school where you discover different cultures, develop new friendships, and become more adventurous and easygoing. Out of your comfort zone, you have an opportunity to be surprised by how much more you can be, and you fill your life with more adventure, discovery, and excitement.

Discover Different Cultures – As a student of the travel school, you expand your mind. You see the richness of different cultures, with their amazing history and unique geography. There is nothing like seeing the world with your own eyes and interacting directly with other ethnicities. You are reminded that while we have different physical appearances and cultural environments, we are all one.

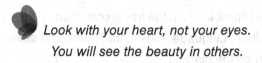

Look with your heart, not your eyes.
You will see the beauty in others.

Develop New Friendships – Reaching out to someone else sets the stage for expansion to take place in both your and the other person's life. There is joy in developing new friendships and mutual sharing. A big smile with a thank you or hello said in another language is all you need to create a connection.

I feel blessed to have visited a few foreign countries over the years. I have met great people who have become friends and enriched my life. Travel has truly made me see the world as my home and mankind as my brethren.

As a travel school student, you get to develop new skills, especially if you are volunteering in underprivileged countries. You may find yourself digging holes or being part of a team rebuilding homes and schools. The end result is simply amazing: increased confidence, new skill sets, and a great contribution in improving the lives of others.

Become Adventurous – Travel means time for more adventures. Don't be shy to fill your days with exciting activities that bring more fun into your life. Try climbing a mountain, canoeing down a river, or going on a safari. Be adventurous with your taste buds and enjoy other countries' delicacies. Say to yourself, "I will be curious and open-minded, and I will discover all the beauties that life has to offer."

Sometimes travel comes with challenges, like a late airplane departure, a missed airline connection, or lost luggage. Do not let these annoyances negatively impact your adventure. Unplanned situations make amusing tales to tell your friends, and memories you will never forget. They bring flavor to your trips. Thus, no need to get angry about a situation you have no control over.

Life has surprised me with so many travel adventures, and they made each of my trips even more unique. You are the *Marvelous You*, and you know how to make the best out of any circumstances. Just go with the flow to make your trip more enjoyable.

Get ready, and enroll today in the travel school and enrich your life with other people's culture, language, music, traditions, and beliefs. Have fun, and see you soon on the plane!

Have a Marvelous Day

Making room in your day for caring time invigorates your life. The easiest way to do this is by having your *Fun and Play* app activated each and every day. In doing so, you recognize that you are of great value and worthy of your love.

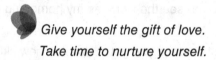

Give yourself the gift of love.
Take time to nurture yourself.

Short escapes a few times a day will ease your body and mind. These can be as simple as doing a few exercises, closing your eyes, taking deep breaths, reading your affirmations, practicing visualization, or reading a book. One hour in your day can transform your day into a marvel experience.

	Let Your Day Be a Marvel Experience	
	Timing	**Activity**
M	15 minutes	**Moment of Silence** – Take a *thought* break for a few minutes, several times a day. Sit comfortably with your eyes closed and simply relax.
A	5 minutes	**Affirmations** – Read your vision of success statement and *Marvelous You* affirmations.
R	15 minutes	**Rest and Relaxation** – Take several mini *Me* times during the day when you take a few deep breaths and stretch your body.
V	5 minutes	**Visualization** – Visualize the actualization of your vision of success statement and each attribute of your *Marvelous Nature*.
E	10 minutes	**Exercise** – Tone your body and relax your mind with light exercises.
L	10 minutes	**Learning and Reading** – Read a book or a magazine and listen to inspiring messages and music.

Start your day with some light exercises to warm up your muscles. You will experience a greater connection with your body, even a sense of gratefulness and respect for the vehicle that allows you to be. At the end of the day, take a few minutes to relax your body with stretches and light exercises.

Your mind cannot be on high speed all day. To keep it vibrant, take a few moments of silence during the day. Simply close your eyes and relax. Try not to give attention to your thoughts. Let them go as they come to your mind. There will be time later to deal with today's worries. This is your time to replenish and gain more clarity. These moments of quietness enrich your spiritual connection and open the door to more inspiration and intuition.

Reading your vision of success affirmations daily is a great way to remind yourself of who you are and where you are going. Don't overlook visualization to feel the deep joy of moving in the direction of your aspirations.

Mini-breaks during the day make all the difference in energizing your body and mind. A few deep breaths are all you need to bring your shoulders down and relax your tense muscles. A warm cup of tea or a walk around the house or office also has a calming effect. Your body feels recharged and ready for the next task ahead.

Don't forget to wind down at the end of the day with a good book or a magazine. Listen to music and inspiring videos or messages that uplift your spirit.

Make the decision to enjoy life, learn, and expand your mind. All it takes is one hour of *Me* time to transform your day into a marvel experience with more well-being, energy, and harmony.

CHAPTER 13

Power Up Your Environment

Home is a reflection of who you are.
Let it be enjoyable and filled with love.

Activate Your *Green Thumb* App

Is your house a mess, with mountains of clothes and toys everywhere? Are bills and untouched mail piling up? How about your office? Are you lost in your mess, with paperwork accumulating? Are you overwhelmed, but not eager to tidy up? If you have answered yes to some of these questions, it is time to turn on your *Green Thumb* app.

With children and pressing demands at work, there is little time for a tidy and pleasant home and workspace. First thing you know, dirty clothes are left for days in the laundry basket, empty plates sit on the living room table, and trash cans are full.

Home is a place of comfort and warmth where you celebrate life.

Green Thumb is wonderful to help you de-clutter and clean your home. Homemaking is simplified with a proper hygiene strategy as you transform your home into a heavenly place, and your workspace becomes an inspiring oasis. That's right, you are inspired to create a home that is both welcoming and pleasant for yourself, your family, and your guests. A nice scent, organized wardrobes, storage areas, and a little decoration here and there make your home an enjoyable living place.

With *Green Thumb*, you enjoy living in a workspace that promotes creativity and inspiration. You want your work environment to be conducive to more productivity and make you feel better connected to your work.

To top it off, with *Green Thumb*, you green your life and make a big difference in preserving planet earth. You love and help care for God's creation. Not only do you green at home and at the office, but you are involved in green initiatives in the community.

If you feel scattered and want to better organize your space at home and at work, turn on your *Green Thumb* app today! Over time, your congestion will be under control for a more pleasant, open, and welcoming environment.

Resolve to De-clutter

There is pleasure in coming home after a hard day at work to find a place that does not look like a flea market. It's true, an uncluttered home has a peaceful, homey, and welcoming feeling. With our busy lives, tidying up just seems impossible. To help you simplify the process, let me give you answers to your *how* questions about de-cluttering.

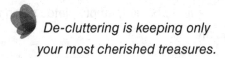

*De-cluttering is keeping only
your most cherished treasures.*

How can I resolve to de-clutter?

Simple. You need to activate your *Green Thumb* app. Seeing the benefits of de-cluttering your space simply sparks your desire for a better organized space. With *Green Thumb*, you are no longer overwhelmed, and you are ready to invest time in giving your home or office space the make-over it deserves. You are excited about the idea of a clean home or work space. You are open to creative ideas to make your environment a more welcoming place.

How do I get better organized?

First, walk around the house and the office to identify areas most in need of tidying. Prepare a list of all the areas up for a make-over: garage, basement, office shelves, filing cabinets, closets, and drawers.

Have a look around to see how much you can throw away and what storage solutions you need: shelves, drawers, bookshelves, folders, coat stands, hangers, etc. The whole idea is to de-clutter and find room for your treasures to be easily found. Lastly, prepare a schedule, with time required to unclutter and names of helpers. Once done, prioritize areas on your list.

How much time should I invest in the task?

Fifteen minutes a day as a family project during the week is enough to keep you all engaged in the process. If it makes sense, half-days during the weekend would speed up the process. Once time is allocated to each task, identify the start and end date of the tasks at hand. Office de-cluttering can be done during lunch hours.

Breaking the uncluttering process into mini weekly projects is all you need to stay encouraged and move forward. Celebrate along the way as each mini-project is completed

How do I get started?

First, activate your *Green Thumb* app. Next, as noted on your schedule, start with one room and sort shelf-by-shelf, closet-by-closet, and drawer-by-drawer. The process is the same when it comes to de-cluttering your office space. Keep only items you really love and are necessary. You want to get rid of as much junk as possible. Pick up each item and ask yourself:

- Have I used this in the past year?
- Will I use this in the next year?

If the answer is yes, then keep it.
If the answer is no, then ask yourself:

- Do I really need this?
- Do I expect to use this in the next year or so?

If the answers to these two questions are no, either give the item away, put it in the garbage, or set it aside for a garage sale.

Have a look at how you use your space to best store items for easy access:

- Keep all your gardening tools together.
- Place your sports items on the same shelf.
- Place small items like screws or hair rollers in transparent plastic bags or containers on shelves to locate them easily.
- Put elastic bands around extension cords.
- Put all your books on a bookshelf.
- Use named folders to file your documents.

While obvious to some, you would be surprised at how many people do not have systems to store their belongings. You simplify your life when items are handy and easily accessible. Remember to not overload your storage space, and keep some empty space for future needs.

When you look at documents, keep important ones like birth, marriage, and death certificates, major suppliers and vaccination invoices, guaranties, loan and legal documents, insurance policies, will, investment statements, tax returns, and tax-related documents in a safe place, preferably in a fireproof box.

How can I avoid cluttering in the future?

Sit down with your family and get everyone to agree on solutions for a clean and tidy home. Without an agreement, you may end up having to soon de-clutter again. With your family on board, everyone de-clutters on a regular basis. Here are some ideas to share with your family:

- Have the children make their beds and throw dirty clothes in the laundry basket.
- Get everyone to leave dirty shoes at the door and hang coats in the closet.
- To simplify everyone's life, put items back where they belong.

To maintain a tidy office space, have a look at documents in your basket and new magazines once a week. File documents in relevant folders and classify magazines in a *To Read* pile, a *To Be Kept* pile or a *Throw Away* pile. If any are classified, ensure that you store them in approved secured filing cabinets.

If you find magazine articles you need to hold onto for future reference, place them in named folders for easy access. Work with your administrative assistant to de-clutter regularly if more convenient.

Whether you de-clutter your home or office, stay motivated and have fun at the tossing game. Your hard work will pay off, and your home and work area will smile right back at you and be much more inviting and inspiring.

Complete the Incompletes

Are you a member of the *Home Procrastination Club*? "I don't think so, what is this club?" you might answer. Well, you are a member of the club when willingness to complete the incompletes is present, but actions are invisible. Here are a few hints:

- You have decided to clean up your car every week, but two weeks later, your car still looks like a garbage bin with empty soft drink cans, old newspapers, dirty tissues, and candy wrapping on the floor.
- You have started the installation of a new hardwood floor in the basement, but a month later, it still looks like a construction site with new uninstalled floorboards in the middle of the room and piles of used materials all over your work area, just waiting to be dumped.
- You have decided to create a garden this year, but a few months later, all you're getting are weeds with some flowers blooming here and there.
- You say you would love to have a tidy home, but the vacuum cleaner has been safely hidden in a basement closet for two weeks.
- You started repainting a bedroom, but you keep finding excuses for not completing the project.

Simply put, you are a member of the *Home Procrastination Club* when you keep putting off your good intentions to make your home a clean and enjoyable place.

"Why do we procrastinate in the first place?" you might ask.

All sorts of reasons are behind procrastination. It may signal you aren't really serious in the first place about your intention, or you are not well-organized. It may mean you are not comfortable with the task at hand or prefer to spend time on more enjoyable tasks.

Perhaps it says you enjoy a little power trip over your spouse by setting aside a task that was asked of you. Whatever the reason behind your procrastination, know that you can triumph over this annoying habit.

Turn on your *Green Thumb* app and deactivate your membership to the *Home Procrastination Club.* Over time, by following this four-step method, you will put little feet under your willingness to change.

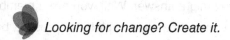 *Looking for change? Create it.*

Step 1: Resolve to Change – Change comes when you first recognize that you are a member of the *Home Procrastination Club.* Reflect as to why you enrolled in the club in the first place. With a better understanding of what causes your lack of motivation to move forward, you will be better equipped to succeed over procrastination.

Below is a table with the most common causes of procrastination. Write down on a card two reasons why you think deactivating your membership will make your life more enjoyable. If you do not see any benefits, change will not come to pass. Each time procrastination knocks at your door, read your card all over again and close the door.

Step 2: Get Going – Overcoming procrastination takes discipline and willingness. In the end, only you can spur yourself into action. To help you transform your powerful intentions into actions, you need an approach that addresses the root causes of your procrastination.

Some people simply need to set realistic goals and a proper plan of action broken down in mini-steps. Others are looking for more motivation, and a helping hand is the answer for gaining momentum. For some others, improving their skills and knowledge with books and instructional videos is the confidence booster that will move them into action.

If you are serious about crushing procrastination, take a look at the table below for practical strategies that address the most common causes of this bad habit.

Mastering Procrastination	
Causes	**Procrastination Stoppers**
You are not serious about your intentions.	■ Take time to reflect on what your goals are and why they are important to you. ■ Be smart and set goals that will move you to success. Unrealistic goals will set you up for failure. ■ Set a plan with realistic time frames, taking into account work and family considerations. ■ Tell a friend to whom you will be accountable.
You are disorganized.	■ Prepare a to-do list, breaking down all the tasks to be done. ■ Cross off completed tasks and reevaluate your plan regularly. ■ Do the activity with a friend who is well-organized and can give you tips to ease the task. ■ Read a book and speak with inspiring people to learn more about the task at hand.
You are not comfortable with the task at hand.	■ Talk to an expert. ■ Watch an instructional video. ■ Do the task with a friend from whom you can learn.
You prefer to spend time on more enjoyable tasks.	■ Break down the project into mini-tasks and limit your time on each one, knowing that soon there will be free time for more enjoyable activities. ■ Do the hardest tasks first while you are less tired. ■ Celebrate your mini-successes with a treat.
You have a little power trip.	■ Understand that you work as a team with your spouse. No one wins or loses; it's all about doing the right thing for the betterment of the family.

Step 3: Be Cautious of Procrastination Traps – Beware of procrastination traps. They are quite subtle, and the first thing you know, you are caught up in answering e-mails, calling a friend, talking to a neighbor, reading the newspaper, watching TV, or chatting on the Internet.

Set some time for such activities, but not all day, leaving you time to get going with home projects. By scheduling time for them as if they were important appointments, you will get nudged into action. Being accountable to a friend is a great deterrent to keep going and turn your projects into reality.

Step 4: Celebrate Your Successes – Get a motivation boost by taking a few minutes to look around and simply enjoy seeing your hard work. Reward yourself with a relaxing treat once you have completed a scheduled task. You will find pleasure in both the treat and the joy that comes with a completed task.

With *Green Thumb*, you will see that overcoming procrastination was not so difficult after all. It's all a matter of putting your mind into it and having a realistic approach that moves you to success.

Transform Your Home into a Heaven

Looking to transform your home into a little heaven? With your *Green Thumb* app well activated, you can turn your home into something you love, with rooms that show your personality and creativity. From bathroom to living room and bedrooms, you can use your own unique touch to give plenty of style to your refuge. Here are some tips you might want to pay attention to as you move ahead in your heavenly transformation.

First, ask yourself if you have a preference for a specific decorating style. Some may want to transform their home into a spa refuge. For others, the country or Cape Cod style is the way to go. Still others might be looking for a more conventional, contemporary, or modern look. With your décor style in mind, you can add the right colors, fabrics, piece of furniture, and accessories to each room to really accentuate your preferred style.

Home is a little piece of heaven you create.

Learn more about your favorite decorating style and look for ideas to guide you in your choices of fabrics, furniture lines, wall decorating, and colors for a more cohesive look. Wall painting is a wonderful tool to complement your furniture, bedspread, and curtains. Thus, it is best to start painting only when you have purchased these items. Bring fabric samples with you to help find the right paint color.

Whatever style you choose to go for, there is always potential to add something for a more relaxing touch. Houseplants bring life to your home, and they are touted to be air purifiers. If you travel a lot and can't care for your plants, then pick artificial plants. There is a great selection to choose from, and they sure can trick the eyes.

Add some scent around the house for a more homey feeling. Fill your bedroom with lavender for its calming and soothing effect, and you won't need to count sheep to fall asleep. Spicy aromas are fun in the kitchen. You can add a bowl of potpourri or a basil plant on the kitchen counter. Scented candles bring romance to the bedroom and tranquility in the living room as you are listening to music or reading your favorite book. Scented soap makes the morning shower more agreeable.

When it comes to your bedroom, make sure to suppress light as much as possible for a good night's sleep. Create tranquil moments before bedtime with dimmed lights or candles for more relaxation.

More and more people enjoy creating a Zen space in their home where they can retreat to for an hour or so to relax, listen to music, or simply read a book. Away from the family noise, you can create a heavenly place in your home. Some like to decorate their room with inspiring pictures and quotes. Others like to add candles, plush pillows, plants, or a plug-in tabletop water fountain. Choose whatever inspires you and leads to serenity.

When it comes to your living room, less furniture is better. You want space to move around easily and avoid a visual tornado effect. Family pictures and art pieces are great accessories to give your home a personal touch. Remember that the midline of your paintings should be approximately 60 inches from the floor. Add some nice lighting as a finishing touch.

Have fun creating your heavenly place. Let your creativity take the stage. After all, are you not the *Marvelous You*, a powerful creator? I can already hear you shout, "Hello, sweet home!" as you step foot in your house after a long day.

Save on Household Bills

With prices going up and salary increments being modest, many families are struggling to make ends meet. Managing a budget is more and more a headache. With *Green Thumb*, home economics is no longer a burden. One approach to trim your monthly spending is by lowering your household bills. Weaving these tips into your life is the analgesic you need for more peace of mind.

Utilities – The following are great energy savers that are part of my daily life and help keep my monthly utility bills down:

- Reduce heating while at work or sleeping. Just cuddle more and pull out a few more blankets for a good night's sleep.
- Do not heat the whole house when at home. Heat only the rooms you are most likely to go to. Keep the heat in by closing the doors.
- Turn off the lights when you leave a room, and use energy-efficient lighting.
- Wash your clothes in cold water. Not only are you saving on utility costs, but you also minimize the possibility of shrinking your clothes.
- In the morning, open the curtains to let the sun warm your house, and take shorter showers. This helps you save on both heat and water usage.
- Replace your appliances with energy saving ones that give you more efficiency options.
- No need to do the laundry every day. Wait for a full load.

- Operate the dishwasher only when fully loaded. Use the timer on your appliance and run it late at night when electricity rates are lower.
- Limit water usage by not watering your lawn every night.
- When the hot summer sun is beaming in, close the shades or blinds to keep your home cool and give a rest to your air conditioning.
- Do a home inspection and look for windows and doors that need new seals and areas that need additional insulation. Perhaps window replacement is a solution for more energy efficiency.

 Making more with less is called ingenuity.

Insurance – You want to slash your auto and home insurance costs? These tips may help you keep a few more dollars in your pocket:

- When you shop around, pay attention to a few factors before making a change. Inquire as to the company's reputation. Look for discounts being offered, impact on rates of past accidents, deductible amount, new policy fees, coverage offered for valuables, etc.
- Consider having your car and home insurance with the same provider for more savings.
- If you are a member of a professional organization, inquire about special discounts you may be entitled to for home and car insurance.
- Reevaluate your home insurance coverage if you discarded several items in the past year.
- Consider cancelling appliance and cell phone insurance when possible.

Cable, Internet and Phone – With so many cable and telephone company offerings, you need to really be clear on your needs and find the plans that best suit your lifestyle. Here are a few tips to lower your monthly bills:

- Bundle up your cable, Internet, and home phone services with one provider when possible.
- Decide what TV channels you are really going to watch. Premium channels and satellite packages can be costly.
- Go to the library to use the Internet if you are not a regular Internet user.
- Use Skype on the Internet for free conversations with anyone around the world who has the software.
- Get rid of phone features such as caller ID and call waiting. If urgent, you know the caller will call you back.
- With so many plans being offered, choosing the right cell phone plan is not easy. Look carefully at your needs in terms of long distance, Internet data (e-mail and web surfing), talk minutes, and texting. Make sure to buy a data roaming plan when you travel out of the country.
- Forego your home phone and use only your cell phone if this option results in more savings. Look carefully at both your plans and needs before making a final decision. If using strictly a cell phone is the answer, play it safe and use headsets when talking on the phone for long periods.

With a few changes in your lifestyle, you will surely create some breathing room in your budget, and managing your budget will no longer be such a tedious task.

Create an Inspiring Workspace

For many of us, our office is our second home, with a third of our weekdays spent working. A welcoming feeling in the morning really sets the tone for the day. Needless to say, an inspiring workspace where we feel comfortable positively impacts our productivity and creativity.

While you may not have a say about the office wall color and design, there are some areas where you can add your personal touch to transform your workspace into a more appealing and inspiring place. If your office feels lifeless, add some greens on your desk and shelves. Plants bring life in the workplace and create a homey feeling. Once in a while, buy yourself some fresh flowers. After all, you have worked hard and deserve a treat. Choose artificial plants and flowers if you find them more convenient.

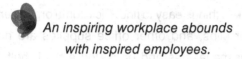

*An inspiring workplace abounds
with inspired employees.*

To revive your workplace, add some artwork on the wall and photographs on your desk. Display travel souvenirs that enhance good-feeling memories. Being surrounded by things you love ignites a sense of well-being. Remember to not overly clutter your space to keep it inspiring and appealing.

Pull your office shades up. Natural light is touted to have a positive effect on the brain and immune system. Sunlight exposure is associated with good feelings and positively influences your alertness, cognitive abilities, concentration, and performance.

In the absence of natural light in your office, ensure that you have ample, adequate lighting. Poor lighting can cause eyestrain, fatigue, and even headaches that will negatively impact your productivity. If needed, invest in a desk lamp and place it for minimum glare on your monitor to avoid squinting.

Sitting on a comfortable chair influences your productivity and creativity. With less muscle spasms and reduced back and neck problems, you can sustain your energy level throughout the day. An ergonomic chair is a great tool to reduce physical distress. Set the arm rest for your elbows to be at a 90 degree angle, with your lower arms at the height of your desk and your upper arms in the vertical position.

Adjust the chair height for your thighs to be parallel to the floor. Your feet should be flat on the floor. If needed, get a footstool. The back rest should be set to avoid slouching. A great way to keep your posture up is with lumbar support. If you don't have the luxury of an ergonomic chair, do your best to maintain good posture and add lumbar support and a footstool as needed.

Your monitor should generally be positioned for your eye level to be two to three inches below the top of the monitor, unless you are wearing bifocals or trifocals. In such cases, position your monitor a few inches lower. Keep your mouse and keyboard close together for less strain on your arms and shoulders.

A tidy place makes things easy to find. Pick some organizers for drawers where pens, paper clips, and other office supplies are neatly placed. You can store your magazines and books on a bookshelf. Unclassified documents that require action or are on hold can be placed on a desk tray while others can be filed in filing cabinets.

With these tips in mind, you will make wonders in creating a workspace for greater energy, creativity, and productivity. When you come in early in the morning, you will feel some pleasure in being in your office, likely thinking, *I enjoy being here, this place is inspiring, and I'll have a great day.*

Green your Life

With your *Green Thumb* app activated, you will happily green your life. Over time, you will become green-savvy. You will have a better understanding as to why your actions matter.

A small green action today is a significant contribution to tomorrow.

You have probably heard of the 3 R's of the environment – reduce, reuse, and recycle. Embracing them is a good start to adding more green to your life and making a difference in preserving the planet for a better tomorrow.

Go Green at Home – A green lifestyle at home is all about practicing the 3 R's and choosing chemical-free household products.

- Reduce – Use online banking and favor rechargeable batteries. Buy products in reusable containers or with little packaging to help in waste reduction. Use an all-purpose cleaner rather than different ones to reduce plastic containers. Choose toxic-free household products to not only preserve the environment but your family's health. Follow my simple energy and water saving tips noted in the section *Save on Household Bills.*

- Reuse – Reuse grocery bags, glass jars, plastic containers, paper boxes, and gift packaging. Donate goods like clothing, home accessories, and old cell phones. Build or buy a compost bin that transforms some waste items into garden and grass enhancer.

- Recycle – Recycle glass, newspaper, plastic bottles, soft drink cans, wire hangers, paper, cardboard, food and paint cans, and foil packaging to reduce the amount of waste sent to landfills. Buy a water filter and drink tap water rather than drinking bottled water. Glass and plastic bottles take years to decompose.

Go Green at Work – Embracing green at the office can easily be done by adopting these green measures:

- Reduce – Make use of technology to file your documents to help in paper reduction. Review draft reports online and print final reports on both sides to reduce paper consumption. Download software from the Internet rather than buying a compact disc. Turn off the lights and shut down your computer and printer at night. Green the employee kitchen by providing mugs instead of disposable cups and towels. Encourage the use of cloth towels rather than paper towels. Offer filtered water to reduce bottled water consumption. Provide air dryers in the restroom.

- Reuse – Donate old furniture, obsolete computers, and printers to schools, senior's organizations, and non-profit organizations that provide technology to underprivileged people around the world.

- Recycle – Make recycling easy by placing bins in convenient locations to collect paper products, plastic, cans, and glass. Place shredder bins near printers or photocopiers for future recycling.

Collect rechargeable batteries, newspapers, and business magazines for recycling.

Go Green in the Community – By following these actions, you will bring more green into your community:

- Reduce – Commute to work, walk, or cycle to reduce carbon dioxide emissions, thus slowing global warming. Plant a tree to create oxygen and absorb carbon dioxide in the environment. Buy local products to help in reducing greenhouse gas created by transporting goods.
- Reuse – Reduce waste by using reusable bags and less paper napkins when dining on take-out food.
- Share – Share green tips with your neighbors and friends and support green initiatives in your community.

With your *Green Thumb* app activated, taking action to live green will be fun and easy. Start today and make an impact! Mother earth will thank you for caring and preserving the environment.

CHAPTER 14

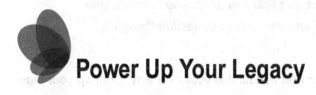

Power Up Your Legacy

Let your legacy be a song that others
will sing forever.

Live with Soulful Purpose and Passion

While you may not be clear on what comes after life, one thing is sure, you are here today, and your presence does matter. You are here to affirm all that you are, and your contribution to this world is totally unique. No one else sees the world with your eyes. No one else smells the roses with your nose. No one else sings like you do. No one else hears the thunder with your ears. No one else feels the wind like you do.

Being from God and in God, your life has great meaning to Him. You are an expression of His life, beauty, grace, and love. He is alive through you and co-creates with you. He wants nothing less than for your life to be a great adventure with meaning and value for yourself, those around you, and those that will come after you.

Your legacy is the footprint you leave behind at the end of your life's journey. You have this amazing potential to create a beautiful legacy of purpose, love, and excellence, and to be remembered forever by your family, friends, colleagues, and many others who have known you or were inspired by your life.

Legacy is not just about material possessions. Central to creating your legacy is living life to the fullest and pursuing your aspirations. You don't want to wake up one day and have regrets for not having followed your hopes and aspirations. You don't want to have to sadly say, "I did not live the life I wanted to. I did not do what I wanted to do. I was too afraid to fail, and I gave up on my dreams."

Create a legacy of purpose and passion. Follow your heart, put little feet under your desires, and feed your mind with good-feeling thoughts.

You are awesome and beautiful in your own way. Light up your inner fire today with a simple thought. Live with a purpose that ignites your passion and drive. Show the world that you are the *Marvelous You*, and let your life shine in the universe forever.

Activate your *True Inspiration* app and listen to the still, small voice of your heart where your aspirations are waiting to come alive. Reflect on your gifts and talents. Reflect on what you want to be remembered for. What does your heart say? What excites you? What ignites passion within you? What is meaningful to you?

Let yourself be guided by your intuition and inspiration. Let your life make a difference in this world. Listen to what your heart is whispering. Once you have found what makes you happy, you will live with a purpose that moves you, and you will find great life satisfaction.

There is divinity in each one of us, with no purpose in life greater than another. There are simply different purposes, with each one as important as another. It is through diversity that the universe finds harmony and wholeness. What matters is to follow your heart and your direction. Direct your energies to what you enjoy doing, not to what others are telling you to do.

Desires with no little feet will get you nowhere. Simply drifting along will not bring excitement, passion, and success into your life. Activate your *Be Happy* app and feed your mind with good-feeling thoughts. Achieve your goals one step at a time with a positive attitude, and you will progress with less effort.

A bad day today is not the premise for a bad one tomorrow. Keep your *Dynamo* app activated and maintain control over your negative emotions. By celebrating your small victories and expressing gratitude daily, you make the journey much more enjoyable and keep the excitement alive.

When you live your truth, you make your greatest contribution, the gift of all that you are. As you live your life with purpose and passion, you will be remembered for your strength, perseverance, drive, and will. You will be a drop in the ocean of life that makes a difference.

Create an Awe-Inspiring Legacy

No dream is ever too big. No dream is impossible. With every desire that is in your heart comes the drive and the will to bring it to light. Activate your *High Drive* app and craft a plan to pursue your aspirations. Be daring! Dare to try! Dare to succeed! Success comes when you believe your best days are ahead of you, not behind you. Believing in the goodness of tomorrow gives you the power and momentum to create an awe-inspiring legacy.

You are gifted with talents, skills, and capacities to make a great contribution to this world. You alone hold the key that unlocks your full potential. You are born to evolve and become all that you can be. To ignore your calling to live to the fullest is to say no to life and yes to the death of your soul.

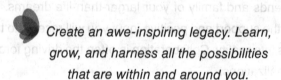

Create an awe-inspiring legacy. Learn, grow, and harness all the possibilities that are within and around you.

Why would you limit yourself? Live to know all that you can be and do. Learn something new, try something new. Each new step allows you to expand. With each victory comes more confidence. Activate your *Dynamo* app and crush the fear of failure and not being good enough. Fear is a lie of your mind. Guess what? Stop listening to those lies. You are not fear; you are the *Marvelous You*, fearless, and peaceful. Get out there and show the world what you are capable of doing.

Let living to your full potential be part of your legacy. Dare to expand and be more than what you are today. If you miss the mark and get hurt, then learn from the experience and try again. Most successful people and great leaders have stories of trials and tribulations, and they all share the same determination, courage, and resilience to pursue their desires.

You are born to be a success and a great leader. Affirm your *Marvelous Essence*; be resilient and courageous. Be willing to take a risk and embrace the unknown. Ask yourself: What did I learn from this? What can I do better next time? Be remembered as a conqueror who was willing to learn and overcame fears and mistakes.

Embrace challenges. Don't just give up in the face of glitches. Be patient with yourself and others. Obstacles are nothing more than opportunities for growth. Turn on your *True Inspiration* app and let solutions be revealed. If you want to create an awe-inspiring legacy, stay on course day after day. Pause momentarily to deal with the obstacles, and then move ahead. Simply put, stand strong, and keep a positive attitude.

Activate your *Go Getter* and *Fly High* apps and move forward with assertive actions to turn your professional aspirations into reality. Pursue your dreams tirelessly. Don't be afraid to knock on doors and get help. Let your passion, inspiration, and excitement transform the impossible into the possible.

Tell your friends and family of your larger-than-life dreams. You may be surprised at the support and positive input you will receive to transform your aspirations into reality. Collaboration is often the driving force behind awe-inspiring realizations.

You are living in your comfort zone right now, but deep down you want change? It's never too late to turn your life around. Forget the excuses and dare to get going. Doors are to be opened, not stared at. Be bold; open the door.

Who knows? You may find something really great waiting for you on the other side of the door. It is only through willingness to expand that you discover your full potential. By taking small steps, you will get to your destination. You will feel alive and be proud of yourself.

See each day as an opportunity to grow. What you do today brings into the universe something that wasn't there yesterday. Be remembered for the beauty your life has brought to the world.

Let Wisdom Be Your Signature

You are the *Marvelous You*, connected to All-That-Is, Infinite Wisdom. With your *Be Happy* app activated, your attitude is one that manifests joyful wisdom, a treasure present in you that comes to light while listening, inquiring, learning, growing, and seeing life's beauty.

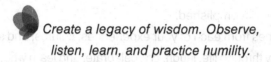

Create a legacy of wisdom. Observe,
listen, learn, and practice humility.

Listen to Your Inner Voice – Wisdom comes when you pause and listen to your inner voice, letting Infinite Consciousness flow within your heart and guide you while you journey through life. In nourishing your connection to God, you are attuned to His voice, not strictly acting on your own knowledge and judgment.

Question Life – Wisdom stems from questioning life, nudging you to find its true meaning. As you create your legacy of wisdom, reflect on the beauties and wonders of life. Reflect on how you have grown and what you have learned over the years. Reflect on where you are and the direction you want to take.

Pause, listen, and look within and around you. What do you hear? What do you see? How do you feel? Don't be afraid to ask yourself some hard questions: What is my life purpose? What can I do to make my life better? Why do I do the things I do? Through your own reflection, you will find who you are and where you are at this point in your life. When you pray and meditate on your life, you find the truths of life hidden in the depth of your higher conscious mind.

Learn – Wisdom comes when you reckon you know so little and there is always more to learn. Read inspirational books and fill your mind with wisdom shared by others. Be receptive to what your friends, family, colleagues, coach, and mentors have to say.

Keep an open mind and learn from those around you. Be wise enough to follow the path of great teachers of wisdom. While you journey in their footsteps, you travel with more ease, as they have opened the way for you.

Grow More – Wisdom comes when you accept that you are a work in progress. You are a beautiful being in the making. Love yourself, with all your strengths and weaknesses. Know what you like and do not like. Be willing to learn and grow. Strive for excellence, not perfection. Give yourself and others some room to explore and make mistakes. Celebrate all that you are and have accomplished.

Wisdom comes from each of your experiences, failures, and successes. While you journey through life, laugh, cry, celebrate, and learn what works and what doesn't. Gaining wisdom means recognizing you know little and there is always more to learn. If you fall, get up and find something positive to learn from the situation. More patience, more compassion, more courage perhaps? Be open to new or different ideas. Change is good, it enriches your life.

See Life's Beauty – With wisdom comes the ability to see the beauty in each moment and each person. It also shows up with a few wrinkles on your face. Aging is a gift of life that makes the next day much easier, as it does bring experience and acumen. Through each moment you observe, learn, and gain greater insights. As time goes by, you better understand life and know what to focus on and overlook. You are better equipped to journey, with less suffering and more inner joyousness.

As you progress in wisdom, share your insights with others. You will be a source of inspiration to someone else in need of a response.

Cultivate Self-Love

You are the *Marvelous You*, an extension of Infinite Love. With your *Love Power* app, not only do you have this capacity to radiate love to others, but you practice self-love. You say, "I am unique, and no one else is like me. I am a beautiful human being, worthy of love, and especially worthy of *my* love."

Being a creature of love, you have been longing for love from the moment you were born. As a child, you longed for the love of your mother and father. As an adolescent, you strove to be accepted by your peers and sports team players. As you mature, your need of belongingness is reflected in your relationships with your friends, family, and colleagues. Loving and being loved makes you feel alive, and both bring forth a sense of belonging and safety.

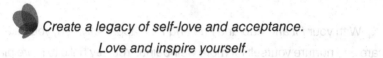

Create a legacy of self-love and acceptance.
Love and inspire yourself.

Unfortunately, your desire for being loved by others may lead you to forget to practice self-love. You may endure verbal or physical abuse for fear of being alone. You may not say what you really think or how you feel for fear of not being loved. You may constantly seek the approval of others for fear of being rejected. You may sabotage your success, thinking you are not worthy or good enough.

As a being of love, you deserve to cultivate self-love and let it be a part of your legacy. Loving yourself is honoring all that you are, with your body, soul, and spirit. In doing so, you are telling the world that you are a beautiful and worthy human being. Let me remind you of the true definitions of self-love:

- Self-love is seeing yourself through the eyes of God. It is knowing that you are worthy to live, create, and have a voice.
- Self-love is a celebration of yourself and your life.
- Self-love is unconditional acceptance of all that you are, with your strengths, weaknesses, and physical traits you love, and those you try to hide.
- Self-love is not letting yourself be drowned by negative comments.
- Self-love is supporting yourself when someone else is not, whether that someone is a colleague, your spouse, a family member, or a supposed friend.
- Self-love is honoring your aspirations and trusting in your own judgment and intuition.

- Self-love is the force that makes you say no to verbal and physical abuse.
- Self-love is embracing each of your life's experiences, the good and not so good, knowing that you are a work in progress.
- Self-love is taking care of yourself day in and day out and bringing more fitness, vigor, and well-being into your life.

With your *Fit and Fab* and *Fun and Play* apps activated, you take time to care and nurture yourself for more well-being. You say hello to more playtime, relaxation, and quietness that energize your body and ease your mind.

Do you still feel uncomfortable or unworthy of self-love? Reflect on what self-love is all about and give yourself a hug today. Shower yourself with the love and affection you deserve, and let your life be a celebration of all that you are.

Be a Light of Love and Gratitude

Love is the greatest legacy of all, as it nourishes the soul of those who receive it. It gives life and warmth, and it comes with beautiful moments that live on in our hearts forever. Those we remember and continue to celebrate are those who have touched our hearts with their love.

Think for a moment of Mother Teresa's gift of her life to the poorest of the poor, Martin Luther King's gift of love for African-Americans, and Nelson Mandela's gift of hope. Our hearts continue to celebrate and be inspired by their lives. There are no riches as deep as love.

Create a legacy of love and gratitude.
Cultivate goodness and forgiveness.
Let the past go to enjoy the present.

When you express love and kindness, you animate the divine force that is in you. A legacy of love develops with each of your smiles, uplifting words, and kind acts of love. Love is a helping hand. Love is taking time out of your schedule for someone in need. Love is a call to say I love you. Love is a little surprise to cheer someone. Love is listening. Love is being open to the ideas of others. Love is being patient. Love is respecting others. Love is giving back with a smiling heart. Love is supporting others in their efforts to become all that they can be.

A legacy of love means respecting differences. Diversity is what makes us stronger. It enriches our lives and expands our view of the world. Being respectful does not mean you agree, it means you allow others to be.

Relationships are precious. They are a gift to be cared for with loyalty, kind words, understanding, and compassion. Don't be shy to thank and compliment someone. You have no idea how words of wisdom and kindness can work wonders in someone else's existence. You may alleviate their burdens and light a spark of hope and encouragement in their life.

Gratitude is an expression of love. It's a thank you note to God and life. Just as you appreciate receiving thank you notes, God does, too. There are so many things and people to be grateful for in your life: your family, job, health, pets, teachers, coaches, mentors, seasons, good food, flowers, movies, taking a walk, traveling, and the list goes on and on.

As you create your legacy of love, activate your *Love Power* app. Take time each day to reflect on your life, and fill your heart with love and gratefulness for all that you are and have.

Extending gratitude for all situations, good or bad, will help you rise above issues with more ease. Disappointments will bear less pain. As you grasp the significance of your true nature, you radiate your light of love and gratitude to others. You let it shine forever in the hearts of those you have touched over the years.

Stay away from anger, sarcasm, and oppressive power; they are love's poisons. They are the agents that extinguish the flames of love. They are the clips that take the power out of your wings.

Create a legacy of beautiful memories, wisely spoken words, kind actions, and genuine love that continue to live forever. You will always be cherished for your contribution to making this world a better place to live, and your life will be a great source of inspiration.

Let Your Riches Live On

With your *Financial Tycoon* app turned on, you have worked hard to create wealth and share it with those around you. A well-thought-out estate plan helps you preserve your wealth to later pass it on to your loved ones with tax efficiency and minimum hurdles as per your wishes.

Estate planning involves, amongst other things, preparing a power of attorney and will, naming your beneficiaries and executor, choosing a guardian for minor children, naming beneficiaries of retirement plans, taking advantage of all tax measures, creating trusts if warranted, reviewing insurance policies to secure your family's future, making funeral arrangements, and putting all your documents in order. Let's have a closer look at these aspects.

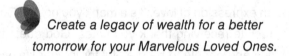

Create a legacy of wealth for a better tomorrow for your Marvelous Loved Ones.

Power of Attorney and Will – A power of attorney is a legal document that enables another person to take care of your affairs on your behalf in the event you become incapacitated. You can choose from either a limited power of attorney or a full one.

A will lets you decide how your wealth will be managed and distributed. Essentially, you get to choose your executor, heirs, and asset allocation. You select a guardian for your young children and document your bequest decisions. As measures may vary from one country to another, it is best to consult an estate professional to fully understand the requirements for a valid will.

Conditions for a valid will may include being executed with sound intent and capacity, created without fraud, drug influence, undue pressure, and mistake, and be formally documented and signed by both the testator and a witness. Someone with no valid will may be subject to the laws of distribution in their residential area. This measure emphasizes the importance of creating a valid will.

For greater tax-efficiency, consult an estate planning expert with tax expertise who can help you develop your will, and best advise you on estate planning to minimize the taxes to be collected on the transfer of your assets to your loved ones.

Prior to the visit, have a list of your assets and liabilities handy. Write down the location of your assets, as they may be subject to a foreign country's estate tax. If you are the owner of an incorporated business, don't overlook adding the company's shares on your asset list. If self-employed, prepare a list of your business assets and liabilities.

Don't be shy about sharing your objectives. With a better understanding of your intentions, the estate planning expert will guide you on an estate structure that takes advantage of current tax measures for more wealth to be distributed to your spouse, children, and other heirs. If you are in a position to distribute part of your wealth while alive, you may wish to donate to charities or make tax-free gifts to family members or political organizations, subject to related tax considerations. Joint custody of assets is another option to consider.

I encourage you to have a lawyer or notary draft your will and have it reviewed by your estate planning expert for consistency with your wishes. As measures may vary from one country to another, inquire if getting married or divorced revokes your current will. In such an instance, you will need to prepare a new one.

Family Trust – To preserve your wealth, you may establish a family trust, which is a legal document that allows the transfer of ownership of certain assets under the control of a trustee for the benefit of trust beneficiaries. The trust document details how and when assets are to be distributed to beneficiaries. You have two options to choose from: a living trust, which is one set up during your lifetime, and a testamentary trust, which is prescribed in your will.

There are legal costs associated with setting up a trust, and possibly recurring trustee management fees and other administration costs. It is best to consult with an estate planning professional who can determine whether or not a trust would provide tax advantages, and in the affirmative, what would be the best structure.

Insurance – Review your life insurance policies to help ensure that sufficient funds are available to safeguard the financial stability of your spouse and children. If you have underage children, you need to think of a guardian upon the death of both you and your spouse. It's a good idea to plan funeral arrangements well in advance to ensure that your wishes are followed.

Estate Documentation – To facilitate an orderly estate process, I encourage you to inform your will executor of the location of the estate-related documents noted below to facilitate the work at hand. As said, keep important documents like your will, birth and marriage certificates, loan documents, insurance policies, investment statements, and tax returns in a safe place, preferably in a fireproof box.

Estate-Related Documents	
• Will and power of attorney	• Loan agreements
• List of assets and liabilities	• Mortgage documents
• Birth and marriage certificates	• Past income tax returns
• Marriage contract	• Children's guardians (names and addresses)
• Safety box	• Pre-planned funeral arrangements
• Insurance policies	• Name of estate planning professional
• Retirement plan documents	• Names of notary, investment advisor, and lawyer
• Investment statements	• Name of accountant or auditor
• Real estate deeds	• Business-related documents
• Trust documents	• Social media accounts and passwords for account closing

Don't forget that creating a better tomorrow for your family is an act of love. So put your heart into it!

Care for Future Generations

Caring for tomorrow is an expression of love towards the universe, your children, your community, your country, and generations to come. It is conscious awareness that what you do today lives on, and that your thoughts and actions make a difference. It is the understanding that planet earth is not yours, and you are simply a visitor for a brief time.

You have the freedom to choose what tomorrow will be. What will you choose? What do you want to be remembered as? My wish is for you to be known as someone who contributed in making this world a better place to live, not someone who lived carefree and left it to future generations to fix issues.

 Create a legacy of care for tomorrow. Be a giver, not a taker. Sow good seeds for future generations to reap the benefits.

It is your responsibility to use planet earth wisely and care for air, land, water, human life, and all land and marine species. Caring for tomorrow extends not only to your children and grandchildren, but to all those to come. Caring about future generations means setting aside your personal needs for the greater good. It's all about those daily green gestures that will make a difference in future people's lives.

And why would you do this? Because you wish future generations to see with their own eyes the beauty that is around you: the flowers, plants, wilderness, mountains, lakes, rivers, and oceans. Your desire is for them to have access to non-contaminated water and air. You want them to have financial resources to live their best lives and not be crushed by debts. You hope they live in a peaceful environment where respect and equality prevail. You want them to say that life on earth is a great experience, challenging but all worthwhile. Simply put, you wish for them that they value life as much as you do, and that in turn they will preserve Mother Earth.

The Greek philosopher Plato once said: "The measure of a man is what he does with his power." It was true then, and even truer today. If you are a government leader, not only do you have an obligation to make decisions for the betterment and protection of your country and its people, but you are responsible to take measures that will benefit future generations. As a government leader, you are responsible to educate people, and support values and initiatives that will increase their well-being and the happiness of those to come. Being a true leader is all about having a positive influence for the benefit of all. As you create your legacy, activate your *Green Thumb* app and care for tomorrow. Your role today is to increase the ability of future generations to live in peace and sustain their existence, physically, and financially. This is the essence of a great leader who will be remembered for generations to come.

Let Your Faith Shine

Faith is a celebration of life, of who you are, a powerful creator connected to other human beings and God. Faith is a gift that you receive upon birth; it's an amazing force that lives in you. With *Higher Power* activated, you simply open this gift. Through expanded consciousness, let faith in yourself, in others, in tomorrow, and in the impossible evolve and grow.

> *Create a legacy of faith. Believe in yourself. Believe in others. Believe in tomorrow. Believe in All-That-Is.*

Faith in Yourself – Faith in yourself is an expression of self-love. It means you have captured the beauty of all that you are with your unique talents, capabilities, and potential. You are a wondrous being born to achieve your aspirations with your body, soul, and spirit. Not only do you have freedom to choose who you want to be and where you want to be, but you are fully equipped with faith to move forward to your destination.

Faith in Others – Faith in others denotes that you trust in the kindness and goodness of people, and your heart is open to forgive their mishaps.

Just as you cultivate self-love, you recognize the same beauty in others. You see others as pure potential who, just like you, experience life with its good and not-so-good moments.

Faith in Tomorrow – Faith in tomorrow is an expression of hope. It says to the world that you do not quit in the face of adversity. You lost your job? Your dream of promotion has been crushed? Your heart well-anchored in faith, you stand firm. Faith in tomorrow keeps you walking, knowing there is light at the end of the tunnel. It keeps your heart hopeful for a better tomorrow as you go through life's dark moments. It makes you see each experience as an opportunity for personal growth and new awareness.

Faith in All-That-Is – Faith in All-That-Is conveys your hope that God has the ultimate power to turn the impossible to possible. It keeps your heart at peace when the storm hits, knowing that He will calm the sea in due time. It crushes heaviness in your heart and replaces it with inner joyousness, calmness, and gratitude. It keeps your lips praising His greatness. It whispers in your ears that you belong to a higher purpose, even though your human consciousness cannot grasp it all at this time.

You can boldly say, "I trust in the power of God and I am no longer afraid of tomorrow. Together, we can bring to life the seeds of greatness that He has placed in me. I know He has the power to align people and events for the realization of my *Marvelous Nature*."

As you journey through life, let your faith shine and be a source of inspiration to others. Not only will faith change your world, but it will change the world. When you will close your eyes to this life, you won't be shy to hold your *Marvelous You Award* for all your stellar accomplishments, small and grand, and for how much you've learned and grown, the love you've shared, the fears you've conquered, the courage you've shown, the riches you've created, the wisdom you've gained, and most importantly, the faith that has driven your life.

Have an amazing life, *MARVELOUS YOU*!

Notes

Chapter 1: Turn On the Power

1. Wikipedia. "Tripartite (Theology)." Accessed December 17, 2013.
   http://en.wikipedia.org/wiki/Tripartite_(theology)
   Wikipedia. "Soul." Accessed December 17, 2013.
   http://en.wikipedia.org/wiki/Soul

2. Wikipedia. "Bipartite (Theology)." Accessed December 17, 2013.
   http://en.wikipedia.org/wiki/Bipartite_(theology)

3. Wikipedia. "Sigmund Freud." Accessed December 17, 2013. http://en.wikipedia.org/
   wiki/Sigmund_Freud
   Wikipedia. "Consciousness." Accessed December 17, 2013. http://en.wikipedia.org/
   wiki/Consciousness
   Wikipedia. "Preconscious." Accessed December 17, 2013. http://en.wikipedia.org/
   wiki/Preconscious
   Wikipedia. "Unconscious Mind." Accessed December 17, 2013. http://en.wikipedia.
   org/wiki/Unconscious_mind

4. Wikipedia. "Sigmund Freud." Accessed December 17, 2013. http://en.wikipedia.org/
   wiki/Sigmund_Freud

5. Tad James. *Lost Secrets of Ancient Hawaiian Huna.* Honolulu: Enlightened
   Spirituality, 1997.

6. Wikipedia. "Subconscious." Accessed December 17, 2013.
   http://en.wikipedia.org/wiki/Subconscious

7. Psych-K ®. "The Psychology and Spirituality of Personal Change." Accessed
   November 18, 2014.
   http://yearning4learning.co.uk/psych-k/

8. Alan Boyle, Science Editor. "Mind Meld? Scientist Uses His Brain to Control Another
   Guy's Finger." *NBC News,* August 2013. Accessed December 19, 2013.
   http://www.nbcnews.com/science/science-news/
   mind-meld-scientist-uses-his-brain-control-another-guys-finger-f8C11015078

9. Craig Weiler. "Telepathy Has Been Scientifically Proven to Be Real." *The Weiler Psi,*
   December 2012. Accessed December 19, 2013.
   http://weilerpsiblog.wordpress.com/2012/12/14/
   telepathy-has-been-scientifically-proven-to-be-real/
   Wikipedia. "Telepathy." Accessed December 19, 2013.
   http://en.wikipedia.org/wiki/Telepathy

10. Wikipedia. "Neuroimaging." Accessed December 19, 2013. http://en.wikipedia.org/wiki/Neuroimaging
   Wikipedia. "Functional Magnetic Resonance Imaging." Accessed December 19, 2013. http://en.wikipedia.org/wiki/Functional_magnetic_resonance_imaging

11. Wikipedia. "Electroencephalography." Accessed December 19, 2013. http://en.wikipedia.org/wiki/Electroencephalography

12. Wikipedia. "Gama Wave." Accessed December 19, 2013. http://en.wikipedia.org/wiki/Gamma_wave
   Wikipedia. "Beta Wave." Accessed December 19, 2013. http://en.wikipedia.org/wiki/Beta_wave
   Wikipedia. "Alpha Wave." Accessed December 19, 2013. http://en.wikipedia.org/wiki/Alpha_wave
   Wikipedia. "Theta Wave." Accessed December 19, 2013. http://en.wikipedia.org/wiki/Theta_rhythm
   Wikipedia. "Delta Wave." Accessed December 19, 2013. http://en.wikipedia.org/wiki/Delta_wave

13. Hyperphysics. "The SQUID Magnetometer and Josephson Junctions." Accessed December 19, 2013.
   http://hyperphysics.phy-astr.gsu.edu/hbase/solids/squid.html
   Wikipedia. "Electrocardiogram." Accessed December 19, 2013.
   http://simple.wikipedia.org/wiki/Electrocardiogram

14. Dr. Korotkov's Lab. "Biofield Research." Accessed December 19, 2013.
   http://www.korotkov.eu/dr-konstantin-g-korotkov/

15. Wikipedia. "Brain." Accessed December 23, 2013.
   http://en.wikipedia.org/wiki/Brain
   Wikipedia. "Mind." Accessed December 23, 2013.
   http://en.wikipedia.org/wiki/Mind
   Philippa Norman, "Healthy Brain for Life." Accessed December 2, 2014.
   http://www.healthybrainforlife.com/articles/about-the-brain/about-your-brain

16. Dr. Korotkov's Lab. "Biofield Research." Accessed December 19, 2013.
   http://www.korotkov.eu/dr-konstantin-g-korotkov/
   Healthy.net. "Energy Medicine." Accessed December 2, 2014.
   http://www.healthy.net/scr/therapy.aspx?Thid=9

17. Wikipedia. "Happiness." Accessed December 23, 2013.
   http://en.wikipedia.org/wiki/Happiness

18. PsiTek. "Creative Visualization. Your Mind Can Keep You Well." Accessed November 18, 2014.
   http://www.psitek.net/pages/PsiTek-creative-visualization12.html#gsc.tab=0

19. Goalop. "On Wayne Rooney and Free Throws: Visualization in Sports." June 2012. Accessed December 23, 2013.
   https://goalop.wordpress.com/2012/06/13/visualize-your-sports/

20. Wikipedia. "Biometrics." Accessed December 2, 2014.
   http://en.wikipedia.org/wiki/Biometrics

Chapter 2: Power Up Your Thoughts

1. Wikipedia. "." Accessed January 2, 2014. http://en.wikipedia.org/wiki/Isaac_Newton
2. Wikipedia. "Archimedes." Accessed January 2, 2014. http://en.wikipedia.org/wiki/Archimedes
3. Wikipedia. "Dreams." Accessed January 2, 2014. http://en.wikipedia.org/wiki/Dream
4. S. Stawski et al. "Jack Welsh and the Motivation of General Electric." University of Chicago Graduate School of Business. Accessed November 28, 2014. http://www.sstawski.com/download/GE.pdf
    ECoach. "Stretch Goals, Achieve Impossible." Accessed December 4, 2014. http://www.1000ventures.com/business_guide/goals_stretch.html
5. Wikipedia. "Subliminal Stimuli." Accessed January 10, 2014. http://en.wikipedia.org/wiki/Subliminal_stimuli
    History. "The Roots of Subliminal Perception." Accessed November 19, 2014. http://www.umich.edu/~onebook/pages/tablepages/history.html
6. Wikipedia. "Self-Hypnosis." Accessed January 13, 2014. http://en.wikipedia.org/wiki/Self-hypnosis
    Wikipedia. "Hypnosis." Accessed January 13, 2014. http://en.wikipedia.org/wiki/Hypnosis
7. Wikipedia. "Hypnosis." Accessed January 13, 2014. http://en.wikipedia.org/wiki/Hypnosis
8. Wikipedia. "Ultimate Fate of the Universe." Accessed January 17, 2014. http://en.wikipedia.org/wiki/Ultimate_fate_of_the_universe

Chapter 3: Power Up Your Strategy

1. Dr. Gail Matthews, PhD. "Goal Research Summary." Dominican University of California. Accessed January 20, 2014. http://www.dominican.edu/academics/ahss/undergraduate-programs-1/psych/faculty/fulltime/gailmatthews/researchsummary2.pdf

Chapter 4: Power Up Your Emotions

1. Wikipedia. "Emotional Freedom Techniques." Accessed February 10, 2014. http://en.wikipedia.org/wiki/Emotional_Freedom_Techniques
    Wikipedia. "Nick Ortner." Accessed February 10, 2014. http://en.wikipedia.org/wiki/Nick_Ortner
2. Wikipedia. "Anxiety Disorder." Accessed February 19, 2014. http://en.wikipedia.org/wiki/Anxiety_disorder
    Wikipedia. "Social Anxiety." Accessed February 19, 2014.

http://en.wikipedia.org/wiki/Social_anxiety

Wikipedia. "Obsessive-Compulsive Disorder." Accessed February 19, 2014. http://en.wikipedia.org/wiki/Obsessive%E2%80%93compulsive_disorder

Wikipedia. "Posttraumatic Stress Disorder." Accessed February 19, 2014. http://en.wikipedia.org/wiki/Posttraumatic_stress_disorder

Wikipedia. "Social Anxiety Disorder." Accessed February 19, 2014. http://en.wikipedia.org/wiki/Separation_anxiety_disorder

3.   Wikipedia. "Anxiety Disorder." Accessed February 20, 2014. http://en.wikipedia.org/wiki/Anxiety_disorder

Wikipedia. "Psychodynamics." Accessed February 20, 2014. http://en.wikipedia.org/wiki/Psychodynamics

Wikipedia. "Cognitive Behavioral Therapy." Accessed February 20, 2014. http://en.wikipedia.org/wiki/Cognitive_behavioral_therapy

Wikipedia. "Interpersonal Psychotherapy." Accessed February 20, 2014. http://en.wikipedia.org/wiki/Interpersonal_psychotherapy

4.   Wikipedia. "Depression." Accessed February 21, 2014. http://en.wikipedia.org/wiki/Depression_(mood)

Chapter 5: Power up Your Faith

1.   Wikipedia. "Universe." Accessed April 7, 2014.
http://en.wikipedia.org/wiki/Universe

2.   Wikipedia. "Near-Death Experience." Accessed April 8, 2014. http://en.wikipedia.org/wiki/Near-death_experience

Wikipedia. "Sleep Paralysis." Accessed April 8, 2014. http://en.wikipedia.org/wiki/Sleep_paralysis

Wikipedia. "Rapid Eye Movement Sleep." Accessed April 8, 2014. http://en.wikipedia.org/wiki/Rapid_eye_movement_sleep

Amy Wilson. "Scientific Light Put on Near-Death Experiences." *Kentucky.com*, January 2011. Accessed April 8, 2014.
http://www.kentucky.com/2011/01/01/1584036/university-of-kentucky-neurologist.html

3.   Wikipedia. "Brain Stem Death." Accessed April 8, 2014. http://en.wikipedia.org/wiki/Brain_stem_death

BBC News. "Near Death has Biological Basis." April 2006. Accessed April 8, 2014. http://news.bbc.co.uk/2/hi/health/4898726.stm

Wikipedia. "Rapid Eye Movement Sleep." Accessed April 8, 2014. http://en.wikipedia.org/wiki/Rapid_eye_movement_sleep

4.   Wikipedia. "Near-Death Experience." Accessed April 8, 2014. http://en.wikipedia.org/wiki/Near-death_experience

5.   Wikipedia. "Out-of-Body Experience." Accessed April 8, 2014.
http://en.wikipedia.org/wiki/Out-of-body_experience

Chapter 7: Power up Your Health

1. U. S. Department of Agriculture and U.S. Department of Health and Human Services. *Dietary Guidelines for American, 2010.* 7th edition. Washington, DC: U.S. Government Printing Office, December 2010. Accessed May 5, 2014. www.dietaryguidelines.gov

2. Wikipedia. "Vitamin." Accessed May 6, 2014. http://en.wikipedia.org/wiki/Vitamin

3. Tanya Brown. "List of Dark Green Leafy Vegetables." Healthy Eating. Accessed November 21, 2014.
http://healthyeating.sfgate.com/list-dark-green-leafy-vegetables-1647.html

4. Michael Ash. "Low Fat Milk – Too Much Too Often – No Evidence of Benefit." *Clinical Education,* August 2013. Accessed May 6, 2014.
http://www.nleducation.co.uk/resources/abstracts/
low-fat-milk-too-much-too-often-no-evidence-of-benefit/
Wikipedia. "Walter Willett." Accessed May 6, 2014.
http://en.wikipedia.org/wiki/Walter_Willett
Eat and Beat Cancer. "Anti-Cancer Diets: What's the Deal with Dairy?" July 2014. Accessed November 21, 2014.
https://eatandbeatcancer.wordpress.com/2014/07/23/
anti-cancer-diets-whats-the-deal-with-dairy/

5. Wikipedia. "Protein." Accessed May 6, 2014.
http://en.wikipedia.org/wiki/Protein
Wikipedia. "Amino Acid." Accessed May 6, 2014.
http://en.wikipedia.org/wiki/Amino_acid
Wikipedia. "Essential Amino Acid." Accessed May 6, 2014.
http://en.wikipedia.org/wiki/Essential_amino_acid

6. Wikipedia. "Creatine." Accessed May 6, 2014.
http://en.wikipedia.org/wiki/Creatine
Wikipedia. "Carnosine." Accessed May 6, 2014.
http://en.wikipedia.org/wiki/Carnosine

7. Physicians Committee for Responsible Medicine. "Meat Consumption and Cancer Risk." Accessed November 21, 2014.
http://www.pcrm.org/health/cancer-resources/
diet-cancer/facts/meat-consumption-and-cancer-risk

8. FDA U.S. Food and Drug Administration. *What You Need to Know about Mercury in Fish and Shellfish (Brochure).* March 2014. Accessed May 6, 2014.
http://www.fda.gov/food/resourcesforyou/consumers/ucm110591.htm
U. S. Department of Agriculture and U.S. Department of Health and Human Services. *Dietary Guidelines for American, 2010.* 7th edition. Washington, DC: U.S. Government Printing Office, December 2010. Accessed May 6, 2014.
www.dietaryguidelines.gov

Natural Resources Defense Council. "Consumer Guide to Mercury in Fish." Accessed in May 6, 2014.
http://www.nrdc.org/health/effects/mercury/guide.asp

9. Wikipedia. "Saturated Fat." Accessed May 7, 2014.
http://en.wikipedia.org/wiki/Saturated_fat
Wikipedia. "Polyunsaturated Fat." Accessed May 7, 2014.
http://en.wikipedia.org/wiki/Polyunsaturated_fat
Wikipedia. "Monounsaturated Fat." Accessed May 7, 2014.
http://en.wikipedia.org/wiki/Monounsaturated_fat
Wikipedia. "Omega-9." Accessed May 7, 2014.
http://en.wikipedia.org/wiki/Omega-9_fatty_acid
Wikipedia. "Essential Fatty Acids." Accessed May 7, 2014.
http://en.wikipedia.org/wiki/Essential_fatty_acid

10. Wikipedia. "Trans Fat." Accessed May 7, 2014.
http://en.wikipedia.org/wiki/Trans_fat
Wikipedia. "Hydrogenation." Accessed May 7, 2014.
http://en.wikipedia.org/wiki/Hydrogenation

11. Wikipedia. "Cooking Oil." Accessed May 7, 2014.
http://en.wikipedia.org/wiki/Cooking_oil
Wikipedia. "Smoke Point." Accessed May 7, 2014.
http://en.wikipedia.org/wiki/Smoke_point

12. Wikipedia. "Omega-6 Fatty Acid." Accessed May 7, 2014.
http://en.wikipedia.org/wiki/Omega-6_fatty_acid

13. Goodnet. "11 Essential Vitamins and Minerals your Body Needs." October 2013.
http://www.goodnet.org/articles/11-essential-vitamins-minerals-your-body-needs
Centers for Disease Control and Prevention. "Vitamins and Minerals." February 2011. Accessed May 9, 2014.
http://www.goodnet.org/articles/11-essential-vitamins-minerals-your-body-needs

14. Wikipedia. "Alkaline Diet." Accessed May 9, 2014.
http://en.wikipedia.org/wiki/Alkaline_diet

15. Christopher Vasey. "Controversy about the Acid-Alkaline Balance: Are Fruits Alkalizing or Acidifying?" Health and Self-Knowledge. Accessed December 8, 2014.
http://www.christophervasey.ch/anglais/articles/controversy_about_the_acid.html

16. Essence of Life. "A List of Acid / Alkaline Forming Foods." Accessed May 9, 2014.
http://www.rense.com/1.mpicons/acidalka.htm

17. Wikipedia. "Free-Radical Theory of Aging." Accessed May 9, 2014.
http://en.wikipedia.org/wiki/Free-radical_theory_of_aging
Wikipedia. "Polyphenol." Accessed May 9, 2014.
http://en.wikipedia.org/wiki/Polyphenol

18. Wikipedia. "Probiotic." Accessed May 9, 2014.
http://en.wikipedia.org/wiki/Probiotic

19. Wikipedia. "Bloating." Accessed May 9, 2014.
http://en.wikipedia.org/wiki/Bloating

Wikipedia. "Digestive Enzymes." Accessed May 9, 2014.
http://en.wikipedia.org/wiki/Digestive_enzyme

20. Wikipedia. "Polyphenol." Accessed May 9, 2014.
http://en.wikipedia.org/wiki/Polyphenol

21. Wikipedia. "Coffee." Accessed May 9, 2014.
http://en.wikipedia.org/wiki/Coffee
Wikipedia. "Caffeine." Accessed May 9, 2014.
http://en.wikipedia.org/wiki/Caffeine

22. Kristin Kirkpatrick, M.S., R.D., L.D. "6 Amazing Benefits of Tea." *HuffPost Healthy Living,* June 2013. Accessed May 9, 2014.
http://www.huffingtonpost.com/kristin-kirkpatrick-ms-rd-ld/tea-health-benefits_b_3504917.html
Wikipedia. "Polyphenol." Accessed May 9, 2014.
http://en.wikipedia.org/wiki/Polyphenol
Wikipedia. "Tea." Accessed May 9, 2014.
http://en.wikipedia.org/wiki/Tea
Wikipedia. "Green Tea." Accessed May 9, 2014.
http://en.wikipedia.org/wiki/Green_tea

23. Wikipedia. "Diet Soda." Accessed May 9, 2014.
http://en.wikipedia.org/wiki/Diet_soda

24. Wikipedia. "Monosaccharide." Accessed May 12, 2014.
http://en.wikipedia.org/wiki/Monosaccharide
Wikipedia. "Disaccharide." Accessed May 12, 2014.
http://en.wikipedia.org/wiki/Disaccharide
Wikipedia. "Polysaccharide." Accessed May 12, 2014.
http://en.wikipedia.org/wiki/Polysaccharide
Wikipedia. "Oligosaccharide." Accessed May 12, 2014.
http://en.wikipedia.org/wiki/Oligosaccharide

25. Wikipedia. "Sugar." Accessed May 12, 2014.
http://en.wikipedia.org/wiki/Sugar

26. World Health Organization. "WHO Opens Public Consultation on Draft Sugars Guideline." March 2014. Accessed May 12, 2014.
http://www.who.int/mediacentre/news/notes/2014/consultation-sugar-guideline/en/

27. American Heart Association. "About Sodium (Salt)." Accessed November 21, 2014.
http://www.heart.org/HEARTORG/GettingHealthy/NutritionCenter/HealthyEating/About-Sodium-Salt_UCM_463416_Article.jsp

28. Wikipedia. "Allergy." Accessed May 12, 2014.
http://en.wikipedia.org/wiki/Allergy

29. American Association of Acupuncture and Bio-Energetic Medicine. "Bio-Energetic Medicine: Basic Explanation of the Electrodermal Screening Test and the Concepts of Bio-Energetic Medicine." Accessed November 21, 2014.

http://www.healthy.net/Health/Article/Basic_Explanation_of_the_Electrodermal_Screening_Test_and_the_Concepts_of_Bio_Energetic_Medicine/1085/1

30. American Lung Association. "What's in a Cigarette?" Accessed May 14, 2014. http://www.lung.org/stop-smoking/about-smoking/facts-figures/whats-in-a-cigarette.html

31. Wikipedia. "Hypnosis." Accessed November 21, 2014. http://en.wikipedia.org/wiki/Hypnosis
Wikipedia. "Self-Hypnosis." Accessed November 21, 2014. http://en.wikipedia.org/wiki/Self-hypnosis

32. D. S. M. Chan et al. "Red and Processed Meat and Colorectal Cancer Incidence: Meta-Analysis of Prospective Studies." *PLOS ONE* (June 6, 2011): e20456. Accessed May 14, 2014. doi:10.1371/journal.pone.0020456. http://www.plosone.org/article/info%3Adoi%2F10.1371%2Fjournal.pone.0020456
Physicians Committee for Responsible Medicine. "Meat Consumption and Cancer Risk." Accessed November 21, 2014. http://www.pcrm.org/health/cancer-resources/diet-cancer/facts/meat-consumption-and-cancer-risk

33. Rebecca Viksnins Snowden. "Eating Charred, Well-done Meat May Increase Pancreatic Cancer Risk." American Cancer Society. April 2009. Accessed November 21, 2014. http://www.wilderness-survival.net/forums/showthread.php?11654-Eating-Charred-Well-done-Meat-May-Increase-Pancreatic-Cancer-R

34. Berkeley Education. "About Organic Produce." Accessed May 15, 2014. https://www.ocf.berkeley.edu/~lhom/organictext.html

35. Meat Poultry Nutrition. "Are Organically Produced Foods More Nutritious?" Accessed May 15, 2014. http://www.meatpoultrynutrition.org/ht/d/Faqs/pid/26093

36. Canadian Cancer Society. "Sugar and Cancer." Accessed May 15, 2014. http://www.cancer.ca/en/prevention-and-screening/be-aware/cancer-myths-and-controversies/sugar-and-cancer/?region=on

37. Wikipedia. "Endocrine Disruptor." Accessed May 15, 2014. http://en.wikipedia.org/wiki/Endocrine_disruptor

38. American Cancer Society. "Cellular Phone Towers." Accessed May 15, 2014. http://www.cancer.org/cancer/cancercauses/othercarcinogens/athome/cellular-phone-towers
National Cancer Institute. "Cell Phones and Cancer Risk." Accessed May 15, 2014. http://www.cancer.gov/cancertopics/factsheet/Risk/cellphones

39. Wikipedia. "Dietary Fiber." Accessed May 16, 2014. http://en.wikipedia.org/wiki/Dietary_fiber

40. Wikipedia. "Detoxification." Accessed May 16, 2014. http://en.wikipedia.org/wiki/Detoxification_(alternative_medicine)

41. Wikipedia. "Goldenseal." Accessed May 16, 2014.

http://en.wikipedia.org/wiki/Goldenseal

Wikipedia. "Silybum Marianum." Accessed May 16, 2014.

http://en.wikipedia.org/wiki/Silybum_marianum

Elizabeth Walling. "Kill Candida Overgrowth with These Nine Powerful Herbs." *Natural News,* August 2011. Accessed November 24, 2014.

42. National Cancer Institute. "What is Cancer Screening?" Accessed May 16, 2014.
    http://www.cancer.gov/cancertopics/screening

43. Wikipedia. "Essential Oil." Accessed May 16, 2014.
    http://en.wikipedia.org/wiki/Essential_oil
    Scents of Peace. "Essential Oils & Fragrance Profiles." Accessed May 16, 2014.
    http://www.scentsofpeace.co.nz/aromatherapy-oils.aspx

44. Wikipedia. "Relaxation Technique." Accessed May 16, 2014.
    http://en.wikipedia.org/wiki/Relaxation_technique
    Wikipedia. "Relaxation (Psychology)." Accessed May 16, 2014.
    http://en.wikipedia.org/wiki/Relaxation_(psychology)

45. Wikipedia. "Physical Exercise." Accessed May 19, 2014.
    http://en.wikipedia.org/wiki/Physical_exercise
    Tuberose. "Sweating." Accessed May 19, 2014.
    http://www.tuberose.com/Sweating.html

46. Organic Facts. "Health Benefits of Laughter." Accessed May 19, 2014.
    https://www.organicfacts.net/health-benefits/other/health-benefits-of-laughter.html

47. M. Boschmann et al. "Water-induced thermogenesis (Abstract)." *Journal of Clinical Endocrinology and Metabolism.* 2003 Dec; 88 (12):6015-9. National Center for Biotechnology. PubMed. Accessed November 24, 2014.
    http://www.ncbi.nlm.nih.gov/pubmed/14671205

48. Alzheimer Association. "Adopt a Brain-Healthy Diet." Accessed December 8, 2014.
    http://www.alz.org/we_can_help_adopt_a_brain_healthy_diet.asp

49. Washington State Department of Health. "Health Benefits of Fish." Accessed December 8, 2014.
    http://www.doh.wa.gov/CommunityandEnvironment/Food/Fish/HealthBenefits

50. Karen Merzenich. "Garlic, Onions, Rosemary, and Sage – Interesting Health Findings for Brain and Body." *Brain HQ,* June 2010. Accessed November 21, 2014.
    http://blog.brainhq.com/2010/06/02/
    garlic-onions-rosemary-and-sage-interesting-health-findings-for-brain-and-body/

51. Wikipedia. "Flavonoid." Accessed May 19, 2014.
    http://en.wikipedia.org/wiki/Flavonoid
    University of California. Berkeley Wellness. "Chocolate on the Brain." November 2012. Accessed November 21, 2014.
    http://www.berkeleywellness.com/healthy-eating/nutrition/article/chocolate-brain

52. The Water Cure. "Frequently Asked Questions. How Much Water Do You Need to Drink?" Accessed May 21, 2014.
    http://www.watercure.com/faq.html

53. Wikipedia. "Stretching." Accessed May 23, 2014.
    http://en.wikipedia.org/wiki/Stretching
    Centers for Disease Control and Prevention. "Physical Activity and Arthritis
    Overview." Accessed May 23, 2014.
    http://www.cdc.gov/arthritis/pa_overview.htm
54. Wikipedia. "Strength Training." Accessed May 23, 2014.
    http://en.wikipedia.org/wiki/Strength_training
55. A Workout Routine. "Does Building Muscle Burn Fat, Burn Calories & Increase
    Metabolism?" Accessed May 23, 2014.
    http://www.aworkoutroutine.com/does-building-muscle-burn-fat/
56. American Heart Association. "Target Heart Rates." Accessed May 23, 2014.
    http://www.heart.org/HEARTORG/GettingHealthy/PhysicalActivity/FitnessBasics/
    Target-Heart-Rates_UCM_434341_Article.jsp#
57. Wikipedia. "Energy Medicine." Accessed May 23, 2014.
    http://en.wikipedia.org/wiki/Energy_medicine
    Healthy.net. "Energy Medicine Resource Center." Accessed May 23, 2014.
    http://www.healthy.net/scr/MainLinks.aspx?Id=35
    Mary Kurus. "Energy Healing – Energy Healing of Auras, Chakras and Energy
    Systems." *The Home of Vibrational Health,* 2009. Accessed May 23, 2014.
    http://www.mkprojects.com/fa_EnergyHealing.html

Chapter 9: Power Up Your Finances

1. Wikipedia. "Permanent Life Insurance." Accessed October 13, 2014.
   http://en.wikipedia.org/wiki/Permanent_life_insurance
2. Wikipedia. "Health Insurance." Accessed October 13, 2014.
   http://en.wikipedia.org/wiki/Health_insurance
   Wikipedia. "Life Insurance." Accessed October 13, 2014.
   http://en.wikipedia.org/wiki/Life_insurance
3. Wikipedia. "Annuity (US Financial Products)." Accessed October 13, 2014.
   http://en.wikipedia.org/wiki/Annuity_(US_financial_products)
4. Wikipedia. "Stock Market Index." Accessed October 16, 2014.
   http://en.wikipedia.org/wiki/Stock_market_index
   Wikipedia. "S&P/TSX Composite Index." Accessed October 16, 2014.
   http://en.wikipedia.org/wiki/S%26P/TSX_Composite_Index
   Wikipedia. "Dow Jones Industrial Average." Accessed October 16, 2014.
   http://en.wikipedia.org/wiki/Dow_Jones_Industrial_Average
   Wikipedia. "S&P 500." Accessed October 16, 2014.
   http://en.wikipedia.org/wiki/S%26P_500
5. Wikipedia. "Money Market." Accessed October 17, 2014.
   http://en.wikipedia.org/wiki/Money_market
   Wikipedia. "Eurodollar." Accessed October 17, 2014

http://en.wikipedia.org/wiki/Eurodollar

6. Wikipedia. "Capital Market." Accessed October 17, 2014.
   http://en.wikipedia.org/wiki/Capital_market
   Wikipedia. "Debenture." Accessed October 17, 2014.
   http://en.wikipedia.org/wiki/Debenture
   Wikipedia. "Derivatives Market." Accessed October 17, 2014.
   http://en.wikipedia.org/wiki/Derivatives_market

7. Wikipedia. "Bond (Finance)." Accessed October 17, 2014.
   http://en.wikipedia.org/wiki/Bond_(finance)

8. Wikipedia. "Derivative (Finance)." Accessed October 17, 2014.
   http://en.wikipedia.org/wiki/Derivative_(finance)

9. Wikipedia. "Mutual Fund." Accessed October 20, 2014.
   http://en.wikipedia.org/wiki/Mutual_fund

10. Wikipedia. "Exchange-Traded Fund." Accessed October 20, 2014.
    http://en.wikipedia.org/wiki/Exchange-traded_fund

11. Wikipedia. "Private Equity Fund." Accessed October 20, 2014.
    http://en.wikipedia.org/wiki/Private_equity_fund

12. Wikipedia. "Hedge Fund." Accessed October 20, 2014.
    http://en.wikipedia.org/wiki/Hedge_fund

13. Wikipedia. "Investment Club." Accessed October 20, 2014.
    http://en.wikipedia.org/wiki/Investment_club

Chapter 11: Power Up Your Business

1. Wikipedia. "Pay Per Click." Accessed November 10, 2014.
   http://en.wikipedia.org/wiki/Pay_per_click

Chapter 12: Power Up Your Leisure Time

1. Wikipedia. "Sleep." Accessed November 20, 2014.
   http://en.wikipedia.org/wiki/Sleep

Index

248, 284, 287, 290, 291, 292,
  296, 299, 301, 306, 313
boredom 37, 73
Boschmann, Michael 154
boundary 110, 175, 179, 185
bowel 143
brain
    consciousness 11
    damage 109, 150
    function 11, 130, 138
    improvement 144
    performance 156, 157
    protecting your 156
brainstorming 267, 269, 279
brainwave 13, 29, 151
brand 144, 156, 197, 261, 262,
  263, 264, 265, 266, 279
break 42, 61, 97, 100, 102, 124,
  143, 157, 165, 175, 179, 231,
  248, 252, 285, 291, 299
break-up 102, 165
breath 8, 99, 111, 113, 228, 286
breathing 80, 81, 86, 109, 130,
  146, 151, 160, 201, 285, 304
Brennan Healing Science 164
brethren 6, 183, 289
brochure 264, 329
brokenness 169
broker
    broker-dealer 210, 213, 214,
      215, 216
    derivative 210
    discount 210, 222
    full-service 210
    insurance 193, 204
    investment 210, 211, 213, 214,
      215, 216, 221
    online 214, 215, 222
brokerage 214, 215, 222
bruise 82, 83
Bruner, Pamela 74

buddy 154
budget 174, 189, 190, 191, 194,
  197, 198, 200, 201, 205, 257,
  258, 262, 264, 266, 270,
  273, 278, 279, 302, 304
buff 154
bug 187, 192, 199
bullying 84, 169
burden 7, 198, 200, 302, 317
business
    card 185, 264, 276
    communication 274
    contact 240, 279
    new 114, 193, 205, 251, 255
    plan 60, 255, 256, 257, 258,
      259, 278
    processes 270
    proposal 120
    signature of excellence 239,
      269, 270
    succession planning 210
busyness 281
butterflies 171

C

cable 197, 303, 304
calorie 41, 132, 133, 134, 140,
  143, 144, 145, 146, 149, 153,
  154, 155, 159, 160, 334
Canadian Cancer Society
  149, 332
cancer 105, 134, 135, 136, 139,
  140, 142, 144, 146, 147, 148,
  149, 150, 151, 152, 157, 287,
  329, 332, 333
candida 150, 333
Canfield, Jack 74
capacity 32, 34, 49, 53, 93, 181,
  227, 259, 283, 311, 314, 318
capital
    gain 217

freedom
    emotional 16, 74, 75, 82,
        164, 327
    financial 186, 188, 190, 194,
        202, 207
free radical 134, 141, 142,
    143, 144
Freud, Sigmund 9, 325
friend v, xviii, 5, 21, 22, 30, 33, 41,
    45, 50, 51, 61, 64, 65, 67, 68,
    74, 76, 79, 84, 86, 88, 90,
    96, 101, 102, 103, 105, 114,
    115, 116, 121, 126, 151, 152,
    155, 161, 162, 163, 166, 167,
    172, 173, 181, 183, 184, 198,
    209, 221, 228, 233, 237, 238,
    282, 288, 289, 290, 299,
    300, 308, 309, 312, 313, 315
friendship v, 26, 48, 120, 152, 165,
    167, 176, 178, 185, 195, 287,
    288, 289
fruit 45, 106, 121, 133, 134, 135,
    140, 141, 142, 143, 145, 146,
    148, 149, 150, 153, 156, 206,
    224, 237, 250, 330
frustration 37, 69, 73, 76, 98, 114,
    161, 173, 174
fulfillment vii, xvii, xviii, 4, 10, 27,
    30, 37, 54, 76, 92, 93, 102,
    115, 118, 124, 125, 127, 165,
    166, 167, 170, 185, 227, 228
fun
    family 198, 287
funding 205, 211, 218
fundraising 184, 225, 243
funeral arrangement 318, 320
fungus 150
fun spending 198
furniture 189, 203, 284, 300,
    301, 307
futures 5, 19, 27, 30, 39, 48, 54,
    61, 70, 78, 82, 84, 95, 156,

    165, 176, 181, 185, 186, 188,
    192, 193, 194, 196, 199, 200,
    205, 206, 213, 215, 216, 217,
    219, 220, 221, 244, 246, 254,
    259, 277, 296, 297, 307, 318,
    321, 322

G

galaxies 107
gambling 161
game
    acting 96
    business 262
    changer 255
    of winning 252
gaming 47
gap 232
garden 76, 77, 78, 81, 82, 90, 110,
    171, 187, 194, 208, 209, 210,
    284, 297, 307
gastro-intestinal discomfort 143
gender 166, 170
generalization 174
generation xviii, 5, 186, 264,
    321, 322
generosity 5, 17, 33, 180, 209,
    225, 276
germ 163
gestures 172, 198, 276, 321
gift v, 5, 17, 23, 26, 32, 44, 49, 50,
    53, 54, 65, 66, 86, 92, 93,
    95, 102, 113, 116, 117, 124,
    127, 129, 132, 166, 176, 180,
    184, 185, 198, 235, 241, 285,
    290, 307, 310, 314, 316, 317,
    319, 322
giftedness 233, 235
giggle 182, 183
giver 224, 321
gland 80

glee xvii, 5, 25, 46, 53, 71, 75, 76,
    81, 91, 94, 95, 99, 107, 115,
    125, 196, 228
glitch 60, 69, 97, 312
globalization 260
glow 160, 173, 185
glucose 135, 145
glycogen 145, 160
goal
    achievement 50, 65, 233
God
    connectedness to 9, 10, 11
    embraced by 35, 46, 162
    faith in 67, 91, 94, 95, 104, 108
    from God and in God 4, 38,
        52, 87, 110, 309
    oneness with 6, 76, 78, 79,
        83, 109
    praise 151
    relationship with 7, 8
    trust in 67, 98, 188
    united to 4
good-feeling thoughts xvii, 4, 7,
    22, 38, 42, 46, 71, 74, 75,
    79, 97, 98, 103, 114, 120,
    123, 124, 152, 157, 187, 208,
    209, 310
goodness 25, 52, 74, 90, 99, 105,
    115, 157, 162, 166, 181, 186,
    188, 209, 311, 316, 322
goodwill spending 198
Google + 265
government leader 170, 322
grace 51, 76, 92, 101, 103, 106,
    107, 108, 110, 309
grain 133, 135, 136, 140, 142, 145,
    146, 148, 153, 219
gratefulness 6, 50, 88, 92, 125,
    181, 209, 228, 291, 317
gratitude
    journal 61, 103, 146, 151

greatness 4, 6, 17, 24, 28, 29, 32,
    33, 35, 40, 44, 45, 46, 91,
    92, 106, 108, 114, 115, 118,
    127, 168, 177, 180, 226, 227,
    228, 231, 235, 239, 245,
    260, 261, 267, 268, 274, 323
grief 71, 73, 89, 90, 102, 165
growth
    body 138
    business 259, 261
    career 236
    financial 7, 188, 209
    hormone 148
    opportunities 256, 278
    social 261
    spiritual 35
guardian 108, 318, 320
guidance v, 25, 28, 30, 40, 56, 57,
    73, 91, 114, 122, 209, 234,
    235, 250, 274, 286
guide xvii, 5, 10, 86, 95, 150, 166,
    178, 193, 196, 210, 261, 272,
    301, 313, 319, 327, 330
guided imagery 16, 151
guideline 132, 133, 135, 145, 248,
    329, 330, 331
gym 56, 57, 62, 63, 159, 160,
    161, 195

H

habit
    eating 101, 123, 141, 152
hallucination 109
hand shaking 131
happiness xvii, 5, 23, 46, 70, 82,
    99, 102, 103, 104, 108, 113,
    115, 118, 183, 233, 241, 281,
    282, 283, 285, 287, 288,
    322, 326
harassment 84
harmonization 245

I

newsletter 244, 246, 264, 265
Newton, Isaac 29, 30, 327
New York Stock Exchange 212
non-resistance 70
non-violence 170
norepinephrine 159
notoriety 169
nurturer 4, 5, 17
nut 133, 136, 138, 139, 142, 143,
    148, 153, 173
nutrient 129, 134, 135, 141, 143,
    148, 149, 150, 155, 186
nutrition 36, 86, 135, 149, 164,
    330, 332, 334
nutritional plan 15, 129, 133, 149,
    152, 153, 154
nutritionist 141, 149, 163

O

obedience 121
obesity 139, 145, 149
objective
    strategic 254, 256, 257, 258
observer 28, 54, 93, 117
obsessive-compulsive disorder
    79, 80, 328
obstacle 46, 50, 52, 57, 58, 59, 63,
    69, 70, 97, 99, 105, 107, 312
offering 120, 221, 253, 255, 256,
    257, 258, 262, 264, 265,
    266, 270, 273, 276, 303
office 60, 61, 96, 157, 172, 195,
    197, 247, 283, 292, 293, 294,
    295, 296, 297, 304, 305,
    306, 307, 329, 330, 375
oil 133, 137, 138, 139, 150, 151,
    153, 218, 330, 333
omega 91, 108, 136, 137, 138,
    139, 140, 156, 330
oneness 6, 7, 14, 76, 78, 79, 83, 91,
    106, 109, 110, 125, 185, 224

One Step Plus One 46, 47
online
    brokerage 214, 215, 222
    store 256, 273
openness 106, 166, 174, 183, 248
operation 204, 253, 260, 269, 270
opinion 68, 122, 142, 172, 173,
    181, 212, 246
opportunity
    emerging 252, 253
    growth 256, 278
oppression vii, 25, 70, 72, 75, 118,
    169, 170
optimism 72, 97, 101, 152, 252,
    277, 279
option
    career 33, 230
    insurance 203, 204
    investment 211, 212, 218, 223
    marketing 264
options and swaps 215
organization 47, 64, 90, 145, 169,
    210, 217, 230, 232, 241, 242,
    244, 246, 249, 250, 254,
    255, 267, 272, 274, 303, 307,
    319, 331, 375
Ortner, Nick 74, 327
osteoporosis 142, 146, 159
outcome 19, 21, 23, 32, 35, 47, 69,
    94, 155, 174, 240, 247, 248,
    254, 256, 257, 258
outlook 16, 50, 55, 69, 75, 113,
    114, 115, 123, 124, 228, 282
output 132, 247
overeating 154
oversight 250
owner 40, 203, 256, 319
ownership 18, 19, 21, 24, 212, 319
oxygen 109, 134, 152, 308

P

pain
    back and neck 158
    emotional 84, 88, 161, 165
    physical 73, 85
painting 195, 284, 301, 302
panic attack 79
paperless 240
parasite 148, 150, 163
parent 18, 36, 45, 82, 88, 121,
    126, 166, 167, 177, 179, 180,
    183, 206, 225, 283
Parkinson disease 144
participant 64, 248
participation 56, 248, 265, 288
partnership 217, 255, 256,
    260, 264
passion xvii, 3, 4, 5, 7, 8, 17, 21,
    24, 27, 28, 33, 34, 37, 38, 39,
    45, 46, 48, 49, 52, 54, 55,
    71, 72, 76, 88, 92, 94, 95,
    96, 98, 100, 113, 114, 121,
    177, 178, 226, 227, 228, 229,
    231, 236, 248, 254, 259,
    262, 276, 279, 281, 309, 310,
    312, 375
patent 256
path 4, 10, 16, 19, 24, 30, 33, 40,
    45, 47, 55, 57, 58, 59, 63, 67,
    75, 76, 77, 78, 81, 86, 87, 90,
    105, 110, 118, 122, 126, 163,
    166, 168, 180, 185, 201, 224,
    227, 228, 229, 233, 235,
    236, 239, 245, 259, 277,
    286, 288, 313
Path to Serenity Technique 75,
    76, 77, 78, 81, 86, 90, 168
patience xviii, 5, 7, 94, 119, 166,
    186, 194, 208, 283, 314
payback 119
pay incentive 278

payment 101, 190, 191, 199, 200,
    201, 203, 205, 206, 214,
    273, 279
pay per click 335
peace xvii, xviii, 4, 5, 6, 7, 17, 26,
    30, 31, 46, 58, 67, 69, 72, 75,
    76, 77, 78, 81, 82, 88, 92,
    93, 94, 98, 100, 102, 108,
    110, 123, 125, 130, 151, 162,
    163, 166, 167, 170, 171, 176,
    193, 203, 205, 218, 281, 286,
    302, 322, 323, 333
peer 7, 19, 20, 21, 67, 230,
    239, 315
penalty 207, 220
pension fund 207
people v, vii, 7, 16, 18, 19, 22, 34,
    36, 41, 43, 44, 47, 49, 51, 54,
    56, 57, 63, 65, 67, 68, 69, 77,
    82, 83, 84, 85, 87, 88, 89,
    90, 92, 98, 99, 105, 106, 107,
    108, 109, 115, 118, 119, 120,
    121, 122, 123, 132, 135, 136,
    144, 147, 150, 157, 159, 163,
    169, 170, 173, 175, 181, 184,
    185, 196, 197, 199, 203, 209,
    217, 220, 224, 225, 226, 227,
    228, 229, 233, 235, 245,
    246, 247, 249, 260, 261, 264,
    265, 270, 276, 280, 282,
    283, 285, 289, 290, 296,
    298, 299, 301, 307, 311, 317,
    321, 322, 323
perception 9, 11, 243, 327
performance
    cognitive 156
    fee 217
    feedback 68
    improvement 227, 267
    indicator 256, 257
    issue 243
    management 232, 234, 261

promotion 114, 117, 237, 238, 241, 246, 256, 265, 267, 279, 323

prop 96, 178

property tax 197

prospect 120, 183, 263, 264, 265, 266, 274, 276

prosperity 46, 115, 186, 187, 188, 198, 224, 225

protector 92, 156

protein 86, 129, 132, 133, 135, 136, 139, 140, 142, 143, 148, 150, 153, 329

prototype 256

provider 5, 64, 131, 141, 149, 166, 273, 303, 304

psychiatrist 87

psychologist 9, 16, 64, 87, 163

public corporation 214

public relation 264

punishment 121, 179

Pure Creativity 4, 38, 48, 118, 229, 259, 267

purpose
    core 254
    life 4, 28, 33, 36, 39, 40, 88, 122, 227, 228, 230, 313
    true vii, 3, 91, 102, 107, 169

Q

Qi Gong 159

qualification 47, 221, 233

quality 16, 44, 181, 197, 237, 242, 243, 244, 250, 259, 262, 263, 270, 275, 288

question 9, 19, 20, 28, 34, 35, 39, 41, 55, 68, 70, 78, 143, 174, 176, 184, 191, 203, 229, 230, 232, 234, 236, 238, 246, 251, 252, 254, 260, 261, 262, 263, 267, 275, 276, 279, 280, 288, 293, 294, 295, 313, 334

quietness xviii, 5, 7, 76, 108, 192, 280, 285, 286, 287, 291, 316

R

3R – Reduce, reuse and recycle 306

race 55, 166, 170, 179

rage 20, 72, 73

Rao, Rajesh 12

rapid eye movement 109, 328

rate of return 41, 189, 193, 207, 214, 220, 222, 223, 256

reaction 15, 21, 37, 73, 146, 222, 247

real estate
    fund 206
    investment group 206

reality 18, 19, 21, 23, 27, 33, 37, 38, 51, 58, 92, 104, 106, 126, 130, 172, 194, 211, 231, 241, 255, 271, 300, 312

receiver 224

reconciliation 174

recovery program 152, 163

reference 9, 11, 221, 240, 246, 297

reflection 28, 39, 67, 68, 73, 176, 229, 232, 245, 254, 259, 268, 293, 313

reishi mushroom 143

rejection 49, 73, 121, 122, 167

relationship
    client 230, 279

relaxation 5, 7, 13, 31, 81, 86, 118, 130, 146, 151, 152, 157, 280, 281, 285, 291, 301, 316, 333

relaxin 151

religion 18, 166, 170, 284

remembrance 89

remote viewing 9

rental property 206

S

sadness 58, 73, 83, 85, 87, 102, 117, 167
safety 100, 148, 162, 315, 320
salary increment 302
sale
  manager 261
salesforce 256, 261
salt 146, 331
sarcasm 173, 174, 317
satisfaction
  customer 270
savings
  account 191, 205, 206, 213, 218, 220
  bond 220
  plan 41, 57, 63, 189, 191, 203, 207
  retirement 191
scale 154, 155, 193, 229
scarcity 17, 18, 48, 102, 165, 187, 194, 208, 279
schedule
  accounts receivable
      aging 273
  repayment 200
  weekly 240
school
  administration 84
  counselor 88
screening test 151, 332
search engine 265
seasonal 256
Securities and Exchange
    Commission 216
security 20, 162, 174, 210, 213, 214, 215, 216, 217, 223
seed
  seeds of greatness 6, 28, 32, 44, 46, 91, 92, 106, 114, 127, 227, 239, 323

wealth seeds 186, 199, 208, 209
self xvii, xviii, 3, 4, 5, 6, 8, 17, 21, 24, 28, 29, 31, 44, 45, 46, 47, 48, 50, 55, 58, 62, 66, 69, 72, 75, 76, 77, 78, 79, 82, 83, 85, 86, 90, 91, 92, 93, 99, 104, 110, 114, 118, 119, 122, 127, 129, 147, 162, 164, 167, 179, 181, 194, 207, 222, 228, 239, 248, 280, 288, 314, 315, 316, 319, 322, 323, 327, 330, 332
self-confidence 50
self-control 4, 44, 55, 62, 92, 118, 207
self-development 239
self-discipline 21, 129, 162, 194, 228
self-doubt 48, 50, 69, 118, 167
self-efficacy 248
self-esteem 4, 47, 85, 122, 127, 179, 288
self-hypnosis 46, 47, 147, 327, 332
selfie 172
self-image 119
selfishness 165, 281
self-love 5, 76, 85, 86, 90, 314, 315, 316, 322, 323
self-oppression 72, 118
self-pity 69, 114
self-protection 167
self-rejection 167
self-repression 167
self-worth 181
senior leadership 241, 258
sensation 11, 15, 73
sense
  better 42, 265
  inner 30
  of accomplishment 61, 284

Toronto Stock Exchange 212
touch
     therapeutic 164
toxin 141, 147, 150, 152, 158, 160, 163, 164
traditions 8, 290
training
     cardio 160
     strength 159, 282, 334
transaction fee 200, 222
trans fat 137, 139, 330
transformation
     Power Tool 20
     process 37, 117
transport spending 194
trauma 109, 176
travel 58, 59, 67, 122, 166, 193, 198, 202, 203, 284, 288, 289, 290, 301, 304, 305, 314
treasure
     chest 22, 23, 50, 90, 103, 106, 178, 183, 186, 288
Treasury bills 189, 213, 218, 220
trend 249, 253, 257, 258, 259, 263, 270, 278
tripartite nature 8
true self xviii, 6, 8
trust
     living 319
     testamentary 319
trustee 319
truth 10, 92, 122, 162, 238, 310
truthfulness 171
tumor
     killing cell 130
tunnel 89, 109, 161, 224, 272, 323
turmoil vii, 48, 58, 78, 121
Twitter 265, 266

U

understanding 7, 11, 18, 25, 31, 51, 70, 73, 83, 88, 91, 94, 108, 110, 151, 166, 170, 174, 175, 209, 213, 228, 233, 237, 244, 245, 246, 249, 252, 263, 271, 272, 274, 283, 298, 306, 317, 319, 321
uneasiness 80
union 172, 213
uniqueness 39, 42, 90, 117, 229, 230, 231, 233, 239, 263
unit 145, 206, 222, 223, 256, 258, 278
United States Department of Agriculture's National Organic Program 148
unity 8, 26, 125, 152, 170
Universal Resource Locator 246
universe xvii, 3, 4, 13, 17, 22, 23, 28, 31, 34, 47, 52, 76, 81, 91, 93, 94, 104, 107, 108, 117, 119, 124, 125, 169, 170, 259, 310, 312, 321, 327, 328
University of Minnesota 148
unworthiness 45, 179
upset 15, 72, 73, 78, 144, 173, 243
Up to The Top Technique 51, 52
Up You Go
     attitude 231, 239, 242, 249
     Career Pillars 230, 242
     Career Plan 226, 229, 231, 233, 236
     questions 232, 267
urgencies 59, 282

V

value
     proposition 264
variance 243, 270, 273

vegetable 133, 134, 135, 136,
    137, 138, 139, 140, 141, 142,
    143, 145, 146, 148, 150, 153,
    156, 329
veggie 133, 134, 142, 148,
    153, 156
vehicle 32, 189, 197, 291
venture 44, 206, 251, 264, 265
vibration
    mode 248
    of energy 22, 92
    positive 76, 282
victim 24, 38, 70, 82, 84, 162, 167
victory 47, 51, 52, 69, 79, 85, 86,
    92, 94, 114, 152, 310, 311
video 12, 264, 265, 266, 287, 299
view 8, 10, 11, 12, 36, 116, 170,
    173, 176, 178, 184, 185, 189,
    199, 255, 259, 317
viewpoint 172
vigor 164, 228, 316
violence vii, 25, 169, 170
virus 168, 169, 170
vision
    of success 19, 30, 31, 34,
        35, 38, 39, 40, 41, 42,
        55, 59, 60, 62, 65, 95,
        96, 97, 99, 101, 227,
        236, 291
visionary 28, 54, 117, 277
visualization 13, 16, 22, 43, 46,
    78, 96, 99, 130, 151, 208,
    290, 291, 326
Visual Motor Rehearsal
    Program 16
vitality xviii, 7, 31, 56, 62, 85, 129,
    130, 131, 132, 134, 140,
    160, 164
vitamin 81, 86, 129, 134, 135, 136,
    139, 141, 142, 147, 149, 150,
    156, 329, 330

vlog 265
voice
    inner 20, 28, 29, 30, 33, 39,
        40, 57, 122, 176, 178,
        233, 313
    mail 61, 264
volltlon 122
volunteer 33, 184
volunteering 88, 185, 225,
    239, 289

W

waiting ix, 54, 83, 92, 94, 96, 106,
    108, 119, 120, 121, 221, 246,
    297, 304, 310, 312
Waitley, Denis 16
walk 29, 76, 77, 81, 86, 113, 114,
    115, 124, 146, 151, 157, 159,
    172, 178, 180, 181, 183, 198,
    200, 227, 239, 243, 249, 251,
    277, 284, 291, 295, 308, 317
war vii, 17, 25, 177, 215, 224
warmth 69, 152, 171, 182,
    293, 316
water
    retention 154
    troubled 174
W. D. Factor 30, 31, 32, 35,
    239, 249
weakness 38, 49, 86, 226, 229,
    231, 253, 257, 261, 268,
    314, 315
wealth xviii, 25, 31, 36, 46, 48, 57,
    63, 130, 186, 187, 188, 190,
    191, 194, 195, 197, 198, 199,
    202, 203, 204, 205, 206,
    207, 208, 209, 211, 212, 218,
    221, 259, 284, 318, 319
weapon 169, 174
website 60, 144, 210, 246, 248,
    264, 265

weight
    goal 155
    lifting 159
    management 47
weighting 211, 218, 219, 220, 221
Welch, Jack 43
well-being vii, xviii, 5, 7, 8, 10, 13,
    16, 22, 30, 35, 43, 46, 53,
    71, 72, 73, 74, 75, 76, 77,
    78, 79, 80, 81, 82, 85, 86,
    87, 90, 91, 99, 100, 103, 114,
    115, 124, 125, 129, 132, 146,
    151, 152, 157, 163, 164, 170,
    171, 250, 280, 281, 282, 285,
    292, 305, 316, 322
wellness 7, 16, 17, 80, 86, 129,
    130, 131, 162, 163, 164,
    281, 334
wholeness 7, 14, 45, 46, 76, 82,
    87, 88, 89, 92, 130, 166, 310
wholesale 256
wholesaler 256
Willett, Walter 135, 329
will executor 320
willingness 90, 236, 297, 298, 312
willpower 130
wing 4, 5, 24, 46, 90, 94, 110, 115,
    118, 177, 178, 251, 317
wisdom v, xvii, xviii, 3, 4, 5, 17, 28,
    29, 38, 46, 99, 101, 106, 107,
    114, 127, 128, 178, 248, 278,
    313, 314, 317, 323
wit 259
Wolfgang von Goethe, Johann 44
wonder 1, 5, 93, 102, 117, 125,
    141, 160, 171, 228, 282, 306,
    313, 317
word 7, 8, 16, 19, 35, 46, 47, 69,
    75, 76, 83, 89, 98, 99, 113,
    114, 115, 127, 138, 139, 147,
    166, 171, 172, 173, 174, 175,
    177, 180, 181, 205, 222, 227,

233, 245, 248, 249, 263,
    267, 268, 271, 275, 276, 277,
    279, 317
work
    excellence 239, 241
    expectation 232, 287
    hard 58, 194, 257, 297, 300
    instruction 246
    quality 44
    team v, 44, 99, 238, 240,
        243, 244, 252, 255, 267,
        268, 270
    work-life harmony 31, 35,
        39, 229, 230, 236, 239,
        240, 241
workforce 278
working condition 233
working paper 240
work in progress 314, 316
work-life harmony 31, 35, 39, 229,
    230, 236, 239, 240, 241
workout 159, 160, 284, 334
workplace 196, 202, 203,
    229, 305
workshop 210, 236, 239, 248, 269
workspace 268, 293, 294,
    304, 306
world
    betterment of the 94
    of possibilities 93
World Cancer Research Fund 147
World Health Organization
    145, 331
worry 10, 25, 47, 73, 77, 78, 80,
    81, 120, 122, 123, 154, 196,
    276, 291
worth xvii, 78, 102, 117, 181, 189,
    190, 192, 194, 199, 200
wound 73, 74, 83, 86, 88, 89, 90,
    118, 127, 166, 167, 244
wrinkle 144, 314

Y

yeast 150
youthfulness 144, 230, 280, 282
YouTube 265, 266

Z

zen 301
zone
    comfort 28, 43, 123, 288, 312
    well-being 7, 71, 72, 73,
        81, 114

About the Author

Jocelyne F. Lafrenière is an international management consultant, executive coach, corporate trainer, and keynote speaker. She holds a bachelor of commerce degree and is a Chartered Professional Accountant. She is a Certified Professional Success Coach and Neuro-Linguistic Programming Practitioner.

For more than 25 years, Jocelyne has served as an advisor to United Nations agencies, government departments and agencies, businesses, and non-profit organizations around the world. She is known for her business acumen and her drive and passion. She is a former partner of KPMG Canada, one of the world's largest professional services firms, where she led the International Development Assistance Services and Compliance Services in their Ottawa office. She is currently the president of JFL International Inc., a management consulting, coaching, and training firm.

Throughout her career, Jocelyne has actively championed for the empowerment of women, the protection of children, and education. Jocelyne is the founder of the JFL Foundation, which advances the lives of underprivileged people around the world through education and entrepreneurship. She defends human rights through the JFL Peace Movement. She is a recipient of the Queen Elizabeth II Diamond Jubilee Medal for her significant contribution to the community in Canada and abroad.

Printed in the United States
by Baker & Taylor

Printed in the United States
By Bookmasters